**Student's Solutions Manual and
Study Guide to Accompany**

BUSINESS

STATISTICS

An Introductory Course

KEN BLACK
University of Houston at Clear Lake

West Publishing Company

St. Paul   New York   Los Angeles   San Francisco

WEST'S COMMITMENT TO THE ENVIRONMENT
In 1906, West Publishing Company began recycling materials left over from the production of books. This began a tradition of efficient and responsible use of resources. Today, up to 95% of our legal books and 70% of our college texts are printed on recycled, acid-free stock. West also recycles nearly 22 million pounds of scrap paper annually—the equivalent of 181,717 trees. Since the 1960s, West has devised ways to capture and recycle waste inks, solvents, oils, and vapors created in the printing process. We also recycle plastics of all kinds, wood, glass, corrugated cardboard, and batteries, and have eliminated the use of styrofoam book packaging. We at West are proud of the longevity and the scope of our commitment to our environment.

Production, Prepress, Printing and Binding by West Publishing Company.

COPYRIGHT © 1992 by   WEST PUBLISHING CO.
610 Opperman Drive
P.O. Box 64526
St. Paul, MN 55164–0526

ISBN 0–314–00196–4

CONTENTS

Preface

This Solutions Manual and Study Guide has been developed to accompany the text, <u>Business Statistics:</u> <u>An Introductory Course</u>. All materials in this manual have been developed by Ken Black to assure that topics considered and presented here are consistent with the manner of presentation in the main text. This manual has been organized to parallel the twelve chapters of the main text. Each of the chapters in the manual contains six parts: chapter objectives, chapter outline, key words, study questions, answers to study questions, and solutions to the odd-numbered problems in the main text.

The study questions have been prepared in such a way as to guide you, the student, through the chapter. This is accomplished by asking questions about key words and concepts presented in the chapter. Also, additional problems have been created and presented in the study question section to afford you the opportunity for further practice. These problems cover most of the major topics in each chapter. Problem scenarios have been kept to a minimum to allow you to focus on data manipulation and computation. The answers to each of these study questions is given in the next section of the chapter to allow you to evaluate your progress in mastering the chapter material.

Section six of each chapter contains the solutions to the odd-numbered problems from the main text chapter. I have made an attempt to provide you with the maximum amount of detailed information on each problem. I find in teaching statistics that a lot of learning goes on between the student and the solutions manual in wrestling with the whys and wherefores of the printed solution.

I hope that you find this solutions manual and study guide to be an integral part of your learning experience in this course. This book is intended to facilitate the creation of an optimal experience in studying statistics.

I wish to thank Jessica Evans, Developmental Editor of West Educational Publishing Company, for her continued guidance and support in the preparation and publication of this document. I want to give special recognition to Marlene Lewis who has greatly assisted me in bringing this document to publication through her professional expertise and word processing capability.

Finally, to the students, I wish a successful journey into the world of statistics. Keep pushing on! In time, it will come together for you. I hope that this manual assists in making the course a successful one.

INTRODUCTION TO STATISTICS

I. **CHAPTER OBJECTIVES**

The primary objective of chapter one is to introduce you to the world of statistics, enabling you to:

1. Be aware of a wide range of applications of statistics in business.

2. Define statistics.

3. Differentiate between descriptive and inferential statistics.

4. Classify numbers by level of data and understand why doing so is important.

II. **CHAPTER OUTLINE**

1.1   Statistics in Business

       Examples of Statistics in Business

               Accounting
               Finance
               Management
               Management Information Systems
               Marketing

1.2   What is Statistics?

1.3   Descriptive Versus Inferential Statistics

1.4   Levels of Data Measurement

       Nominal Level

       Ordinal Level

       Interval Level

       Ratio Level

       Comparison of the Four Levels of Data

III. **KEY WORDS**

Statistics   Nominal Level Data
Population   Ordinal Level Data
Census   Interval Level Data
Sample   Ratio Level Data
Descriptive Statistics   Metric Data
Inferential Statistics   Nonmetric Data
Parameter   Parametric Statistics
Statistic   Nonparametric Statistics

IV. **STUDY QUESTIONS**

1. A science dealing with the collection, analysis, interpretation, and presentation of numerical data is called _____.

2. One way to subdivide the field of statistics is into the two branches of _____ statistics and _____ statistics.

3. A collection of persons, objects or items of interest is a _____.

4. Data gathered from a whole population is called a _____.

5. If a population consists of all the radios produced today in the Akron facility and if a quality control inspector randomly selects forty of the ratios, the group of forty is referred to as _____.

6. If data are used to reach conclusions only about the group from which the data are gathered, then the statistics are referred to as _____ statistics.

7. If data are gathered from a subgroup of a larger group and the data are used to reach conclusions about the larger group, then the statistics are said to be _____ statistics.

8. Another name for inferential statistics is _____ statistics.

9.   Descriptive measures which are usually denoted by Greek letters are called _____.

10. The highest level of data measurement is _____.

11. The level of data measurement used when ranking items is _____.

12. If a number represents the geographic location of a business, then the level of data represented by the number is probably _____.

13. If the data being gathered are only ordinal level data, then the researcher should only use _____ statistics to analyze the data.

14-25 For each of the following, the data gathered are most likely to be which level of data? Nominal, Ordinal, Interval, or Ratio?

14. The ages of managers of fast-food restaurants.

15. An employee's identification number.

16. The number of freight cars per train for five hundred trains.

17. The elevation of a town.

18. The number of feet it takes a car to stop going fifty miles per hour.

19. The number of ounces of orange juice consumed by each Floridian in the morning.

20. The volume of wheat in each silo in Nebraska in August.

21. A rating scale of the productivity of each worker which has as its adjectives: very poor, poor, average, good, outstanding.

22. A person's religious preference.

23. Weights of statistics' textbooks.

24. Years of experience on the job.

25. Number representing a worker's assignment to the red team, blue team, or green team at work where the red team is considered the top workers and the green team is considered the least productive workers.

V.   **ANSWERS TO STUDY QUESTIONS**

1.	Statistics	13.	Nonparametric
2.	Descriptive, Inferential	14.	Ratio
		15.	Nominal
3.	Population	16.	Ratio
4.	Census	17.	Interval
5.	Sample	18.	Ratio
6.	Descriptive	19.	Ratio
7.	Inferential	20.	Ratio
8.	Inductive	21.	Ordinal
9.	Parameters	22.	Nominal
10.	Ratio	23.	Ratio
11.	Ordinal	24.	Ratio
12.	Nominal	25.	Ordinal

VI.   **SOLUTIONS TO ODD-NUMBERED PROBLEMS IN TEXT.**

1.1   Examples of data in functional areas:

accounting - cost of goods, salary expense, depreciation, utility costs, taxes, equipment inventory, etc.

human resources - salaries, size of engineering staff, years experience, age of employees, years of education, etc.

organizational behavior - measurement of union participation, measurement of employer support, measurement of tendency to control, number of subordinates reporting to a manager, measurement of leadership style, etc.

sales - number of units sold, dollar sales volume, forecast sales, size of sales force, market share, etc.

consumer behavior - measurement of consumer motivation, measurement of consumer frustration, measurement of brand preference, attitude measurement, measurement of consumer risk, etc.

<u>physical distribution</u> - transportation distances, sizes of orders, number and size of storage facilities, transportation costs, storage costs, sizes of inventories, etc.

<u>finance</u> - World bank bond rates, number of failed savings and loans, measured risk of common stocks, stock dividends, foreign exchange rate, liquidity rates for a single-family, etc.

<u>information systems</u> - c.p.u. time, size of memory, number of work stations, storage capacity, percent of professionals who are connected to a computer network, dollar assets of company computing, etc.

1.3 <u>Descriptive statistics</u> in recorded music industry -

1) R.C.A. total sales of compact discs this week, number of artists under contract to a company at a given time.

2) total dollars spent on advertising last month to promote an album.

3) number of units produced in a day.

4) number of retail outlets selling the company's products.

<u>Inferential statistics</u> in recorded music industry -

1) measure the amount spent per month on recorded music for a few consumers then use that figure to infer the amount for the population.

2) determination of market share for rap music by randomly selecting a sample of 500 purchasers of recorded music.

3) Determination of top ten single records by sampling the number of requests at a few radio stations.

4) Estimation of the average length of a single recording by taking a sample of records and measuring them.

The difference between descriptive and inferential statistics lies mainly in the usage of the data. These descriptive examples all gather data from every item in the population about which the description is being made. For example, R.C.A. measures the sales on <u>all</u> its compact discs for a week and reports the total.

In each of the inferential statistics examples, a <u>sample</u> of the population is taken and the population value is estimated or inferred from the sample. For example, it may be practically impossible to determine the proportion of buyers who prefer rap music. However, a random sample of buyers can be contacted and interviewed for music preference. The results can be inferred to population market share.

1.5   a)   ratio

        b)   ratio

        c)   ratio

        d)   ordinal

        e)   nominal

        f)   ratio

        g)   ratio

        h)   ratio

        i)   ordinal

        j)   ratio

        k)   nominal

        l)   nominal

        m)   ratio

CHARTS AND GRAPHS

I. **CHAPTER OBJECTIVES**

The overall objective of chapter two is for you to master several techniques for summarizing and depicting data, enabling you to:

1. Recognize the difference between grouped and ungrouped data.

2. Construct a frequency distribution.

3. Construct a histogram, a frequency polygon, an ogive, a pie chart, and a stem and leaf plot.

II. **CHAPTER OUTLINE**

    2.1   Frequency Distributions

               Class Midpoint

               Relative Frequency

               Cumulative Frequency

    2.2   Graphic Depiction of Data

               Histograms

               Frequency Polygons

               Ogives

               Pie Charts

               Stem and Leaf Plots

III. **KEY WORDS**

Frequency Distribution	Cumulative Frequency
Ungrouped Data	Histogram
Grouped Data	Frequency Pologon
Range	Ogive
Class Midpoint	Pie Chart
Relative Frequency	Stem and Leaf Plot

IV.   **STUDY QUESTIONS**

1.   The following data represents the number of printer ribbons used by each of 28 departments in a company annually. This is an example of _____ data.

```
8    4   5   10   6   5   4   6   3   4   4   6   1   12
2   11   2    5   3   2   6   7   6  12   7   1   8    9
```

2.   Below is a frequency distribution of ages of managers with a large retail firm. This is an example of _____ data.

Age	f
20-29	11
30-39	32
40-49	57
50-59	43
over 60	18

3.   For best results, a frequency distribution should have between _____ and _____ classes.

4.   The difference between the largest and smallest numbers is called the _____.

5.   Consider the values below. In constructing a frequency distribution, the lowest class beginning point should be at least as small as _____ and the highest class endpoint should be at least as large as _____.

```
27   21   08   10   09   16   11   12   21   11   29   19   17   22   28
               28   29   19   18   26   17   34   19   16   20
```

6.   The class midpoint can be determined by _____.

7-8   Examine the frequency below:

class	frequency
5 - under 10	56
10 - under 15	43
15 - under 20	21
20 - under 25	11
25 - under 30	12
30 - under 35	8

7.   The relative frequency for the class 15-20 is

_____.

8.   The cumulative frequency for the class 20-25 is

_____.

9.   The graphical depiction in chapter two which is a type

of vertical bar chart is a _____.

10. The graphical depiction that utilizes cumulative or

decumulative frequencies is a _____.

11. The graph shown below is an example of a

_____.

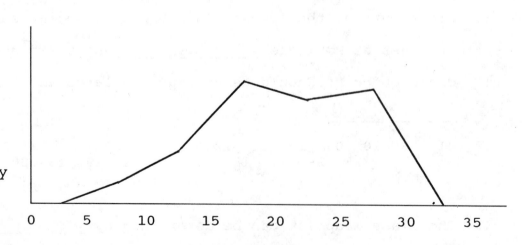

frequency

    0   5   10   15   20   25   30   35

12. Consider the categories below and their relative amounts:

Category	Amount
A	112
B	319
C	57
D	148
E	202

If you were to construct a Pie Chart to depict these categories, then you would allot _____ degrees to category D.

13. Given the values below, construct a stem and leaf plot using two digits for the stem.

346   340   322   339   342   332   338   357
          328   329   346   341   321   332

V. **ANSWERS TO STUDY QUESTIONS**

1. Raw

2. Grouped

3. 5, 15

4. Range

5. 8, 34

6. Averaging the two class endpoints

7. 21/151 = .1391

8. 131

9. Histogram

10. Ogive

11. Frequency Polygon

12. 148/838 of 369° = 63.6°

13.
32	1	2	8	9		
33	2	2	8	9		
34	0	1	2	3	6	6

VI.   **SOLUTIONS TO ODD-NUMBERED PROBLEMS IN TEXT.**

2.1   a) One possible 5 class frequency distribution:

Class Interval	Frequency
10 - under 25	9
25 - under 40	13
40 - under 55	11
55 - under 70	9
70 - under 85	8
	50

b) One possible 10 class frequency distribution:

Class Interval	Frequency
10 - under 18	7
18 - under 26	3
26 - under 34	5
34 - under 42	9
42 - under 50	7
50 - under 58	3
58 - under 66	6
66 - under 74	4
74 - under 82	4
82 - under 90	2

c) The ten class frequency distribution gives a more detailed breakdown of temperatures, pointing out the smaller frequencies for the higher temperature intervals. The five class distribution collapses the intervals into broader classes making it appear that there are nearly equal frequencies in each class.

2.3

Class Interval	Frequency	Class Midpoint	Relative Frequency	Cumulative Frequency
0 - 5	6	2.5	6/86 = .0698	6
5 - 10	8	7.5	.0930	14
10 - 15	17	12.5	.1977	31
15 - 20	23	17.5	.2674	54
20 - 25	18	22.5	.2093	72
25 - 30	10	27.5	.1163	82
30 - 35	4	32.5	.0465	86
TOTAL	86		1.0000	

The relative frequency tells us that it is most probable that a customer is in the 15 - 20 category (.2674). Over two thirds (.6744) of the customers are between 10 and 25 years of age.

2.5   Some examples of cumulative frequencies in business:
            sales for the fiscal year,
            costs for the fiscal year,
            spending for the fiscal year,
            inventory build-up,
            accumulation of workers during a hiring buildup,
            production output over a time period.

2.7   <u>Histogram</u>

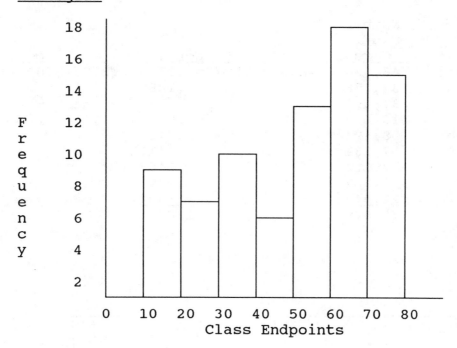

<u>Frequency Polygon</u>

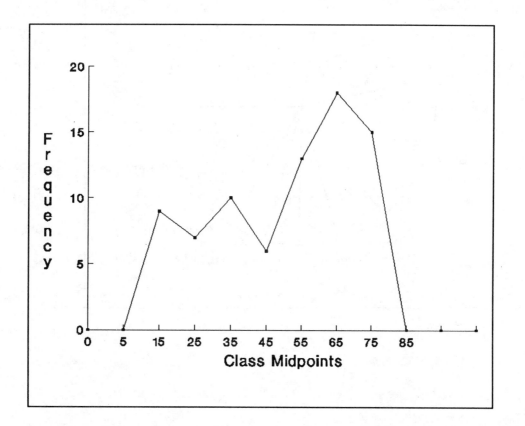

2.9

Company	Number of Cars	Proportion	Number of Degrees
Volkswagen-Audi	48,980	48980/175979= .2783	.2783(360°)=100°
BMW	33,076	.1880	68°
Mercedes-Benz	31,511	.1791	64°
Rover	10,655	.0605	22°
Citreon-Peugeot	8,494	.0483	17°
General Motors	7,231	.0411	15°
Volvo	7,122	.0405	15°
Ford Motor	5,967	.0399	12°
Others	22,943	.1304	47°
TOTAL	175,979	1.0001	360°

Pie Chart

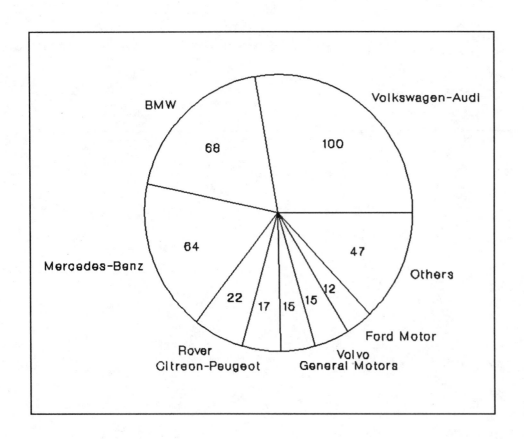

2.11

STEM	LEAF
21	2, 8, 8, 9
22	0, 1, 2, 4, 6, 6, 7, 9, 9
23	0, 0, 4, 5, 8, 8, 9, 9, 9, 9
24	0, 0, 3, 6, 9, 9, 9
25	0, 3, 4, 5, 5, 7, 7, 8, 9
26	0, 1, 1, 2, 3, 3, 5, 6
27	0, 1, 3

2.13 Olson Company
      Frequency distribution

Class Interval	Frequency
32 - under 37	1
37 - under 42	4
42 - under 47	12
47 - under 52	11
52 - under 57	14
57 - under 62	5
62 - under 67	2
67 - under 72	1
TOTAL	50

2.15   Frequency Distribution:

Class Interval	Frequency
10 - under 20	2
20 - under 30	3
30 - under 40	9
40 - under 50	7
50 - under 60	12
60 - under 70	9
70 - under 80	6
80 - under 90	2
	50

HISTOGRAM

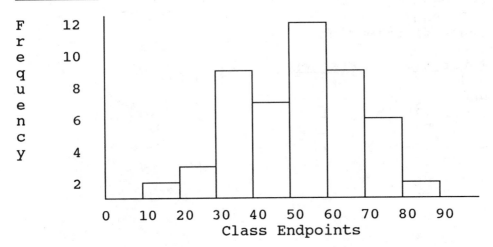

FREQUENCY POLYGON

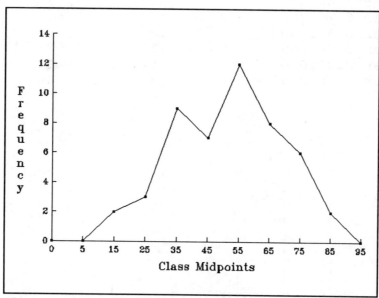

The normal distribution appears to peak near the center and dimish towards the end intervals.

2.17

Asking Price	Frequency	Cumulative Frequency
$ 50,000 - under $ 60,000	21	21
$ 60,000 - under $ 70,000	27	48
$ 70,000 - under $ 80,000	18	66
$ 80,000 - under $ 90,000	11	77
$ 90,000 - under $100,000	6	83
$100,000 - under $110,000	3	86
	86	

HISTOGRAM

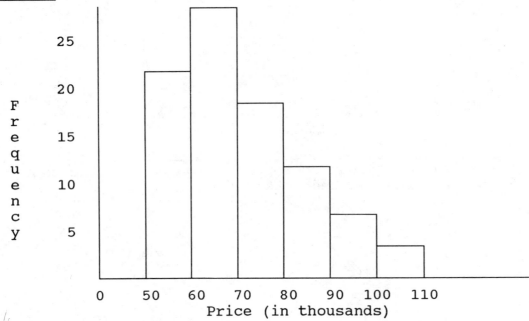

FREQUENCY POLYGON

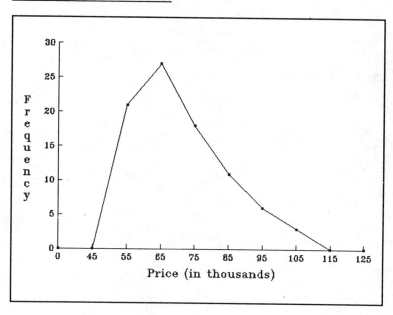

OGIVE

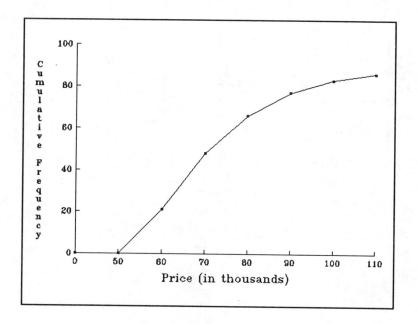

2.19

Price	Cumulative Frequency	Frequency
$1.75 - under $1.90	9	9
$1.90 - under $2.05	14	23
$2.05 - under $2.20	17	40
$2.20 - under $2.35	16	56
$2.35 - under $2.50	18	74
$2.50 - under $2.65	8	82
$2.65 - under $2.80	5	87
	87	

HISTOGRAM

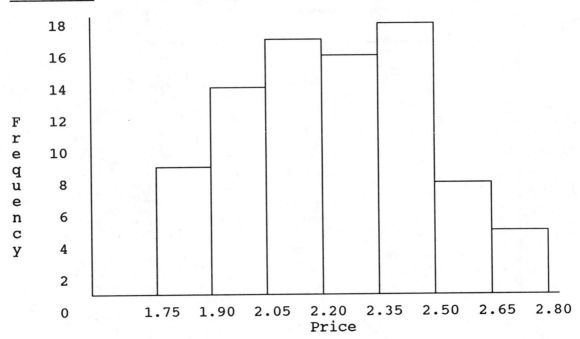

FREQUENCY POLYGON

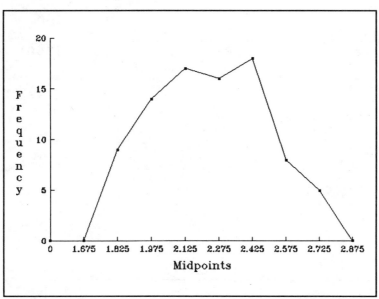

OGIVE

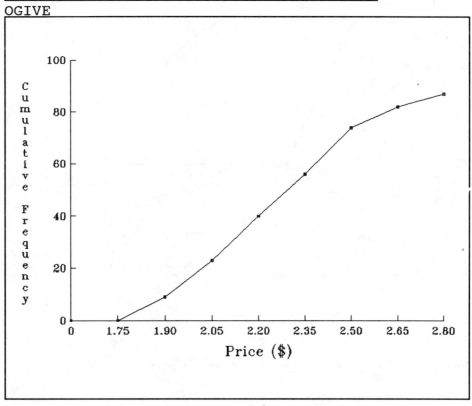

2.21

Company	Number	Proportion		Degrees	
Chevron	1221	1221/3803 =	.3211	.3211(360) =	116°
Amoco	314		.0826		30°
Texaco	500		.1315		47°
Exxon	611		.1607		58°
Shell	567		.1491		54°
Mobil	421		.1107		40°
Arco	24		.0063		2°
Tenneco	145		.0381		14°
TOTAL	3803		1.0001		361°

Pie Chart

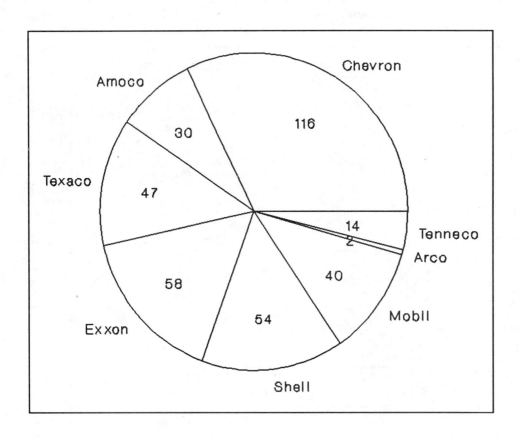

2.23

Country/Continent	Proportion	Degrees
Europe	.512	.512(360) = 184°
Britain	.179	64°
Other	.155	56°
North America	.154	55°
		359°

Pie Chart

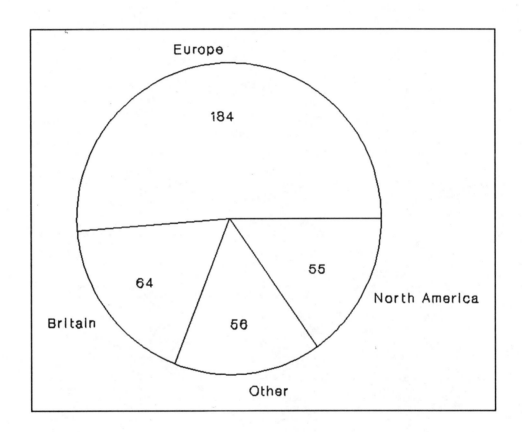

2.25

STEM	LEAF
22	00, 68
23	01, 37, 44, 75
24	05, 37, 48, 60, 68
25	24, 55
26	02, 56, 70, 77
27	42, 60, 64
28	14, 30
29	22, 61, 75, 76, 90, 96
30	02, 10

DESCRIPTIVE STATISTICS

I.   **CHAPTER OBJECTIVES**

The focus of chapter three is on the use of statistical techniques to describe data. Its intent is to enable you to:

1.   Distinguish between central tendency and variability.

2.   Understand conceptually the meaning of mean, median, mode, and range.

3.   Compute a mean, a median, a mode, a range, a variance, a standard deviation, a mean absolute deviation, and a coefficient of variation.

4.   Differentiate between sample and population variance and standard deviation.

5.   Understand the meaning of standard deviation as it is applied using the empirical rule and Chebyshev's theorem.

II. **CHAPTER OUTLINE**

    3.1   Measures of Central Tendency for Ungrouped Data

            Mode

            Median

            Mean

    3.2   Computing the Mean for Grouped Data

    3.3   Measures of Variability for Ungrouped Data

            Range

            Mean Absolute Deviation, Variance, and

                   Standard Deviation

            Population Versus Sample Variance and

                   Standard Deviation

            Computational Formulas for Variance and

                   Standard Deviation

            Meaning of Standard Deviation

               Empirical Rule

               Chebyshev's Theorem

            Z Scores

            Coefficient of Variation

    3.4   Measures of Variability for Grouped Data

    3.5   Skewness

            Skewness and the Relationship of the Mean, Median,

               and Mode

III. **KEY WORDS**

Measures of Central tendency
Mode
Median
Arithmetic Mean
Measures of Variability
Range
Deviations from the Mean
Mean Absolute Deviation

Variance
Standard Deviation
Empirical Rule
Chebyshev's Theorem
Z score
Coefficient of Variation
Skewness

IV.   **STUDY QUESTIONS**

1.   Statistical measures used to yield information about
the center or middle of a group of numbers are called
_____.

2.   The "average" is the _____.

3.   The value occurring most often in a group of numbers is
called _____.

4.   In a set of 110 numbers arranged in order, the median
is located at the _____ position.

5.   If a set of data has an odd number of values, the
median is the middle value.

Consider the data: 5, 4, 6, 6, 4, 5, 3, 2, 6, 4, 6, 3, 5

Answer questions 6-8 using this data.

6.   The mode is _____.

7.   The median is _____.

8.   The mean is _____.

9.   If a set of values is a popoulation, then the mean is
denoted by _____.

10.   In computing a mean for grouped data, the
_____ is used to represent all data in a
given class interval.

11. The mean for the data given below is _____.

Class Interval	Frequency
50 - under 53	14
53 - under 56	17
56 - under 59	29
59 - under 62	31
62 - under 65	18

12. Measures of variability describe the _____ of a set of data.

13. The range of the data given below is _____.

27 65 28 61 34 91 61 37 58 31
43 47 44 20 48 50 49 43 19 52

14. The Mean Absolute Deviation is computed by averaging the _____ of deviations around the mean.

15. Subtracting each value of a set of data from the mean produces _____ from the mean.

16. The sum of the deviations from the mean is always

_____.

17. The variance is the _____ of the standard deviation.

18. The **population** variance is computed by using _____ in the denominator. Whereas, the **sample** variance is computed by using _____ in the denominator.

19. If the sample standard deviation is 9, then the sample variance is _____.

Consider the data below and answer questions 20-22 using the

data: 2, 3, 6, 12

20.   The mean absolute deviation for this data is

      _____.

21.   The sample variance for this data is _____.

22.   The population standard deviation for this data is

      _____.

23.   In estimating what proportion of values fall within so

      many standard deviations of the mean, a researcher

      should use _____ if the shape of the

      distribution of numbers is unknown.

24.   Suppose a distribution of numbers is mound shaped with

      a mean of 150 and a variance of 225. Approximately

      _____ percent of the values fall between 120

      and 180. Between _____ and _____

      fall 99.7% of these values.

25.   The shape of a distribution of numbers is unknown. The

      distribution has a mean of 275 and a standard deviation

      of 12. The value of k for 299 is _____. At

      least _____ percent of the values fall

      between 251 and 299.

26.   Suppose data are normally distributed with a mean of 36

      and a standard deviation of 4.8. The Z score for 30 is

      _____. The Z score for 40 is

      _____.

27. A normal distribution of values has a mean of 74 and a standard deviation of 21. The coefficient of variation for this distribution is _____?

Consider the data below and use the data to answer questions 28-29.

Class Interval	Frequency
2- 4	5
4- 6	12
6- 8	14
8-10	15
10-12	8
12-14	4

28. The sample variance for the data above is

_____.

29. The population standard deviation for the data above is

_____.

30. The distribution _____ is

_____.

31. If a unimodal distibution has a mean of 50, a median of 48, and a mode of 47, the distribution is skewed

_____.

V.   **ANSWERS TO STUDY QUESTIONS**

1. Measures of Central Tendency

2. Mean

3. Mode

4. 55.5^{th}

5. Middle

6. 6

7. 5

8. 4.54

9. μ

10. Class Midpoint

11. 58.11

12. Spread or Dispersion

13. 72

14. Absolute Value

15. Deviations

16. Zero

17. Square

18. N, n-1

19. 81

20. 3.26

21. 20.25

22. 3.897

23. Chebyshev's Theorem

24. 95

25. 2, 75

26. -1.25, 0.83

27. 28.38%

28. 7.54

29. 2.72

30. Skewed Left

31. Right

VI.   SOLUTIONS TO ODD-NUMBERED PROBLEMS IN TEXT.

3.1   Mode

2, 2, 3, 3, 4, 4, 4, 4, 5, 6, 7, 8, 8, 8, 9

The mode = $\boxed{4}$

4 is the most frequently occurring value

3.3   Median
Arrange terms in ascending order:

073, 167, 199, 213, 243, 345, 444, 524, 609, 682
There are 10 terms.
Since there are an even number of terms, the median is the average of the two middle terms:

$$\text{Median} = \frac{243 + 345}{2} = \frac{588}{2} = 294$$

Using the formula, the median is located at the $\frac{n + 1}{2}^{th}$ term

n = 10 therefore $\frac{10 + 1}{2} = \frac{11}{2} = 5.5^{th}$ term.
The median is located halfway between the 5th and 6th terms.

5th term = 243 6th term = 345

Halfway between 243 and 345 is the median = $\boxed{294}$

3.5   Mean

7
-2
5
9
0
-3
-6
-7
-4
-5
2
-8

$\Sigma X = -12$

$$\mu = \frac{\Sigma X}{N} = \frac{-12}{12} = \boxed{-1}$$

$$\overline{X} = \frac{\Sigma X}{N} = \frac{-12}{12} = \boxed{-1}$$

(It is not stated in the problem whether the data represent a population or a sample).

3.7 **Mean and Median**

$$\begin{array}{r} 30{,}000{,}000 \\ 14{,}400{,}000 \\ 5{,}100{,}000 \\ 5{,}000{,}000 \\ 4{,}000{,}000 \\ 3{,}800{,}000 \\ 3{,}500{,}000 \\ \underline{3{,}200{,}000} \end{array}$$

$$\mu = \frac{\Sigma X}{N} = \frac{69{,}000{,}000}{8} = \boxed{8{,}625{,}000}$$

$\Sigma X = 69{,}000{,}000$

Median → There are eight terms.

The median is the $\frac{N + 1}{2}^{th} = \frac{8 + 1}{2}^{th} = 4.5^{th}$ term.

The median is the average of 4,000,000 and 5,000,000 =

$\frac{4{,}000{,}000 + 5{,}000{,}000}{2} = \boxed{4{,}500{,}000}$

The median value can be used to show approximately how much attendance a middle size part of the largest eight parks is. It also demonstrates how large Disney World and Disneyland are compared to the other parks in attendance. (30,000,000 and 14,400,000 compared to the middle size attendance figure, 4,500,000).

The average is useful in determining exact numbers of park attendees in estimating such things as total park potential for concessions, etc.

3.9 Mean and Median of:

167.9
154.5
112.5
106.9
73.4
53.5
45.9
44.3
40.5
40.0

$\Sigma X = 839.4$

$\mu = \dfrac{\Sigma X}{N} = \dfrac{839.4}{10} =$ $\boxed{\text{83.94 tons (100,000)}}$

Median - Since there are ten terms, the median is located at

$$\frac{N + 1^{th}}{2} = \frac{10 + 1^{th}}{2} = \frac{11^{th}}{2} = 5.5^{th} \text{ term}$$

The median is the average of 53.5 and 73.4

Median $= \dfrac{53.5 + 73.4}{2} = \dfrac{126.9}{2} =$ $\boxed{\text{63.45 tons (100,000)}}$

Since the mean (83.94) is larger than the median (63.45), there are more extreme values at the larger end of the values.

3.11 Mean

Class	f	m	fm
0 - 2	39	1	39
2 - 4	37	3	81
4 - 6	16	5	80
6 - 8	15	7	105
8 - 10	10	9	90
10 - 12	8	11	88
12 - 14	6	13	78
	$\Sigma f=121$		$\Sigma fm=561$

$\mu = \dfrac{\Sigma fm}{\Sigma f} = \dfrac{561}{121} =$ $\boxed{4.64}$

3.13 **Mean**

Class	f	m	fm
0 - 1	31	0.5	15.5
1 - 2	57	1.5	85.5
2 - 3	24	2.5	65.0
3 - 4	14	3.5	49.0
4 - 5	6	4.5	27.0
5 - 6	3	5.5	16.5
	Σf=137		Σfm=258.5

$$\mu = \frac{\Sigma fm}{\Sigma f} = \frac{258.5}{137} = \boxed{1.89}$$

3.15

Class	f	m	fm
0 - 20,000	16	10,000	160,000
20,000 - 40,000	11	30,000	330,000
40,000 - 60,000	9	50,000	450,000
60,000 - 80,000	4	70,000	280,000
80,000 - 100,000	7	90,000	680,000
100,000 - 120,000	2	110,000	220,000
120,000 - 140,000	0	130,000	0
140,000 - 160,000	0	150,000	0
160,000 - 180,000	0	170,000	0
180,000 - 200,000	1	190,000	190,000
	Σf=50		Σfm=2,260,000

$$\mu = \frac{\Sigma fm}{\Sigma f} = \frac{2,260,000}{50} = \boxed{45,200 \text{ farms}}$$

The grouped mean (45,200) is greater than the mean (43,464.4) for ungrouped data because the class midpoint is used for each class to·compute the group mean. Apparently, the individual numbers of farms per state per class do not average to the class midpoints in all cases.

3.17

X	$\lvert X-\overline{X} \rvert$	$(X-\overline{X})^2$
4	$\lvert 4-1 \rvert = 3$	9
-3	$\lvert -3-1 \rvert = 4$	16
0	1	1
-5	6	36
2	1	1
9	8	64
-4	5	25
5	4	16
$\Sigma X = 8$	$\Sigma \lvert X-\overline{X} \rvert = 32$	$\Sigma (X-\overline{X})^2 = 168$

$$\overline{X} = \frac{\Sigma X}{n} = \frac{8}{8} = 1$$

a)   Range $= 9 - (-5) =$ $\boxed{14}$

b)   M.A.D. $= \dfrac{\Sigma \lvert X - \overline{X} \rvert}{n} = \dfrac{32}{8} =$ $\boxed{4}$

c) $S^2 = \dfrac{\Sigma (X - \overline{X})^2}{n-1} = \dfrac{168}{7} =$ $\boxed{24}$

d) $S = \sqrt{\dfrac{\Sigma (X-\overline{X})^2}{n-1}} = \sqrt{24}$

$= \boxed{4.899}$

3.19 $s^2 = \boxed{500.671}$ $S = \boxed{22.376}$

3.21

X	$|X-\overline{X}|$	$(X-\overline{X})^2$
4.8	$|4.8-4.933|=$ 0.133	.0177
1.3	3.633	13.1987
6.0	1.067	1.1385
3.6	1.333	1.7769
5.1	0.167	.0279
3.9	1.033	1.0671
6.7	1.767	3.1223
4.8	0.133	.0177
7.1	2.167	4.6959
5.4	0.467	.2181
8.3	3.367	11.3367
2.2	2.733	7.4693
$\Sigma X=$ 59.2	$\Sigma|X-\overline{X}|=$ 18.000	$\Sigma(X-\overline{X})^2=$ 44.0868

$$\overline{X} = \frac{\Sigma X}{n} = \frac{59.2}{12} = 4.933$$

a) $\text{M.A.D.} = \frac{\Sigma|X - \overline{X}|}{n} = \frac{18}{12} = \boxed{1.5}$

b) $S^2 = \frac{\Sigma(X - \overline{X})^2}{n-1} = \frac{44.0868}{11} = \boxed{4.008}$

c) $S = \sqrt{\frac{\Sigma(X-\overline{X})^2}{n-1}}$

$= \boxed{2.002}$

3.23 $\mu = 38$ $\sigma = 6$
            between 26 and 50:

      $X_1 - \mu = 50 - 38 = 12$
      $X_2 - \mu = 26 - 38 = -12$

      $\dfrac{X_1 - \mu}{\sigma} = \dfrac{12}{6} = 2$ Standard deviations

      $\dfrac{X_2 - \mu}{\sigma} = \dfrac{-12}{6} = -2$ Standard deviations

      $K = 2$
      Since the distribution is <u>not</u> normal, use Chebyshev's
      theorem:

$1 - \dfrac{1}{K^2} = 1 - \dfrac{1}{2^2} = 1 - \dfrac{1}{4} = \dfrac{3}{4} = .75$

> at least 75% of the values will fall between 26 and 50

between 14 and 62? $\mu = 38$ $\sigma = 6$

$X_1 - \mu = 62 - 38 = 24$

$X_2 - \mu = 14 - 38 = -24$

$\dfrac{X_1 - \mu}{\sigma} = \dfrac{+24}{6} = 4$

$\dfrac{X_2 - \mu}{\sigma} = \dfrac{-24}{6} = -4$

$K = 4$

$1 - \dfrac{1}{K^2} = 1 - \dfrac{1}{4^2} = 1 - \dfrac{1}{16} = \dfrac{15}{16} = .9375$

> at least 93.75% of the values fall between 14 and 62.

between what 2 values do at least 89% of the values fall?

$$1 - \frac{1}{K^2} = .89$$

$$1 - .89 = \frac{1}{K^2}$$

$$.11 = \frac{1}{K^2}$$

$$.11 \ K^2 = 1$$

$$K^2 = \frac{1}{.11}$$

$$K^2 = 9.09$$

$$K = 3.015$$

With $\mu = 38$, $\sigma = 6$ and $K = 3.015$ at least 89% of the values fall within:

$$\mu \pm 3.015 \ \sigma$$

$$38 \pm 3.015 \ (6)$$

$$38 \pm 18.09$$

$$\boxed{19.91 \text{ and } 56.09}$$

3.25 $\mu = 29$ $\sigma = 4$

$X_1 - \mu = 21 - 29 = -8$
$X_2 - \mu = 37 - 29 = +8$

$\dfrac{X_1 - \mu}{\sigma} = \dfrac{-8}{4} = -2$ Standard deviations

$\dfrac{X_2 - \mu}{\sigma} = \dfrac{+8}{4} = +2$ Standard deviations

---
Since the distribution is normal, the empirical rule
states that 95% of the values fall within $\mu \pm 2\sigma$.

Exceed 37 days:

Since 95% fall between 21 and 37 days, 5% fall outside this
range. Since the normal distribution is symmetrical 2½%
fall below 21 and above 37.

Thus, 2½% lie above the value of 37.

Exceed 41 days:

$\dfrac{X - \mu}{\sigma} = \dfrac{41 - 29}{4} = \dfrac{12}{4} = 3$ Standard deviations

The empirical rule states that 99.7% of the values fall
within $\mu \pm 3\sigma = 29 \pm 3(4) = 29 \pm 12$

between 17 and 41, 99.7% of the values will fall.
0.3% will fall outside this range.

Half of this or .15% will lie above 41.

Less than 25: $\mu = 29$ $\sigma = 4$

$\dfrac{X - \mu}{\sigma} = \dfrac{25 - 29}{4} = \dfrac{-4}{4} = -1$ Standard deviation

According to the empirical rule:

$\mu \pm 1\sigma$ contains 68% of the values
$29 \pm 1(4)$
29 ± 4
from 25 to 33.

32% lie outside this range with ½(32%) = | 16% less than 25.

3.27 $\mu = 17.6$ $\sigma = 2.9$

$Z_1 = \dfrac{X_1 - \mu}{\sigma} = \dfrac{19 - 17.6}{2.9} =$ $\boxed{.48}$

$Z_2 = \dfrac{X_2 - \mu}{\sigma} = \dfrac{22 - 17.6}{2.9} =$ $\boxed{1.52}$

$Z_3 = \dfrac{X_3 - \mu}{\sigma} = \dfrac{15 - 17.6}{2.9} =$ $\boxed{-.9}$

$Z_4 = \dfrac{X_4 - \mu}{\sigma} = \dfrac{10 - 17.6}{2.9} =$ $\boxed{-2.62}$

   The classrooms with positive Z scores are above the national average in size. The classrooms with negative Z scores are below the national average in size. Using the empirical rule as a rough guide, the Z scores give some idea what percentages of classroom sizes lie above or below that particular room.

3.29   <u>Mobile</u>   <u>New York City</u>
            $\mu_1 = 61$ $\mu_2 = 37$
            $\sigma_1 = 12$ $\sigma_2 = 9$

$CV_1 = \dfrac{\sigma_1(100\%)}{\mu_1} = \dfrac{12(100\%)}{61} =$ $\boxed{19.67\%}$ <u>Mobile</u>

$CV_2 = \dfrac{\sigma_2(100\%)}{\mu_2} = \dfrac{9(100\%)}{37} =$ $\boxed{24.32\%}$ <u>New York City</u>

New York has a higher relative variability in January than Mobile.

3.31

Class	f	m	fm	fm^2
5 - 9	20	7	140	980
9 - 13	18	11	198	2,178
13 - 17	8	15	120	1,800
17 - 21	6	19	114	2,166
21 - 25	2	23	46	1,058
	$\Sigma f=$ 54		$\Sigma fm=$ 618	$\Sigma fm^2=$ 8,182

$$S^2 = \frac{\Sigma fm^2 - \frac{(\Sigma fm)^2}{n}}{n-1} = \frac{8,182 - \frac{(618)^2}{54}}{53} = \frac{8,182 - 7,071.7}{53}$$

$$S^2 = \frac{1,109.3}{53} = \boxed{20.9}$$

$$S = \sqrt{S^2} = \sqrt{20.9}$$

$$= \boxed{4.57}$$

3.33

Class	f	m	fm	fm^2
10 - 20	7	15	105	1,575
20 - 30	6	25	150	3,750
30 - 40	3	35	105	3,675
40 - 50	3	45	135	6,075
50 - 60	1	55	55	3,025
	Σf= 20		Σfm= 550	Σfm^2= 18,100

$$\mu = \frac{\Sigma fm}{N} = \frac{\Sigma fm}{\Sigma f} = \frac{550}{20} = \boxed{27.5}$$

$$\sigma = \sqrt{\frac{\Sigma fm^2 - \frac{(\Sigma fm)^2}{N}}{N}} = \sqrt{\frac{18,100 - \frac{(550)^2}{20}}{20}} =$$

$$\sqrt{\frac{18,100 - 15,125}{20}} = \sqrt{\frac{2,975}{20}} = \sqrt{148.75}$$

$$\sigma = \boxed{12.2}$$

3.35

mean = 51
median = 54
mode = 59

The distribution is skewed to the left. More people are older but the most extreme ages are younger ages.

3.37 Arranging the values in an ordered array:

1, 1, 1, 1, 1, 1, 1, 1, 2, 2, 2, 2, 2, 2, 2, 2, 2, 2, 2,
3, 3, 3, 3, 3, 3, 4, 4, 5, 6, 8

$$\overline{X} = \frac{\Sigma X}{n} = \frac{75}{30} = \boxed{2.5}$$

Mode = $\boxed{2}$ (There are eleven 2's)

Median: There are n = 30 terms.

The median is located at $\frac{n + 1}{2}^{th} = \frac{30 + 1}{2} = \frac{21}{2} = 15.5^{th}$ position.

Median is the average of the 15th and 16th value.

However, since these are both 2, the median is $\boxed{2.}$

3.39 Compute the sample variance and standard deviation:

$$\Sigma X = 1,523$$

$$\Sigma X^2 = 65,715$$

$$n = 40$$

$$S^2 = \boxed{198.12}$$

$$S = \boxed{14.08}$$

3.41

X	X^2
17.4	302.76
17.0	289.00
16.5	272.25
16.0	256.00
15.7	246.49
14.7	216.09
14.7	216.09
14.6	213.16
14.2	201.64
13.8	190.44

$\Sigma X = 154.6$ $\Sigma X^2 = 2{,}403.92$

$$\mu = \frac{\Sigma X}{N} = \frac{154.6}{10} = \boxed{15.46}$$

$$\sigma^2 = \frac{\Sigma X^2 - \frac{(\Sigma X)^2}{N}}{N} = \frac{2403.92 - \frac{(154.6)^2}{10}}{10} =$$

$$= \frac{2403.92 - 2390.12}{10} = \frac{13.804}{10} = \boxed{1.3804}$$

$$\sigma = \sqrt{\frac{\Sigma X^2 - \frac{(\Sigma X)^2}{N}}{N}} = \sqrt{1.3804}$$

$$= \boxed{1.175}$$

3.43   Distances ordered in an array:

X	$\lvert X-\mu \rvert$	$(X-\mu)^2$
395	$\lvert 395-403.5 \rvert = 8.5$	72.25
400	3.5	12.25
400	3.5	12.25
400	3.5	12.25
400	3.5	12.25
402	1.5	2.25
404	0.5	.25
404	0.5	.25
405	1.5	2.25
408	4.5	20.25
410	6.5	42.25
414	10.5	110.25
$\Sigma X = 4,842$	$\Sigma \lvert X-\mu \rvert = 48.0$	$\Sigma \lvert X-\mu \rvert^2 = 299.00$

a) $\mu = \dfrac{\Sigma X}{N} = \dfrac{4842}{12} = \boxed{403.5}$

b)   Median: $\dfrac{n + 1^{th}}{2}$ term $= \dfrac{12 + 1^{th}}{2} = 6.5^{th}$ Term

Average 402 and 404 $= \dfrac{402 + 404}{2} = \boxed{403}$

c)   M.A.D. $= \dfrac{\Sigma \lvert X - \mu \rvert}{N} = \dfrac{48}{12} = \boxed{4.0}$

d) $\sigma^2 = \dfrac{\Sigma (X - \mu)^2}{N} = \dfrac{299}{12} = \boxed{24.92}$

$\sigma = \sqrt{\sigma^2} = \sqrt{24.92}$

$= \boxed{4.99}$

e)   X = 400 $Z = \dfrac{X - \mu}{\sigma} = \dfrac{400 - 403.5}{4.99} = \dfrac{-3.5}{4.99} = \boxed{-.70}$

3.45

X	X^2
.94	.8836
.94	.8836
.98	.9604
1.03	1.0609
1.05	1.1025
1.08	1.1664
1.12	1.2544
1.15	1.3225
1.15	1.3225
1.19	1.4161
$\Sigma X = 10.63$	$\Sigma X^2 = 11.3729$

a) mean: $\overline{X} = \dfrac{\Sigma X}{n} = \dfrac{10.63}{10} =$ $\boxed{1.063}$

b) median: $n = 10$ $\dfrac{n + 1^{th}}{2}$ term $= \dfrac{10 + 1}{2} = \dfrac{11}{2} = 5.5^{th}$

median = average 1.05, 1.08 = $\dfrac{1.05 + 1.08}{2} =$ $\boxed{1.065}$

c) Mode: There are two modes: $\boxed{.94 \text{ and } 1.15}$

d) Variance: $s^2 = \dfrac{\Sigma X^2 - \dfrac{(\Sigma X)^2}{n}}{n-1} = \dfrac{11.3729 - \dfrac{(10.63)^2}{10}}{9} =$

$\dfrac{11.3729 - 11.2997}{9}$

$S^2 = \dfrac{.732}{9} =$ $\boxed{.00813}$

e) Standard deviation: $S = \sqrt{s^2}$ $= \sqrt{.00813}$

$=$ $\boxed{.09}$

f) $X_A = .94$ $Z_A = \dfrac{X_A - \mu}{\sigma} = \dfrac{.94 - 1.063}{.09} = \dfrac{-.123}{.09} =$ $\boxed{-1.37}$

The gasoline price in Atlanta is well below the average.

3.47 Arranging the data in an ordered array:

X
179,000
201,900
239,000
250,000
255,000
259,000
261,000
275,000
279,000
297,000
303,000
335,000

$\Sigma X = 3,144,900$

$\Sigma X^2 = 8.3836161 \times 10^{11}$

Mean $= \overline{X} = \dfrac{\Sigma X}{n} = \dfrac{3,133,900}{12} = \boxed{261,158.3}$

Median: $n = 12$ $\dfrac{12 + 1}{2} = \dfrac{13}{2} = 6.5^{th}$ term

$\qquad\qquad$ = average 259,000 and 261,000 =

$\qquad\qquad \dfrac{259,000 + 261,000}{2} = \boxed{260,000}$

Range: $335,000 - 179,000 = \boxed{156,000}$

Standard deviation:

$$S = \sqrt{\dfrac{\Sigma X^2 - \dfrac{(\Sigma X)^2}{n}}{n-1}} = \sqrt{\dfrac{8.3836161 \times 10^{11} - \dfrac{9.82133 \times 10^{12}}{12}}{11}} =$$

$$\sqrt{\dfrac{8.3836 \times 10^{11} - 8.184441 \times 10^{11}}{11}} = \sqrt{1,810,682,652}$$

$$= \boxed{42,552.1}$$

3.49

Class	f	m	fm	fm^2
15 – 20	5	17.5	87.5	1,531.25
20 – 25	12	22.5	270.0	6,075.00
25 – 30	19	27.5	522.5	14,368.75
30 – 35	29	32.5	942.5	30,631.25
35 – 40	44	37.5	1,650.0	61,875.00
40 – 45	37	42.5	1,572.5	66,831.25
45 – 50	18	47.5	855.0	40,612.50
50 – 55	6	52.5	315.0	16,537.50
	$\Sigma f=170$		$\Sigma fm=6,215.0$	$\Sigma fm^2=238,462.50$

a)   Mean: $\overline{X} = \dfrac{\Sigma fm}{n} = \dfrac{\Sigma fm}{\Sigma f} = \dfrac{6,215}{170} =$ $\boxed{36.56}$

b)   Variance: $S^2 = \dfrac{\Sigma fm^2 - \dfrac{(\Sigma fm)^2}{n}}{n-1} =$

$$\dfrac{238,462.5 - \dfrac{(6,215)^2}{170}}{169} = \dfrac{238,462.5 - 227,213.1}{169}$$

$$= \dfrac{11,249.4}{169} = \boxed{66.56}$$

Standard Deviation:

$$S = \sqrt{S^2} = \sqrt{66.56}$$

$$= \boxed{8.16}$$

3.51 $CV_1 = \dfrac{\sigma_1}{\mu_1}(100\%) = \dfrac{8.2}{29}(100\%) =$ $\boxed{28.3\%}$

$CV_2 = \dfrac{\sigma_2}{\mu_2}(100\%) = \dfrac{8.7}{41}(100\%) =$ $\boxed{21.2\%}$

$CV_3 = \dfrac{\sigma_3}{\mu_3}(100\%) = \dfrac{11.0}{37}(100\%) =$ $\boxed{29.7\%}$

Section 3 had the highest coefficient of variation.
Section 2 had the lowest coefficient of variation.

The coefficients of variation tell the variation of each
section's examinations relative to the section's mean.

3.53 CV_x = $\dfrac{\sigma_x}{\mu_x}(100\%)$ = $\dfrac{3.45}{32}(100\%)$ = $\boxed{10.78\%}$

              CV_Y = $\dfrac{\sigma_Y}{\mu_Y}(100\%)$ = $\dfrac{5.40}{84}(100\%)$ = $\boxed{6.43\%}$

Stock X has a greater relative variability.

3.55   Mean $41,600
                Median $35,700
                Mode $33,000

Since these three measures are not equal, the distribution
is skewed.

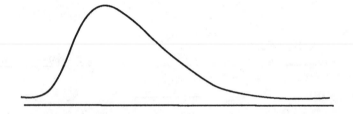

The distribution is skewed to the right. Often, the median
is preferred in reporting income data because it yields
information about the middle of the data while ignoring
extremes.

PROBABILITY

I. **CHAPTER OBJECTIVES**

The main objective of Chapter four is to help you understand the basic principles of probability, specifically enabling you to:

1. Comprehend the different ways of assigning probability.

2. Utilize the four main types of probability.

3. Select the appropriate law of probability to use in solving problems.

4. Solve problems using the laws of probability.

II. **CHAPTER OUTLINE**

4.1 Introduction to Probability

4.2 Methods of Assigning Probabilities

Classical Method of Assigning Probabilities

Relative Frequency of Occurrence

Subjective Probability

4.3 Structure of Probability

Event

Elementary Events

Sample Space

Unions and Intersections

Mutually Exclusive Events

Independent Events

Collectively Exhaustive Events

Complimentary Events

4.4 Four Types of Probability

4.5 Addition Law

Special Rule of Addition

4.6 Multiplicative Law

Special Law of Multiplication

4.7 Law of Conditional Probability

Independent Events

4.8   Revision of Probabilities: Bayes' Rule

4.9   Using the Multiplicative Law with Multiple Trials

      Problems with Replacement

      Problems without Replacement

III. **KEY WORDS**

Classical Probability
Experiment
Event
A Priori
Relative Frequency of Occurrence
Subjective Probability
Elementary Events
Sample Space
Set Notation
Union
Intersection

Mutually Exclusive Events
Independent Events
Collectively Exhaustive
   Events
Complement of an Event
Marginal Probability
Union Probability
Joint Probability
Conditional Probability
Bayes' Rule
Combinations

IV.   **STUDY QUESTIONS**

1.   The _____ method of assigning probabilities
     relies on the insight or feelings of the person
     determining the probabilities.

2.   If probabilities are determined "a priori" to an
     experiment using rules and laws, then the
     _____ method of assigning probabilities is
     being used.

3.   The range of possibilities for probability values is
     from _____ to _____.

4.   Suppose a technician keeps track of all defects in raw
     materials for a single day and uses this information to
     determine the probability of finding a defect in raw
     materials the next day. She is using the
     _____ method of assigning probabilities.

5.   The outcome of an experiment is called a(n)
     _____. If these outcomes cannot be
     decomposed further, then they are referred to as
     _____ _____.

6.   A population consists of the odd numbers between 1 and
     9 inclusive. If a researcher randomly samples numbers
     from the population three at a time, the sample space
     is _____.

7.   Let A = {2,3,5,6,7,9} and B = {1,3,4,6,7,9}
     A U B = _____ and A ∩ B = _____.

8. If the occurrence of one event does not affect the occurrence of the other event, then the events are said to be _____.

9. The outcome of the roll of one die is said to be _____ of the outcome of the roll of another die.

10. The event of rolling a three on a die and the event of rolling an even number on the same roll with the same die are _____.

11. If the probability of the intersection of two events is zero, then the events are said to be _____.

12. If three objects are selected from a bin, one at a time with replacement, the outcomes of each selection are _____.

13. Suppose a population consists of a manufacturing facility's 1600 workers. Suppose an experiment is conducted in which a worker is randomly selected. If an event is the selection of a worker over 40 years old, then the event of selecting a worker 40 years or younger is called the _____ of the first event.

14. The probability of selecting X given that Y has occurred is called a _____ probability.

15. The probability of X is called a _____ probability.

16. The probability of X or Y occurring is called a
     _____ probability.

17. The probability of X and Y occurring is called a
     _____ probability.

18. Only one of the four types of probability does not use
     the total possible outcomes in the denominator when
     calculating the probability. This type of probability
     is called _____ probability.

19. If the $P(A|B) = P(A)$, then the events A, B are
     _____ events.

20. If the $P(X) = .53$, the $P(Y) = .12$, and the
     $P(X \cap Y) = .07$, then $P(X \cup Y) =$ _____.

21. If the $P(X) = .26$, the $P(Y) = .31$, and X, Y are
     mutually exclusive, then $P(X \cup Y) =$ _____.

22. In a company, 47% of the employees wear glasses, 60% of
     the employees are women, and 28% of the employees are
     women and wear glasses. Complete the probability
     matrix below for this problem.

                          WEAR GLASSES
                           YES   NO
                      ┌────────┬────────┐
                Men   │   │   │
        Gender   ├────────┼────────┤
                Women │   │   │
                      └────────┴────────┘

23. Suppose that in another company, 40% of the workers are
     part time and 80% of the part time workers are men.
     The probability of randomly selecting a company worker
     who is both part time and a man is _____.

24. The probability of tossing three coins in a row and getting all tails is _____. This is an application of the _____ law of multiplication because each toss is _____.

25. Suppose 70% of all cars purchased in America are U.S.A. made and that 18% of all cars purchased in America are both U.S.A. made and are red. The probability that a randomly selected car purchased in America is red given that it is U.S.A. made is _____.

Use the matrix below to answer questions 26-35:

	C	D	
A	.35	.31	.66
B	.14	.20	.34
	.49	.51	1.00

26. The probability of A and C occurring is _____.

27. The probability of A or D occurring is _____.

28. The probability of D occurring is _____.

29. The probability of B occurring given C is _____.

30. The probability of B and D occurring is _____.

31. The probability of C and D occurring is _____.

32. The probability of C or D occurring is _____.

33. The probability of C occurring given D is _____.

34. The probability of C occurring given A is _____.

35. The probability of C or B occurring is _____.

36. Another name for revision of probabilities is

    _____.

37. Suppose the prior probabilities of A and B are .57 and
    .43 respectively. Suppose that $P(E|A)$ = .24 and
    $P(E|B)$ = .56. If E is known to have occurred, then the
    revised probability of A occurring is _____
    and of B occurring is _____.

38. Suppose that five items are selected from a population
    and that we want to determine the probability that
    three of these five items have a given characteristic.
    The number of different sequences of five items with
    three having the given characteristic is

    _____.

39. Suppose that 8% of a population purchases brand X
    margarine. If six people are randomly selected from
    the population, the probability that exactly one person
    will be a brand X margarine purchaser is

    _____.

40. There are seven engineers on staff. Five of these
    seven engineers are electrical engineers. Suppose
    three different engineers are randomly selected from
    the staff. The probability that exactly two are
    electrical engineers is _____.

V.   **ANSWERS TO STUDY QUESTIONS**

1. Subjective

2. Classical

3. 0, 1

4. Relative Frequency

5. Event, Elementary Events

6. {(1,3,5), (1,3,7), (1,3,9), (1,5,7), (1,5,9), (1,7,9), (3,5,7), (3,5,9), (3,7,9), (5,7,9)}

7. {1,2,3,4,5,6,7,9}, {3,6,7,9}

8. Independent

9. Independent

10. Mutually Exclusive

11. Mutually Exclusive

12. Independent

13. Complement

14. Conditional

15. Marginal

16. Union

17. Joint or Intersection

18. Conditional

19. Independent

20. .58

21. .57

22.

WEAR GLASSES

Gender		YES	NO	
	Men	.19	.21	.40
	Women	.28	.32	.60
		.47	.53	1.00

23. .32

24. 1/8 = .125, Special, Independent

25. .2571

26. .35

27. .86

28. .51

29. .2857

30. .20

31. .0000

32. 1.00

33. .0000

34. .5303

35. .69

36. Bayes' Rule

37. .3623, .6377

38. $_5C_3$ = 10

39. .3164

40. .5714

VI. SOLUTIONS TO ODD-NUMBERED PROBLEMS IN TEXT

4.1 Sample Space
$\{H_1\ H_2\ H_3,\quad T_1\ H_2\ H_3,\quad H_1\ T_2\ H_3,\quad H_1\ H_2\ T_3,$
$\ \ T_1\ T_2\ H_3,\quad T_1\ H_2\ T_3,\quad H_1\ T_2\ T_3,\quad T_1\ T_2\ T_3\}$

Probability of 1 head = $\dfrac{3}{8}$

$$\boxed{\begin{array}{c}\{H_1\ T_2\ T_3,\quad T_1\ H_2\ T_3,\quad T_1\ T_2\ H_3,\}\\ \text{Out of total sample space}\end{array}}$$

4.3 die 1 → 6 possibilities
die 2 → 6 possibilities
die 3 → 6 possibilities

For each die there are 6 possibilities.

Total possible elementary events:

6 x 6 x 6 = 216 elementary events

One example of mutually exclusive elementary events is:

(2, 3, 4) and (5, 5, 4)

Two outcomes are mutually exclusive if the three digits appearing on the one trial are not exactly the same as the three digits on the second trial.

Each die tossed is independent of the other dice.

4.5 X = {1, 3, 5, 7, 8, 9}, Y = {2, 4, 7, 9}
and Z = {1, 2, 3, 4, 7,}

a) X U Z = $\boxed{\{1,\ 2,\ 3,\ 4,\ 5,\ 7,\ 8,\ 9\}}$

b) X ∩ Y = $\boxed{\{7,\ 9\}}$

c) X ∩ Z = $\boxed{\{1,\ 3,\ 7\}}$

d) X U Y U Z = $\boxed{\{1,\ 2,\ 3,\ 4,\ 5,\ 7,\ 8,\ 9\}}$

e)   X ∩ Y ∩ Z =   {7}

f)   (X U Y)∩ Z = {1, 2, 3, 4, 5, 7, 8, 9)∩

      {1, 2, 3, 4, 7} =   {1, 2, 3, 4, 7}

g)   (Y ∩ Z) U (X ∩ Y) = {2, 4, 7} U {7, 9} =   {2, 4, 7, 9}

4.7   Examples of some every day events that are independent:
       you go to class, a store on the far side of town has a
       sale on milk, four blocks from the court house a cat
       gets caught in a tree, channel 13 takes a station
       break, etc.

       Daily life events that are mutually exclusive:

       1)   you are in class on campus - you are at home watching
             television
       2)   fire truck number one is at the scene of a residential
             house fire, fire truck number one is parked in the
             station.
       3)   the large tree in the backyard is dying - the large
             tree in the backyard is not dying.

4.9   If A = {2, 6, 12, 24} and the population is the positive
       even numbers through 30,

       $\overline{A}$ =   {4, 8, 10, 14, 16, 18, 20, 22, 26, 28, 30}

4.11

	D	E	F	
A	5	8	12	25
B	10	6	4	20
C	8	2	5	15
	23	16	21	60

a) $P(A \cup D) = P(A) + P(D) - P(A \cap D)$

$= \dfrac{25}{60} + \dfrac{23}{60} - \dfrac{5}{60} = \dfrac{43}{60} \qquad = \boxed{.7167}$

b) $P(E \cup D) = P(E) + P(B) - P(E \cap B)$

$= \dfrac{16}{60} + \dfrac{20}{60} - \dfrac{6}{60} = \dfrac{30}{60} \qquad = \boxed{.5000}$

c) $P(D \cup E) = P(D) + P(E) = \dfrac{23}{60} + \dfrac{16}{60} = \dfrac{39}{60} = \boxed{.65}$

d) $P(A \cup B \cup C) = P(A) + P(B) + P(C)$

$= \dfrac{25}{60} + \dfrac{20}{60} + \dfrac{15}{60} = \dfrac{60}{60} \qquad \boxed{1.00}$

e) $P(B \cup E \cup F) = P(B) + P(E) + P(F) - P(B \cap E) - P(B \cap F)$

$= \dfrac{20}{60} + \dfrac{16}{60} + \dfrac{21}{60} - \dfrac{6}{60} - \dfrac{4}{60} = \dfrac{47}{60} = \boxed{.7833}$

4.13   A = event - flown in an airplane at least once
        T = event - ridden in a train at least once

        P(A) = .47
        P(T) = .28

P (ridden either a train or an airplane) =
$P(A \cup T) = P(A) + P(T) - P(A \cap T) = .47 + .28 - P(A \cap T)$

Cannot solve this problem without knowing the probability of the intersection. We need to know the probability of the intersection of A and T, the proportion who have ridden both.

4.15 Of the people in the 25-49 age bracket:

Let WL = Women in Labor force
ML = Men in Labor force
WM = Women married
MM = Men married

P(WL) = .75
P(ML) = .90
P(WM) = .78
P(MM) = .74
P(WM ∩ WL) = .61
P(MM ∩ ML) = .65

a) P(WM U WL) = P(WM) + P(WL) - P(WM ∩ WL)

= .78 + .75 - .61 = $\boxed{.92}$

b) P(WM U WL) - P(WM ∩ WL) = .92 - .61 = $\boxed{.31}$

c) P(MM U ML) = P(MM) + P(ML) - P(MM ∩ ML)
= .74 + .90 - .65 = $\boxed{.99}$

d) P(notMM ∩ notML) = 1 - P(MM U ML) = 1 - .99 = $\boxed{.01}$

e) P(MM ∩ ML) = $\boxed{.65}$

4.17   Let T = review transcript
                        F = consider faculty references

$$P(T) = .54$$
$$P(F) = .44$$
$$P(T \cap F) = .35$$

a)   P(F) = $\boxed{.44}$

b)   P(F ∩ T) = P(T ∩ F) = $\boxed{.35}$

c)   P(F U T) = P(F) + P(T) - P(F ∩ T) = .44 + .54 - .35 = $\boxed{.63}$

d)   P(F U T) - P(F ∩ T) = .63 - .35 = $\boxed{.28}$

e)   1 - P(F U T) = 1 - .63 = $\boxed{.37}$

4.19 Dice are independent

P(5 green ∩ 4 white) = P(5 green) ∩ P(4 white)

$$\frac{1}{6} \cdot \frac{1}{6} = \frac{1}{36} = \boxed{.0278}$$

To compute the probability of a 3 on one die and a 1 on the other, we must understand that it can happen two ways:

(3 green and 1 white) or (1 green and 3 white)

P(3 green ∩ 1 white) U P(1 green ∩ 3 white)

P(3 green) · P(1 white) + P(1 green) · P(3 white)

$$\frac{1}{6} \cdot \frac{1}{6} + \frac{1}{6} \cdot \frac{1}{6} = \frac{2}{36} = \boxed{.0556}$$

4.21 **Without replacement:**

$P(A_1 \cap A_2 \cap A_3) =$

$P(A_1) \cdot P(A_2|A_1) \cdot P(A_3|A_1 \cap A_2)$

$$\frac{4}{52} \cdot \frac{3}{51} \cdot \frac{2}{50} = \frac{24}{132,600} = \boxed{.00018}$$

$P(J_1 \cap Q_2 \cap K_3) =$

$P(J_1) \cdot P(Q_2|J_1) \cdot P(K_3|J_1 \cap Q_2) =$

$$\frac{4}{52} \cdot \frac{4}{51} \cdot \frac{4}{50} = \frac{64}{132,600} = \boxed{.00048}$$

With replacement:

$P(A_1 \cap A_2 \cap A_3) = P(A_1) \cdot P(A_2) \cdot P(A_3) =$

$$\frac{4}{52} \cdot \frac{4}{52} \cdot \frac{4}{52} = \frac{64}{140,608} = \boxed{.00046}$$

The probability of drawing 3 aces in a row increases with replacement.

4.23

	D	E	F	
A	.12	.13	.08	.33
B	.18	.09	.04	.31
C	.06	.24	.06	.36
	.36	.46	.18	1.00

a) $P(E \cap B) =$ $\boxed{.09}$

b) $P(C \cap F) =$ $\boxed{.06}$

c) $P(E \cap D) =$ $\boxed{.00}$

4.25 Let C = cans
         A = aluminum

a) $P(\text{not } C) = P(\overline{C}) = 1 - P(C) = 1 - .48 =$ $\boxed{.52}$

b) $P(\text{not } A) = P(\overline{A}) = 1 - P(A)$
      but $P(A) = P(C) \cdot P(A|C) = .48(.94) =$ $\boxed{.4512}$

      $P(\overline{A}) = 1 - P(A) = 1 - .4512 = \boxed{.5488}$

c) $P(A) = P(C) \cdot P(A|C) = .48(.94) =$ $\boxed{.4512}$
      only cans can be aluminum

d) $P(C) - P(A)$

      $.48 - .4512 = \boxed{.0288}$

e) $P(A \cup \overline{C}) = P(A) + P(\overline{C}) - P(A \cap \overline{C})$

      $.4512 + .52 - .0000$

      NOTE: $P(A \cap \overline{C}) = .0000$ because only cans are aluminum

           $.4512 + .52 = \boxed{.9712}$

4.27

	E	F	G	
A	15	12	8	35
B	11	17	19	47
C	21	32	27	80
D	18	13	12	43
	65	74	66	205

a) $P(G|A) = \dfrac{8}{35} =$ $\boxed{.2286}$

b) $P(B|F) = \dfrac{17}{74} =$ $\boxed{.2297}$

c) $P(C|E) = \dfrac{21}{65} =$ $\boxed{.3231}$

d) $P(E|G) =$ $\boxed{.0000}$

4.29 **without replacement:**

$$P(Q_2|Q_1) = \quad \frac{3}{51} = \boxed{.0588}$$

with replacement:

$$P(Q_2|Q_1) = P(Q_2) = \quad \frac{4}{52} = \boxed{.0769}$$

4.31 Let U = Undersize

$$P(U_2|U_1) = \frac{299}{999} = \boxed{.2993}$$

$$P(U_1 \cap U_2) = P(U_1) \cdot P(U_2|U_1) =$$

$$\frac{300}{1,000} \cdot \frac{299}{999} = \frac{89,700}{999,000} = \boxed{.0898}$$

4.33 Let L = Large Bank
         M = Medium Bank
         S = Small Bank
         F = Bank Failure

a) $P(F) = \dfrac{200}{13,500} = \boxed{.0148}$

b) $P(S|F) = \dfrac{125}{200} = \boxed{.625}$

c) $P(\overline{F}|M \text{ or } L) = ??$
     20% Large + 35% Medium =
     55% = .55 Large or Medium
     13,500(.55) = 7,425 Large or Medium Banks
     200 - 125 = 75 failing banks in the Large and Medium size
     7,425 - 75 = 7,350 non failing Large and Medium Banks

$$P(\overline{F}| M \text{ or } L) = \frac{P(\overline{F} \cap M \text{ or } L)}{P(M \text{ or } L)} =$$

$$\frac{\dfrac{7,350}{13,500}}{\dfrac{7,425}{1,350}} = \boxed{.9899}$$

4.35 Let   M = Move
            T = people in their 20's

a)   for an American

$$P(M|T) = \frac{P(M \cap T)}{P(T)} = \frac{.03}{.14} = \boxed{.2143}$$

b)   for an American:

$$P(T|\overline{M}) = \frac{P(T \cap \overline{M})}{P(\overline{M})} \text{ but}$$

$$P(T \cap M) = .03$$

$$P(T \cap \overline{M}) = .14 - .03 = .11 \text{ and}$$

$$P(\overline{M}) = 1 - P(M) = 1 - .18 = .82$$

$$P(T|\overline{M}) = \frac{P(T \cap \overline{M})}{P(\overline{M})} = \frac{.11}{.82} = \boxed{.1342}$$

c)   for a New Zealander:

$$P(T|M) = \frac{P(T \cap M)}{P(M)} = \frac{.05}{.19} = \boxed{.2632}$$

4.37   Let   A = Alex fills the order
                    B = Alicia fills the order
                    C = Juan fills the order
                    I = order filled incorrectly
                    K = order filled correctly

    $P(A) = .30$ $P(B) = .45$ $P(C) = .25$
    $P(I|A) = .20$ $P(I|B) = .12$ $P(I|C) = .05$
    $P(K|A) = .80$ $P(K|B) = .88$ $P(K|C) = .95$

a) $P(B) = .45$

b) $P(I|C) = .05$

c)

Event	Prior $P(E_i)$	Conditional $P(I|E_i)$	Joint $P(I \cap E_i)$	Revised $P(E_i|I)$	
A	.30	.20	.0600	$.0600/.1265=$	.4743
B	.45	.12	.0540	$.0540/.1265=$	.4269
C	.25	.05	.0125	$.0125/.1265=$	.0988

                              $P(I) = .1265$ 1.000

By Tree:

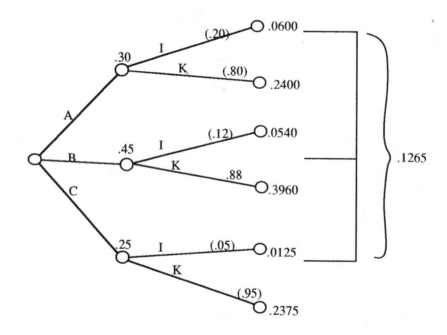

Revised: $P(A|I) = \dfrac{.0600}{.1265} =$ $\boxed{.4743}$

$P(B|I) = \dfrac{.0540}{.1265} =$ $\boxed{.4269}$

$P(C|I) = \dfrac{.0125}{.1265} =$ $\boxed{.0988}$

d)

Event	Prior $P(E_i)$	Conditional $P(K|E_i)$	Joint $P(K \cap E_i)$	Revised $P(E_i|K)$	
A	.30	.80	.2400	$^{.2400}/_{.8735}=$	.2748
B	.45	.88	.3960	$^{.3960}/_{.8735}=$	.4533
C	.25	.95	.2375	$^{.2375}/_{.8735}=$	.2719
			$P(K) = .8735$		1.0000

See previous tree for k branches.

4.39 Let   G = Gomez pitches
           J = Jackson pitches
           S = Smith pitches
           A = Alvarez pitches
           W = wins game
           L = loses game

Event	Prior P(Ei)	Conditional P(W|Ei)	Joint P(W ∩ Ei)	Revised P(Ei|W)	
G	.25	.60	.1500	.1500/.4500=	.3333
J	.25	.45	.1125	.1125/.4500=	.2500
S	.25	.35	.0875	.0875/.4500=	.1944
A	.25	.40	.1000	.1000/.4500=	.2222

$$P(W) = .4500 \qquad\qquad .9999$$

By Tree:

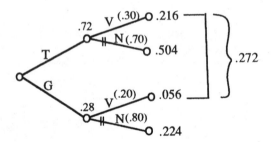

Revised: $P(G|W) = \dfrac{.1500}{.4500} = \boxed{.3333}$

        $P(J|W) = \dfrac{.1125}{.4500} = \boxed{.2500}$

        $P(S|W) = \dfrac{.0876}{.4500} = \boxed{.1944}$

        $P(A|W) = \dfrac{.1000}{.4500} = \boxed{.2222}$

4.41 $P(U) = .17$ $P(NU) = .83$ $n = 5$

$$_5C_2(.17)^2(.83)^3 \qquad = \frac{5!}{2!3!} \; (.17)^2(.83)^3 =$$

$$10(.0289)(.571787) = \boxed{.16525}$$

4.43 $n = 4$ packages

a)   1 sequence $D_1 \cdot A_2 \cdot A_3 \cdot A_4$

$$\frac{6}{30} \cdot \frac{24}{29} \cdot \frac{23}{28} \cdot \frac{22}{27} = .1107827$$

$$_4C_1 = \frac{4!}{1!3!} = 4 \text{ sequences}$$

Probability of 1 defect = $4(.1107827) = \boxed{.44313}$

b)   2 or more requires determining 2, 3, and 4 and summing the answers. A more efficient way is to determine the complement of 2 or more (0, 1) and subtract from 1.

0 defects:

$A_1, \; A_2, \; A_3, \; A_4$

$$\text{Prob (0 defects)} = \frac{24}{30} \cdot \frac{23}{29} \cdot \frac{22}{28} \cdot \frac{21}{27} = \frac{255024}{657720} = \boxed{.38774}$$

Prob (1 defect) - from part (a) = $\boxed{.44313}$

Prob (0 or 1 defect) = $.38774 + .44313 = .83087$

Prob (2 or more) = 1 - Prob(0 or 1) = $1 - .83087 = \boxed{.16913}$

4.45 Let A = alcohol problem; N = no alcohol problem
      $P(A)$ = .18   n = 7
      $P(N)$ = .82

a)   Prob(X=7 with alcohol problems)

      One sequence: A_1 A_2 A_3 A_4 A_5 A_6 A_7

      $P(A_1 \cap A_2 \cap A_3 \cap A_4 \cap A_5 \cap A_6 \cap A_7)$ =

      $(.18)(.18)(.18)(.18)(.18)(.18)(.18)$ = $(.18)^7$ = .000006122

      number of sequences = $_7C_7$ = $\dfrac{7!}{7!0!}$ = 1

      Prob (X=7) = $\boxed{.000006122}$

b)   Prob (X=0 with alcohol problems)

      One sequence: N_1 N_2 N_3 N_4 N_5 N_6 N_7

      $P(N_1 \cap N_2 \cap N_3 \cap N_4 \cap N_5 \cap N_6 \cap N_7)$ =

      $(.82)(.82)(.82)(.82)(.82)(.82)(.82)$ = $(.82)^7$ = .2492855

      Number of sequences = $_7C_0$ = $\dfrac{7!}{0!7!}$ = 1

      Prob (X=0) = $\boxed{.2492855}$

c)   Prob (X=2 with alcohol problems

      One sequence: A_1 A_2 N_3 N_4 N_5 N_6 N_7

      $P(A_1 \cap A_2 \cap N_3 \cap N_4 \cap N_5 \cap N_6 \cap N_7)$ =

      $(.18)(.18)(.82)(.82)(.82)(.82)(.82)$ = .012012

      Number of sequences: $_7C_2$ = $\dfrac{7!}{2!5!}$ = 21

      Prob (X=2) = 21(.012012) = $\boxed{.252255}$

d)   Prob (X≤1 with alcohol problems) =

Prob (X=0) + Prob (X=1)

Prob (X=0) = .2492855 from (b)

for (X=1):   One sequence: $A_1 \ N_2 \ N_3 \ N_4 \ N_5 \ N_6 \ N_7$

$P(A_1 \cap N_2 \cap N_3 \cap N_4 \cap N_5 \cap N_6 \cap N_7) =$

$(.18)(.82)(.82)(.82)(.82)(.82)(.82) = .05472$

Number of sequences: $_7C_1 = \dfrac{7!}{1!6!} = 7$

Prob(X=1) = 7(.05472) = .38305

Prob(X≤1) = Prob(X=0) + Prob(X=1) =

.24929 + .38305 = $\boxed{.63234}$

e)   Expect to get 18% of the seven lawyers: (.18)(7) = 1.26
In the long run out of samples of 7 lawyers, there would be
an average of 1.26 with alcohol problems.   In any particular
sample, 1 is the most likely number.

4.47

Variable 1
D   E

		D	E	
A		10	20	30
B		15	5	20
C		30	15	45
		55	40	95

Variable 2   B

a) $P(E) = \dfrac{40}{95} = \boxed{.42105}$

b) $P(B \cup D) = P(B) + P(D) - P(B \cap D)$

$= \dfrac{20}{95} + \dfrac{55}{95} - \dfrac{15}{95} = \dfrac{60}{95} = \boxed{.63158}$

c) $P(A \cap E) = \dfrac{20}{95} = \boxed{.21053}$

d) $P(B|E) = \dfrac{5}{40} = \boxed{.1250}$

e) $P(A \cup B) = P(A) + P(B) = \dfrac{30}{95} + \dfrac{20}{95} = \dfrac{50}{95} = \boxed{.52632}$

f) $P(B \cap C) = \boxed{.0000 \text{ (mutually exclusive)}}$

g) $P(D|C) = \dfrac{30}{45} = \boxed{.66667}$

h) $P(A|B) = \dfrac{P(A \cap B)}{P(B)} = \dfrac{.0000}{20/95} = \boxed{.0000 \text{ mutually exclusive}}$

i) $P(A) = P(A|D)$??

$\dfrac{30}{95} = \dfrac{10}{55}$??

$.31579 \neq .18182$ No, Variables 1 and 2 are <u>not</u>
independent.

4.49

INCOME

		<15K	15-25K	25-50K	>50K	
	< 21	1,446	655	140	19	2,260
	21 - 34	226	5,295	3,733	1,839	11,093
AGE	34 - 44	207	1,550	5,711	3,514	10,982
	45 - 54	1,026	1,975	2,370	2,528	7,899
	≥ 55	740	3,702	5,922	4,442	14,806
		3,645	13,177	17,876	12,342	47,040

a)

INCOME

		<15K	15-25K	25-50K	>50K	
	< 21	.0307	.0139	.0030	.0004	.0480
	21 - 34	.0048	.1126	.0794	.0391	.2359
AGE	35 - 44	.0044	.0330	.1214	.0747	.2335
	45 - 54	.0218	.0420	.0504	.0537	.1679
	≥ 55	.0157	.0787	.1259	.0944	.3147
		.0774	.2802	.3801	.2623	1.0000

b) $P(21\text{-}34) = \boxed{.2359}$

c) $P(<21 \cap 15\text{-}25K) = \boxed{.0139}$

d) $P(<21 \cup 25\text{-}50K) =$
$P(<21) + P(25\text{-}50K) - P(<21 \cap 25\text{-}50K) =$

$.0480 + .3801 - .0030 = \boxed{.4251}$

e) $(P>50K|35\text{-}44) = \dfrac{P(>50K \cap 34\text{-}44)}{P(35\text{-}44)} = \dfrac{.0747}{.2335} = \boxed{.3199}$

f)   P(35-44 ∩ 45-54) = | .0000 |

      The age categories are <u>mutually exclusive.</u>

g)   P(<21) - P(<21|<15K)??

      .0480 =   <u>.0307</u>
                .0774

      .0480 ≠ .3966   <u>Not independent.</u>

4.51   <u>U.S. Physicians in 1988</u>

		<35	35-44	45-54	55-65	>65	
GENDER	Man	.18	.25	.17	.13	.12	.85
	Woman	.07	.05	.02	.01	.00	.15
		.25	.30	.19	.14	.12	1.00

a)   P(35-55) = | .30 |

b)   P(Woman ∩ 45-54) = | .02 |

c)   P(Man U 35-44) = P(Man) + P(35-44) - P(Man ∩ 35-44) =

      .85 + .30 - .25 = | .90 |

d)   P(<35 U 55-64) = P(<35) + P(55-64) = .25 + .14 = | .39 |

e)   P(Woman|45-54) = <u>P(Woman ∩ 45-54)</u> = <u>.02</u> = | .1053 |
                          P(45-54)   .19

4.53

   without replacement:
   $P(A_1 \cap K_2 \cap Q_3 \cap J_4)$

$$= \frac{4}{52} \cdot \frac{4}{51} \cdot \frac{4}{50} \cdot \frac{4}{49} = \frac{256}{6,497,400} = .0000394$$

   with replacement:

$$= \frac{4}{52} \cdot \frac{4}{52} \cdot \frac{4}{52} \cdot \frac{4}{52} = \frac{256}{7,311,616} = .0000350$$

   without replacement higher.

4.55   Let S = believe SS secure
                   N = don't believe SS will be secure
                 <45 = under 45 years old
                 ≥45 = 45 or more years old

                       P(N) = .51
           Therefore, P(S) = 1 - .51 = .49

                       P(N|<45) = .67
           Therefore, P(S|<45) = 1-P(N|<45) = 1 - .67 = .33

                       P(S|≥45) = .70
           Therefore, P(N|≥45) = 1 - P(S|≥45) = 1 - .70 = .30

                       P(<45) = .57

	S	N	
	S	N	
<45	.189	.381	.57
>45	.301	.129	.43
	.49	.51	1.00

a)   P(>45) = 1 - P(<45) = 1 - .57 = $\boxed{.43}$

b)   P(<45 ∩ S) = P(<45) · P(S|<45) = (.57)(.33) = $\boxed{.188}$

   (Rounding error because 33% should actually be 33.3333% and
     67% is actually 66.6666%)

c)   P(≥45|S) = $\dfrac{P(245 ∩ S)}{P(S)}$ = $\dfrac{P(>45)·P(S|≥45)}{P(S)}$ = $\dfrac{(.43)(.70)}{.49}$

        = $\boxed{.6143}$

d)   P(<45 U N) = P(<45) + P(N) - P(<45 ∩ N) =

     P(<45) + P(N) - [P(<45)·P(N|<45)] = .57 + .51 - (.57)(.67) =

     1.08 - .3819 = $\boxed{.6981}$

4.57   Let M = Mastercard
             A = American Express
             V = Visa Card

             P(M) = .30
             P(A) = .20
             P(V) = .25
          P(M ∩ A) = .08
          P(V ∩ M) = .12
          P(A ∩ V) = .06

a)   P(V U A) = P(V) + P(A) − P(V ∩ A)

              = .25 + .20 − .06 = $\boxed{.39}$

b) $P(V|M) = \dfrac{P(V \cap M)}{P(M)} = \dfrac{.12}{.30} =$ $\boxed{.40}$

c) $P(M|V) = \dfrac{P(V \cap M)}{P(V)} = \dfrac{.12}{.25} =$ $\boxed{.48}$

d)   P(V) = P(V|M)??

      .25 ≠ .40

      Not independent

e)   A not mutually exclusive of V because P(A ∩ V) ≠ .0000

4.59   Let M = expect to save more
                  R = expect to reduce debt
                NM = don't expect to save more
                NR = don't expect to reduce debt

              P(M)   = .43
              P(R)   = .45
           P(R|M)   = .81
        P(NR|M) = 1-P(R|M) = 1 - .81 = .19
           P(NM) = 1 - P(M) = 1 - .43 = .57
           P(NR) = 1 - P(R) = 1 - .45 = .55

a) $P(M \cap R) = P(M) \cdot P(R|M) = (.43)(.81) =$ | .3483 |

b) $P(M \cup R) = P(M) + P(R) - P(M \cap R)$

              $= .43 + .45 - .3483 =$ | .5317 |

c)   P(neither save nor reduce debt) =

      $1 - P(M \cup R) = 1 - .5317 =$ | .4683 |

d) $P(M \cap NR) = P(M) \cdot P(NR|M) = (.43)(.19) =$ | .0817 |

      By Matrix:

                       Reduce

                    Yes   No

            Yes | .3483 | .0817 | .43
      Save
             No | .1017 | .4683 | .57

                   .45   .55 | 1.00

4.61

Event	Prior	$P(\text{has} \mid e_i)$	$P(\text{has} \cap e_i)$	Revised
Soup	.60	.73	.4380	.8456
Breakfast Meats	.35	.17	.0595	.1149
Hot dogs	.05	.41	.0205	.0396
			.5180	

4.63   Let   T = Household has 2 or more TV's
                    N = Household has 1 or less TV's
              P(T) = .63
              P(N) = 1 - P(T) = 1-.63 = .37
            n = 3

a)   Prob(X=3)

      one sequence T_1 T_2 T_3

      Prob($T_1 \cap T_2 \cap T_3$) = (.63)(.63)(.63) = .25005

      Number of sequences = $_3C_3$ = $\dfrac{3!}{3!0!}$ = 1

      Prob(X=3) = 1(.25005) = $\boxed{.25005}$

b)   Prob(X=1)

      one sequence T_1 N_2 N_3

      Prob($T_1 \cap N_2 \cap N_3$) = (.63)(.37)(.37) = .08625

      Number of sequences = $_3C_1$ = $\dfrac{3!}{1!2!}$ = 3

      Prob(X=1) = 3(.08625) = $\boxed{.25875}$

c)   Prob(X≥2) = Prob(X=2) + Prob(X=3)

      Prob(X=2):

      one sequence T_1 T_2 N_3

      Prob($T_1 \cap T_2 \cap N_3$) = (.63)(.63)(.37) = .14685

      Number of sequences = $_3C_2$ = $\dfrac{3!}{2!1!}$ = 3

      Prob(X=2) = 3(.14685)= .44055

      Prob(X=3) = from(a) = .25005

      Prob(X≥2) = .44055 + .25005 = $\boxed{.6906}$

4.65   Let A = American made
                  N = not American made
               P(A) = $\frac{1}{250}$ = .004

               P(N) = 1 - .004 = .996
             n = 10

a)   Prob(X=1):

one sequence A_1 N_2 N_3 N_4 N_5 N_6 N_7 N_8 N_9 N_{10}

Prob($A_1 \cap N_2 \cap N_3 \cap N_4 \cap N_5 \cap N_6 \cap N_7 \cap N_8 \cap N_9 \cap N_{10}$) =

(.004)(.996)(.996)(.996)(.996)(.996)(.996)(.996)(.996)(.996)

=   .003858

Number of sequences = $_{10}C_1$ = $\frac{10!}{1!9!}$ = 10

Prob(X=1) = 10(.003858) = $\boxed{.0386}$

b)   Prob(X=0):

one sequence N_1 N_2 N_3 N_4 N_5 N_6 N_7 N_8 N_9 N_{10}

Prob($N_1 \cap N_2 \cap N_3 \cap N_4 \cap N_5 \cap N_6 \cap N_7 \cap N_8 \cap N_9 \cap N_{10}$) =

(.996)(.996)(.996)(.996)(.996)(.996)(.996)(.996)(.996)(.996)

=   .96071

Number of sequences = $_{10}C_0$ = $\frac{10!}{0!10!}$ = 1

Prob(X=0) = 1(.96071) = $\boxed{.9607}$

c)   Prob(X>2) = Prob(X=3) + Prob(X=4) +... + Prob(X=10)

Prob(X=3):

one sequence A_1 A_2 A_3 N_4 N_5 N_6 N_7 N_8 N_9 N_{10}

Prob($A_1 \cap A_2 \cap A_3 \cap N_4 \cap N_5 \cap N_6 \cap N_7 \cap N_8 \cap N_9 \cap N_{10}$) =

(.004)(.004)(.004)(.996)(.996)(.996)(.996)(.996)(.996)(.996)

=   .000000062

Number of sequences = $_{10}C_3$ = $\dfrac{10!}{7!3!}$ = .0000

Prob(X>2) = $\boxed{.0000}$ because if

P(X=3) = .0000   so are P(X=4), P(X=5), etc.

DISCRETE DISTRIBUTIONS

5

I.   **CHAPTER OBJECTIVES**

The overall learning objective of Chapter five is to help you understand a category of distributions that produces only discrete outcomes, thereby enabling you to:

1.   Distinguish between discrete random variables and continuous random variables.

2.   Identify the type of statistical experiments that can be described by the binomial distribution, and know how to work such problems.

3.   Decide when to use the Poisson distribution in analyzing statistical experiments, and know how to work such problems.

4.   Decide when binomial distribution problems can be approximated by the Poisson distribution, and know how to work such problems.

5.   Decide when to use the hypergeometric distribution, and know how to work such problems.

II. **CHAPTER OUTLINE**

III. **KEY WORDS**

Random Variable

Discrete Random Variables

Continuous Random Variables

Discrete Distributions

Continuous Distributions

Binomial Distribution

Poisson Distribution

Lambda

Hypergeometric
    Distribution

IV. **STUDY QUESTIONS**

1. Variables that take on values at every point over a given interval are called _____ _____ variables.

2. Variables that take on values only at certain points over a given interval are called _____ _____ variables.

3. An experiment in which a die is rolled six times will likely produce values of a _____ random variable.

4. An experiment in which a researcher counts the number of customers arriving at a supermarket checkout counter every two minutes produces values of a _____ random variable.

5. An experiment in which the time it takes to assemble a product is measured is likely to produce values of a _____ random variable.

6. A binomial distribution is an example of a _____ distribution.

7. The normal distribution is an example of a _____ distribution.

8. On any one trial of a binomial experiment, there can be only _____ possible outcomes.

9. Suppose the probability that a given part is defective is .10. If four such parts are randomly drawn from a large population, the probability that exactly two parts are defective is _____ .

10. Suppose the probability that a given part is defective is .04. If thirteen such parts are randomly drawn from a large population, the expected value or mean of the binomial distribution that describes this experiment is _____ .

11. Suppose a binomial experiment is conducted by randomly selecting 20 items where p = .30. The standard deviation of the binomial distribution is

_____ .

12. Suppose forty-seven percent of the workers in a large corporation are under thirty-five years of age. If fifteen workers are randomly selected from this corporation, the probability of selecting exactly ten who are under thirty-five years of age is

_____ .

13. Suppose that twenty-three percent of all adult Americans fly at least once a year. If twelve adult Americans are randomly selected, the probability that exactly four have flown at least once last year is

_____ .

14. Suppose that sixty percent of all voters support the President of the United States at this time. If twenty voters are randomly selected, the probability that at least eleven support the President is _____.

15. The Poisson distribution was named after the French mathematician _____.

16. The poisson distribution focuses on the number of discrete occurrences per _____.

17. The Poisson distribution tends to describe the _____ occurrences.

18. The long-run average or mean of a Poisson distribution is _____.

19. The variance of a Poisson distribution is equal to _____.

20. If Lambda is 2.6 occurrences over an interval of five minutes, the probability of getting six occurrences over one five minute interval is _____.

21. Suppose that in the long-run a company determines that there are 1.2 flaws per every twenty pages of typing paper produced. If ten pages of typing paper are randomly selected, the probability that more than two flaws are found is _____.

22. If Lambda is 1.8 for a four minute interval, an adjusted new Lambda of _____ would be used to analyze the number of occurrences for a twelve minute interval.

23. Suppose a binomial distribution problem has an n = 200
     and a p = .03. If this problem is worked using the
     Poisson distribution, the value of Lambda is _____.

24. Suppose a binomial distribution problem has an n = 500
     and a p = .01. If this problem is worked using the
     Poisson distribution, the value of Lambda is _____.

25. The hypergeometric distribution should be used when a
     binomial type experiment is being conducted without
     replacement and the sample size is greater than or
     equal to _____% of the population.

26. Suppose a population contains sixteen items of which
     seven are X and nine are Y. If a random sample of five
     of these population items is selected, the probability
     that exactly three of the five are X is _____.

27. Suppose a population contains twenty people of which
     eight are members of the Catholic church. If a sample
     of four of the population is taken, the probability
     that at least three of the four are members of the
     Catholic church is _____.

28. Suppose a lot of fifteen personal computer printers
     contains two defective printers. If three of the
     fifteen printers are randomly selected for testing, the
     probability that no defective printers are selected is
     _____.

V.   **ANSWERS TO STUDY QUESTIONS**

1. continuous random

2. discrete random

3. discrete

4. discrete

5. continuous

6. discrete

7. continuous

8. two

9. .0486

10. 0.52

11. 2.049

12. .0661

13. .1772

14. .755

15. Poisson

16. interval

17. rare

18. lambda

19. lambda

20. .0319

21. .1203

22. 5.4

23. 6.0

24. 5.0

25. 5

26. .2885

27. .1531

28. .6286

VI. **SOLUTIONS TO ODD-NUMBER PROBLEMS IN TEXT**

5.1

a) $n = 4$ $p = .10$ $q = .90$ $P(X=3) =$

$_4C_3(.10)^3(.90)^1 = 4(.001)(.90) =$ $\boxed{.0036}$

b) $n = 7$ $p = .80$ $q = .20$ $P(X=4) =$

$_7C_4(.80)^4(.20)^3 = 35(.4096)(.008) =$ $\boxed{.1147}$

c) $n = 10$ $p = .60$ $q = .40$ $P(X \geq 7) =$

$P(X=7) + P(X=8) + P(X=9) + P(X=10) =$

$_{10}C_7(.60)^7(.40)^3 + _{10}C_8(.60)^8(.40)^2 + _{10}C_9(.60)^9(.40)^1 + _{10}C_{10}(.60)^{10}(.40)^0 =$

$120(.0280)(.064) + 45(.0168)(.16) + 10(.0101)(.40) + 1(.0060)(1) =$

$.2150 + .1209 + .0403 = .0060 =$ $\boxed{.3822}$

d) $n = 12$ $p = .45$ $q = .55$ $P(5 \leq X \leq 7) =$

$P(X=5) + P(X=6) + P(X=7) =$

$_{12}C_5(.45)^5(.55)^7 + _{12}C_6(.45)^6(.55)^6 + _{12}C_7(.45)^7(.55)^5 =$

$792(.0185)(.0152) + 924(.0083)(.0277) + 792(.0037)(.0503) =$

$.2225 + .2124 + .1489 =$ $\boxed{.5838}$

$$P = \frac{\lambda^x e^{-\lambda}}{X!}$$

5.3
a) $n = 20$ $p = .70$ $q = .30$

$\mu = n \cdot p = 20(.70) = \boxed{14}$

$\sigma = \sqrt{n \cdot p \cdot q} = \sqrt{20(.70)(.30)} = \sqrt{4.2} = \boxed{2.05}$

b) $n = 70$ $p = .35$ $q = .65$

$\mu = n \cdot p = 70(.35) = \boxed{.245}$

$\sigma = \sqrt{n \cdot p \cdot q} = \sqrt{70(.35)(.65)} = \sqrt{15.925} = \boxed{3.99}$

c) $n = 100$ $p = .50$ $q = .50$

$\mu = n \cdot p = 100(.50) = \boxed{50}$

$\sigma = \sqrt{n \cdot p \cdot q} = \sqrt{100(.50)(.50)} = \sqrt{25} = \boxed{5}$

5.5 $p = .11$ $q = .89$ $n = 20$

a)   Prob(X=0)

$_{20}C_0(.11)^0(.89)^{20} = (1)(1)(.0972) = \boxed{.0972}$

b)   Prob(X=4)

$_{20}C_4(.11)^4(.89)^{16} = (4845)(.0001464)(.1549673) = \boxed{.1099}$

c)   Prob(X≥15) = Prob(X=15) + Prob(X=16) + Prob(X=17)

+ Prob(X=18) + Prob(X=19) + Prob(X=20) =

$_{20}C_{15}(.11)^{15}(.89)^5 + {}_{20}C_{16}(.11)^{16}(.89)^4 + {}_{20}C_{17}(.11)^{17}(.89)^3$

$+ {}_{20}C_{18}(.11)^{18}(.89)^2 + {}_{20}C_{19}(.11)^{19}(.89)^1 + {}_{20}C_{20}(.11)^{20}(.89)^0 =$

$.0000 + .0000 + .0000 + .0000 + .0000 + .0000 = \boxed{.0000}$

d)   Expected number $= \mu = n \cdot p = 20(.11) = \boxed{2.2}$

5.7   n = 25

a)   P = .70   q = .30

Prob (X≥15) =   Prob(X=15) + Prob(X=16) + Prob(X=17) +
      Prob(X=18) + Prob(X=19) + Prob(X=20) + Prob(X=21) +
      Prob(X=22) + Prob(X=23) + Prob(X=24) + Prob(X=25) =

.092 + .134 + .165 + .171 + .147 +
.103 + .057 + .024 + .007 + .001 + .000 = $\boxed{.901}$

b)   p = .70   q = .30

Prob (X>20) = Prob(X=21) + Prob(X=22) + Prob(X=23) +
                    Prob(X=24) + Prob(X=25) =

.057 + .024 + .007 + .001 + .000 = $\boxed{.089}$

c)   P = .30   q = .70

Prob (X≤15) =   Prob(X=15) + Prob(X=14) + Prob(X=13) +
      Prob(X=12) + Prob(X=11) + Prob(X=10) + Prob(X=9) +
      Prob(X=8) + Prob(X=7) + Prob(X=6) + Prob(X=5) +
      Prob(X=4) + Prob(X=3) + Prob(X=2) + Prob(X=1) +
      Prob(X=0) =

.001 + .004 + .011 + .027 + .054 +
.092 + .134 + .165 + .171 + .147 +
.103 + .057 + .024 + .007 + .001 + .000 = $\boxed{1.000}$

5.9   n = 10   p = .20

X	Prob
0	.107
1	.268
2	.302
3	.201
4	.088
5	.026
6	.006
7	.001
8	.000
9	.000
10	.000

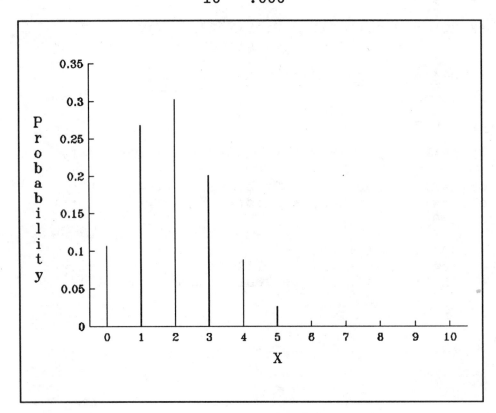

The expected value of this distribution is
$\mu = n \cdot p = 10(.20) = 2$

The answers to 5.8 are relatively obvious since the values
are weighted heavily towards the small values of X.

5.11 n = 15   p = .55   q = .45

a)   Prob(X≥10) = Prob(X=10) + Prob(X=11) + Prob(X=12) +
      Prob(X=13) + Prob(X=14)+ Prob(X=15) =

$_{15}C_{10}(.55)^{10}(.45)^5$ + $_{15}C_{11}(.55)^{11}(.45)^4$ +
$_{15}C_{12}(.55)^{12}(.45)^3$ + $_{15}C_{13}(.55)^{13}(.45)^2$ +
$_{15}C_{14}(.55)^{14}(.45)^1$ + $_{15}C_{15}(.55)^{15}(.45)^0$ =

.1404 + .0780 + .0318 + .0090 + .0016 + .0001 = $\boxed{.2609}$

b)   Prob(X<5) = Prob(X=4) + Prob(X=3) + Prob(X=2) +
                  Prob(X=1) + Prob(X=0) =

$_{15}C_4(.55)^4(.45)^{11}$ + $_{15}C_3(.55)^3(.45)^{12}$ + $_{15}C_2(.55)^2(.45)^{13}$ +
$_{15}C_1(.55)^1(.45)^{14}$ + $_{15}C_0(.55)^0(.45)^{15}$ =

.0191 + .0052 + .0010 + .0001 = $\boxed{.0254}$

c)   Prob(6≤X≤10) = Prob(X=6) + Prob(X=7) + Prob(X=8) +
                     Prob(X=9) + Prob(X=10) =

$_{15}C_6(.55)^6(.45)^9$ + $_{15}C_7(.55)^7(.45)^8$ + $_{15}C_8(.55)^8(.45)^7$ +
$_{15}C_9(.55)^9(.45)^6$ + $_{15}C_{10}(.55)^{10}(.45)^5$ =

.1048 + .1647 + .2013 + .1914 + .1404 = $\boxed{.8026}$

d) μ = n·p = 15(.55) = $\boxed{8.25}$

$\sigma = \sqrt{n \cdot p \cdot q}$ $= \sqrt{15(.55)(.45)}$

= $\boxed{1.93}$

e)   The empirical rule states that 95% of all values fall within
      $\mu \pm 2\sigma$. For this problem,

$\mu \pm 2\sigma$ = 8.25 ± 2(1.93) = 8.25 ± 3.86 = $\boxed{4.39 \leq X \leq 12.11}$

5.13

a) $\text{Prob}(X=5 \mid \lambda=2.3)=$

$$\frac{(2.3^5)(e^{-2.3})}{5!} = \frac{(64.36343)(.1002588)}{(120)} = \boxed{.0538}$$

b) $\text{Prob}(X=2 \mid \lambda=3.9) =$

$$\frac{(3.9^2)(e^{-3.9})}{2!} = \frac{(15.21)(.02024)}{(2)} = \boxed{.1539}$$

c) $\text{Prob}(X\leq3 \mid \lambda=4.1) =$

$\text{Prob}(X=3) + \text{Prob}(X=2) + \text{Prob}(X=1) + \text{Prob}(X=0) =$

$$\frac{(4.1^3)(e^{-4.1})}{3!} = \frac{(68.921)(.016574)}{6} = .1904$$

$$+ \frac{(4.1^2)(e^{-4.1})}{2!} = \frac{(16.81)(.016573)}{2} = .1393$$

$$+ \frac{(4.1^1)(e^{-4.1})}{1!} = \frac{(4.1)(.016573)}{1} = .0679$$

$$+ \frac{(4.1^0)(e^{-4.1})}{0!} = \frac{(1)(.016573)}{1} = .0166$$

$$.1904 + .1393 + .0679 + .0166 = \boxed{.4142}$$

d) $\text{Prob}(X=0 \mid \lambda=2.7) =$

$$\frac{(2.7^0)(e^{-2.7})}{0!} = \frac{(1)(.0672)}{1} = \boxed{.0672}$$

e) $Prob(X=1 \mid \lambda=5.4) =$

$$\frac{(5.4^1)(e^{-5.4})}{1!} = \frac{(5.4)(.0045)}{1} = \boxed{.0244}$$

f) $Prob(4 < X < 8 \mid \lambda = 4.4) =$

$Prob(X=5 \mid \lambda=4.4) + Prob(X=6 \mid \lambda=4.4) + Prob(X=7 \mid \lambda=4.4) =$

$$\frac{(4.4^5)(e^{-4.4})}{5!} + \frac{(4.4^6)(e^{-4.4})}{6!} + \frac{(4.4^7)(e^{-4.4})}{7!} =$$

$$\frac{(1649.162)(.012277)}{120} + \frac{(7256.314)(.012277)}{720} +$$

$$\frac{(31927.781)(.012277)}{5040}$$

$= .1687 + .1237 + .0778 =$ $\boxed{.3702}$

5.15

a) $\lambda = 6.3$

mean = $\boxed{6.3}$

Standard deviation = $\sqrt{6.3}$ = $\boxed{2.51}$

X	Prob
0	.0018
1	.0116
2	.0364
3	.0765
4	.1205
5	.1519
6	.1595
7	.1435
8	.1130
9	.0791
10	.0498
11	.0285
12	.0150
13	.0073
14	.0033
15	.0014
16	.0005
17	.0002
18	.0001
19	.0000

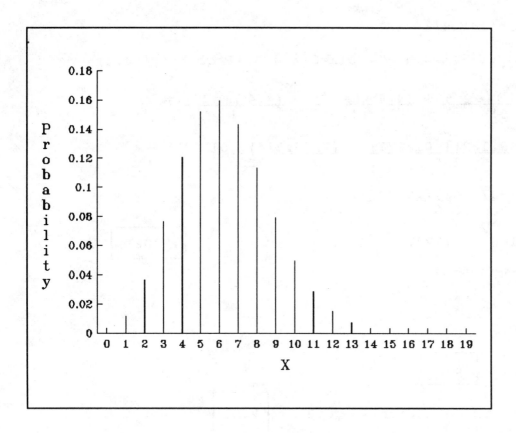

b) $\lambda = 1.3$

mean = $\boxed{1.3}$

standard deviation = $\sqrt{1.3}$ = $\boxed{1.14}$

X	Prob
0	.2725
1	.3542
2	.2303
3	.0998
4	.0324
5	.0084
6	.0018
7	.0003
8	.0001
9	.0000

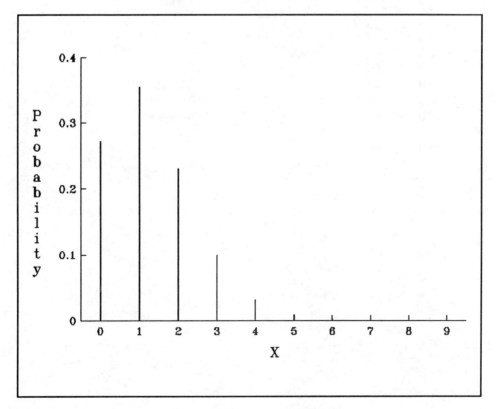

c) λ=8.9

mean = $\boxed{8.9}$

standard deviation = $\sqrt{8.9}$ = $\boxed{2.98}$

X	Prob
0	.0001
1	.0012
2	.0054
3	.0160
4	.0357
5	.0635
6	.0941
7	.1197
8	.1332
9	.1317
10	.1172
11	.0948
12	.0703
13	.0481
14	.0306
15	.0182
16	.0101
17	.0053
18	.0026
19	.0012
20	.0005
21	.0002
22	.0001

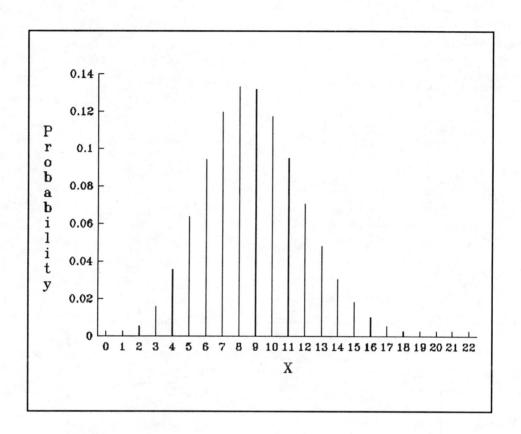

d) $\lambda = 0.6$

mean = | 0.6 |

standard deviation $= \sqrt{0.6} =$ | .775 |

X	Prob
0	.5488
1	.3293
2	.0988
3	.0198
4	.0030
5	.0004
6	.0000

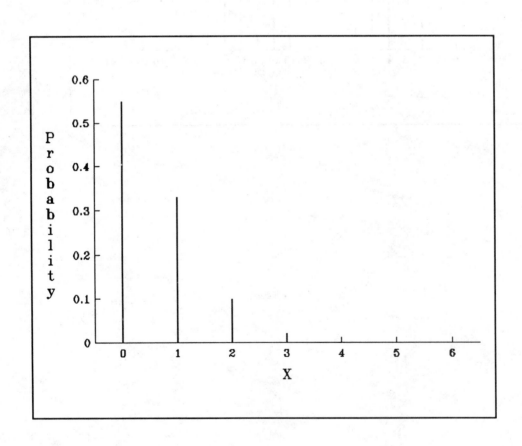

5.17 $\lambda = \mu = \dfrac{\Sigma X}{N} = \dfrac{64}{20} = 3.2 \ no\text{-}hitter/season$

a) $Prob(X=0 \,|\, \lambda=3.2)$

from Table A.3: $\boxed{.0408}$

b) $Prob(X=10/3 \ seasons)$
Different interval (3 times as long)
Change Lambda to:
$\lambda = 9.6$ no-hitters/3 seasons
$Prob(X=10 \,|\, \lambda=9.6) =$

from Table A.3 = $\boxed{.1241}$

5.19 $\lambda = 0.6$ trips/ 1 year

a) $Prob(X=0 \,|\, \lambda=0.6):$

from Table A.3 = $\boxed{.5488}$

b) $Prob(X=1 \,|\, \lambda=0.6):$

from Table A.3 = $\boxed{.3293}$

c) $Prob(X \geq 2 \,|\, \lambda=0.6):$

from Table A.3

X	Prob.
2	.0988
3	.0198
4	.0030
5	.0004
6	.0000
X ≥ 2	.1220

d)   Prob(X≤3/3 year period):

The interval length has been increased (3 times)
New Lambda = λ = 1.8 trips/3 years

$Prob(X{\le}3\,|\,\lambda{=}1.8)$:

from Table A.3

X	Prob.
0	.1653
1	.2975
2	.2678
3	.1607
X ≤ 3	.8913

e)   Prob(X=4/6 years):

The interval has been increased (6 times)
New Lambda = λ =3.6 trips/6 years

$Prob(X{=}4\,|\,\lambda{=}3.6)$:

from Table A.3 = $\boxed{.1912}$

5.21 λ = 1.2 pens/carton

a) $Prob(X{=}0\,|\,\lambda{=}1.2)$:

from Table A.3 = $\boxed{.3012}$

b) $Prob(X{\ge}8\,|\,\lambda{=}1.2)$:

from Table A.3 = $\boxed{.0000}$

c) $Prob(X{>}3\,|\,\lambda{=}1.2)$:

from Table A.3

X	Prob.
4	.0260
5	.0062
6	.0012
7	.0002
8	.0000
X > 3	.0336

5.23 **This is a binomial distribution problem:**
$$\text{Prob}(X \geq 6 \,|\, n = 300 \text{ and } p = .009)$$

$$\lambda = \mu = n \cdot p = 300(.009) = 2.7$$

Since $n > 20$ and $n \cdot p \leq 7$, the Poisson approximation is close enough.

$Prob(X{\geq}6 \,|\, \lambda{=}2.7):$

from Table A.3

X	Prob.
6	.0362
7	.0139
8	.0047
9	.0014
10	.0004
11	.0001
X ≥ 6	.0567

5.25

a) $\text{Prob}(x = 3 \,|\, N = 11, \ X = 8, \ n = 4)$

$$\frac{{}_8C_3 \cdot {}_3C_1}{{}_{11}C_4} = \frac{(56)(3)}{330} = \boxed{.5091}$$

b) $\text{Prob}(x < 2) \,|\, N = 15, \ X = 5, \ n = 6)$

$\text{Prob}(x=1) + \text{Prob }(x=0) =$

$$\frac{{}_5C_1 \cdot {}_{10}C_5}{{}_{15}C_6} + \frac{{}_5C_0 \cdot {}_{10}C_6}{{}_{15}C_6} = \frac{(5)(252)}{5005} + \frac{(1)(210)}{5005} =$$

$.2517 + .0420 = \boxed{.2937}$

c) $\text{Prob}(x = 0 \,|\, N = 9, \ X = 2, \ n = 3)$

$$\frac{{}_2C_0 \cdot {}_7C_3}{{}_9C_3} = \frac{(1)(35)}{84} = \boxed{.4167}$$

d) $\text{Prob}(x>4 \,|\, N = 20, \ X = 5, \ n = 7) =$

$\text{Prob}(x=5) + \text{Prob}(x=6) + \text{Prob}(x=7) =$

$$\frac{{}_5C_5 \cdot {}_{15}C_2}{{}_{20}C_7} + \frac{{}_5C_6 \cdot {}_{15}C_1}{{}_{20}C_7} + \frac{{}_5C_7 \cdot {}_{15}C_0}{{}_{20}C_7} =$$

$$\frac{(1)(105)}{77520} + {}_5C_6(\text{impossible}) + {}_5C_7(\text{impossible}) = \boxed{.0014}$$

5.27

a) $n = 4$ $N = 13$ $X = 5$ more than 28,000

$\text{Prob}(x \geq 2 \mid n = 4, \ N = 13, \ X = 5) =$

$\text{Prob}(x=2) + (\text{Prob}(x=3) + \text{Prob}(x=4) =$

$\dfrac{{}_5C_2 \cdot {}_8C_2}{{}_{13}C_4} + \dfrac{{}_5C_3 \cdot {}_8C_1}{{}_{13}C_4} + \dfrac{{}_5C_4 \cdot {}_8C_0}{{}_{13}C_4} =$

$= \dfrac{(10)(28)}{715} + \dfrac{(10)(8)}{715} + \dfrac{(5)(1)}{715} = \boxed{.5105}$

b) $n = 3$ $N = 13$ $X = 6$ less than 27,000

$\text{Prob}(x=3 \mid n = 3, \ N = 13, \ X = 6) =$

$\dfrac{{}_6C_3 \cdot {}_7C_0}{{}_{13}C_3} = \dfrac{(20)(1)}{286} = \boxed{.0699}$

c) $n = 5$ $N = 13$ $X = 1$ San Diego Mesa College

$\text{Prob}(x=1 \mid n = 5, \ N = 13, \ X = 1) =$

$\dfrac{{}_1C_1 \cdot {}_{12}C_4}{{}_{13}C_5} = \dfrac{(1)(495)}{1287} = \boxed{.3846}$

5.29 $N = 9$ $n = 4$ $X = 3$ Hondas:

a) $\text{Prob}(x = 2 \text{ Hondas}) = \dfrac{{}_3C_2 \cdot {}_6C_2}{{}_9C_4} = \dfrac{(3)(15)}{126} = \boxed{.3571}$

b) $\text{Prob}(x \geq 2 \text{ Hondas}) = \text{Prob}(x=2) + \text{Prob}(x=3) + \text{Prob}(x=4) =$

$\underset{\text{(from a.)}}{.3571} + \dfrac{{}_3C_3 \cdot {}_6C_1}{{}_9C_4} + \dfrac{{}_3C_4 \cdot {}_6C_0}{{}_9C_4} =$

$.3571 + \dfrac{(1)(6)}{126} + (\text{impossible to get 4 Hondas}) =$

$.3571 + .0476 = \boxed{.4047}$

c) $\text{Prob}(x=0 \text{ Hondas}) = \dfrac{{}_3C_0 \cdot {}_6C_4}{{}_9C_4} = \dfrac{(1)(15)}{126} = \boxed{.1190}$

5.31 N = 18   X = 11 Hispanic   n = 5

Prob(x≤1) = Prob(1) + Prob(0) =

$$\frac{_{11}C_1 \cdot {_7}C_4}{_{18}C_5} + \frac{_{11}C_0 \cdot {_7}C_5}{_{18}C_5} = \frac{(11)(35)}{8568} + \frac{(1)(21)}{8568} =$$

.0449 + .0025 = $\boxed{.0474}$

It is fairly unlikely that these results occur by chance. A researcher might investigate further the causes of this result. Were officers selected based on leadership, years of service, dedication, prejudice, or what?

5.33

a)   Prob(X=14|n = 20 and p = .60) = ☐ .124

b)   Prob(X<5|n = 10 and p =.30) =

Prob(X=4) + Prob(X=3) + Prob(X=2) + Prob(X=1) + Prob(X=0) =

X	Prob.
0	.028
1	.121
2	.233
3	.267
4	.200
X < 5	.849

c)   Prob(X≥12|n = 15 and p = .60) =

Prob(X=12) + Prob(X=13) + Prob(X=14) + Prob(X=15)

X	Prob.
12	.063
13	.022
14	.005
15	.000
X ≥ 12	.090

d)   Prob(X>20|n = 25 and p = .40) =

Prob(X=21) = Prob(X=22) = Prob(X=23) + Prob(X=24) +
               Prob(X=25) =

X	Prob.
21	.000
22	.000
23	.000
24	.000
25	.000
X > 20	.000

5.35

a) $Prob(X=3 \mid \lambda=1.8)$

= | .1607 |

b) $Prob(X<5 \mid \lambda=3.3)$ =

Prob(X=4) + Prob(X=3) + Prob(X=2) + Prob(X=1) + Prob(X=0) =

X	Prob.
0	.0369
1	.1217
2	.2008
3	.2209
4	.1823
X < 5	.7626

c) $Prob(X \geq 3 \mid \lambda=2.1)$ =

X	Prob.
3	.1890
4	.0992
5	.0417
6	.0146
7	.0044
8	.0011
9	.0003
10	.0001
11	.0000
X ≥ 5	.3504

d) $Prob(2<X\leq5\,|\,\lambda=4.2)$ =

= Prob(x=3) + Prob(x=4) + Prob(x=5) =

X	Prob.
3	.1852
4	.1944
5	.1633
2 < X ≤ 5	.5429

5.37 Prob(X≤3) |n = 8 and p = .60)
      From Table A.2

X	Prob.
0	.001
1	.008
2	.041
3	.124
X ≤ 3	.174

17.4% of the time in a sample of eight, three or fewer
customers are walk-ins by chance. Other reasons for such a
low number of walk-ins might be that she is retaining more
old customers than before or perhaps a new competitor is
attracting walk-ins away from her.

5.39 Prob$(X \geq 13 | n = 25$ and $p = .50) =$
from Table A.2

X	Prob.
13	.155
14	.133
15	.097
16	.061
17	.032
18	.014
19	.005
20	.002
21	.000
22	.000
23	.000
24	.000
25	.000
$X \geq 13$	.499

Prob$(X \geq 20 | n = 25$ and $p = .50) =$

X	Prob.
20	.002

Values >20 Prob. = .0000 $\boxed{.002}$

Expected number = $\mu = n \cdot p = 25(.50) = \boxed{12.5}$

5.41 n = 20 and p = .70
    Expected number = μ = n·p = 20(.70) = $\boxed{14}$

The mean = μ = $\boxed{14}$

The standard deviation = $\sigma = \sqrt{n \cdot p \cdot q} = \sqrt{20(.70)(.30)}$

= $\boxed{2.05}$

from Table A.2:	X	Prob.
	0	.000
	1	.000
	2	.000
	3	.000
	4	.000
	5	.000
	6	.000
	7	.001
	8	.004
	.9	.012
	10	.031
	11	.065
	12	.114
	13	.164
	14	.192
	15	.179
	16	.130
	17	.072
	18	.028
	19	.007
	20	.001

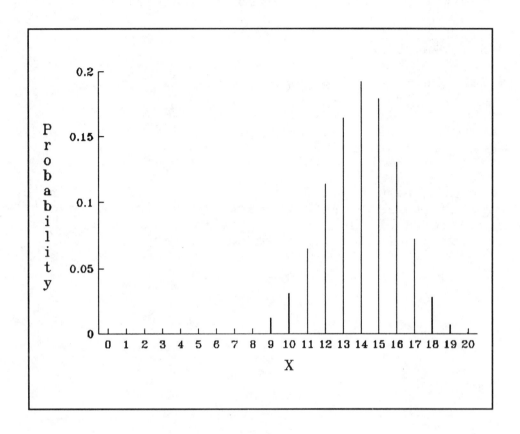

Prob(X=10│n = 20 and p = .70) = from Table A.2:   .031

When 20 calls are selected, only 3.1% of the time would exactly ten be AT&T calls. This outcome is unlikely but possible.

5.43 n = 25   p = .20

a)   Prob(X=8|n = 25 and p = .20) from Table A.2: | .062 |

b)   Prob(X>10)|n=25 and p = .20)

       from Table A.2 _X_   _Prob._
                        11   .004
                        12   .001
                        13   .000
                  X > 10   .005

c)   Since such a result would only occur 0.5% of the time by
       chance, it is likely that the analyst's list was not
       representative of the entire state of Idaho or the 20%
       figure for the Idaho census is not correct.

5.45 λ =1.8 tests/5 minutes.

a) $Prob(X=4 \mid \lambda=1.8)$

       from Table A.3 = $\boxed{.0723}$

b)   The interval has been increased 3 times to 15 minutes.
       Change λ to 5.4 tests/15 minutes.

       $Prob(X \geq 9 \mid \lambda=5.4)$ =
       from Table A.3

X	Prob.
9	.0486
10	.0262
11	.0129
12	.0058
13	.0024
14	.0009
15	.0003
16	.0001
X ≥ 9	.0972

c)   New interval of 10 minutes is twice the length of the
       original interval.

       New Lambda = λ = 3.6 tests/10 minutes

       $Prob(X=0 \mid \lambda=3.6)$

       from Table A.3 = $\boxed{.0273}$

       for 5 minutes:

       $Prob(X=0 \mid \lambda=1.8)$

       from Table A.3 = $\boxed{.1653}$

d)   Expected number of examinations per 5 minutes = λ =

1.8

from Table A.3

X	Prob.
0	.1653
1	.2975
2	.2678
3	.1607
4	.0723
5	.0260
6	.0078
7	.0020
8	.0005
9	.0001

Graph λ = 1.8

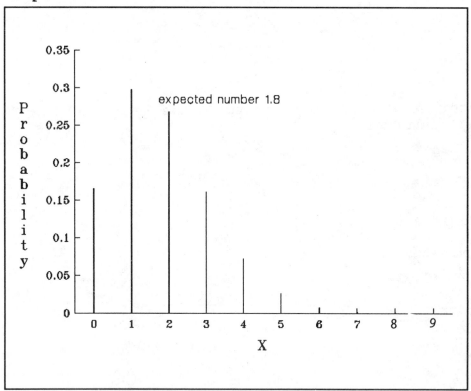

The value of 1 has the highest frequency of occurence.

5.47 $\lambda = 2.4$ calls/1 minute

a) $Prob(X=0\,|\,\lambda=2.4)$

from Table A.3 = $\boxed{.0907}$

b)   Can handle   X ≤ 5 calls
      Cannot handle   X > 5 calls

   $Prob(X>5\,|\,\lambda=2.4)$ =

   from Table A.3

X	Prob.
6	.0241
7	.0083
8	.0025
9	.0007
10	.0002
11	.0000
X > 5	.0358

c)   Prob(X = 3 calls per 2 minutes)

   The interval has been increased 2 times.
   New Lambda = $\lambda = 4.8$ calls/2 minutes.

   from Table A.3: $\boxed{.1517}$

d)   Prob(X ≤ 1 calls per 15 secondths)

   The interval has been decreased by ¼.
   New Lambda = $\lambda = 0.6$ calls/15 seconds.

   $Prob(X \leq 1\,|\,\lambda=0.6)$

   from Table A.3
       Prob(X = 1) =   .3293
       Prob(X = 0) =   .5488
       Prob(X ≤ 1) =   .8781

5.49 $\lambda = 1.4$ defects / 1 lot

If X > 3, buyer rejects
If X ≤ 3, buyer accepts

$Prob(X \le 3 \mid \lambda = 1.4)$

from Table A.3

X	Prob.
0	.2466
1	.3452
2	.2417
3	.1128
X ≤ 3	.9463

5.51   Prob(X=0 | n = 10,000 and p = .0002)

$\lambda = \mu = n \cdot p = (10,000)(.0002) = 2$

Since $\lambda < 7$ and n > 20,

the Poisson distribution is close enough.

$Prob(X=0 \mid \lambda = 2)$ =

from Table A.3 =   .1353

$Prob(X \ge 3 \mid \lambda = 2)$ =

from Table A.3

X	Prob.
3	.1804
4	.0902
5	.0361
6	.0120
7	.0034
8	.0009
9	.0002
10	.0000
X ≥ 3	.3232

5.53

a)   n = 5   N = 26   X = 5 (>40,000)

Prob(x=3|N = 26, n = 5, X = 5) =

$$\frac{_5C_3 \cdot _{21}C_2}{_{26}C_5} = \frac{(10)(210)}{65,780} = \boxed{.0319}$$

b)   n = 8   N = 26   X = 7 (Ariz. or Calif.)

Prob(x≤2|N = 26, n = 8, X = 8) =

Prob(x+2) + Prob(x+1) + Prob(x=0) =

$$\frac{_7C_2 \cdot _{19}C_6}{_{26}C_8} + \frac{_7C_1 \cdot _{19}C_7}{_{26}C_8} + \frac{_7C_0 \cdot _{19}C_8}{_{26}C_8} =$$

$$\frac{(21)(27,132)}{1,562,275} + \frac{(7)(50,388)}{1,562,275} + \frac{(1)(75,582)}{1,562,275} =$$

.3647 + .2258 + .0484 = $\boxed{.6389}$

c)   P(Texas) = $\frac{3}{26}$

<u>with</u> replacement, use the binomial distribution.   n=5, X=2

$$_5C_2 \left(\frac{3}{26}\right)^2 \left(\frac{23}{26}\right)^3$$

$$(10)(.0133)(.69225) = \boxed{.0922}$$

5.55 N = 14   n = 4

a)   Prob(x=4|N = 14, n = 4, X = 10 - Northside)

$$\frac{_{10}C_4 \cdot _4C_0}{_{14}C_4} = \frac{(210)(1)}{1001} = \boxed{.2098}$$

b)   Prob(x=4|N = 14, n = 4, X = 4 - West)

$$\frac{_4C_4 \cdot _{10}C_0}{_{14}C_4} = \frac{(1)(1)}{1001} = \boxed{.0010}$$

c)   Prob(x=2|N = 14, n = 4, X = 4 - West)

$$\frac{_4C_2 \cdot _{10}C_2}{_{14}C_4} = \frac{(6)(45)}{1001} = \boxed{.2697}$$

5.57 n = 13   X = 6 Toshiba   N - X = 7 Zenith   n = 5

a)   Prob(x=5|N = 13, n = 5, X = 7 Zeniths) =

$$\frac{{}_7C_5 \cdot {}_6C_0}{{}_{13}C_5} = \frac{(21)(1)}{1,287} = \boxed{.0163}$$

b)   Prob(x=5|N = 13, n = 5, X = 6 Toshiba) =

$$\frac{{}_6C_5 \cdot {}_7C_0}{{}_{13}C_5} = \frac{(6)(1)}{1,287} = \boxed{.0047}$$

c)   Prob(x=3|N = 13, n = 5, X = 6 Toshiba) =

$$\frac{{}_6C_3 \cdot {}_7C_2}{{}_{13}C_5} = \frac{(20)(21)}{1,287} = \boxed{.3263}$$

6

CONTINUOUS DISTRIBUTIONS

I. **CHAPTER OBJECTIVES**

The primary objective of Chapter six is to help you understand continuous distributions, thereby enabling you to:

1. Appreciate the importance of the normal distribution.

2. Recognize normal distribution problems and, know how to solve such problems.

3. Decide when to use the normal distribution to approximate binomial distribution problems, and know how to work such problems.

4. Decide when to use the exponential distribution to solve problems in business, and know how to work such problems.

II. **CHAPTER OUTLINE**

   6.1 Normal Distribution

              History of the Normal Distribution

              Probability Density Function of the

                 Normal Distribution

              Standardized Normal Distribution

              Working Normal Curve Problems

   6.2 Using the Normal Curve to Work Binomial

              Distribution Problems

              Correcting for Continuity

   6.3 Exponential Distribution

              Probabilities of the Exponential Distribution

III. **KEY WORDS**

Normal Distribution   Z Distribution
Standardized Normal Distribution   Correction for Continuity
Z Score   Exponential Distribution

IV. **STUDY QUESTIONS**

1. Probably the most widely known and used of all distributions is the _____ distribution.

2. Many human characteristics can be described by the _____ distribution.

3. The area under the curve of a normal distribution sums to _____.

4. In working normal curve problems using the raw values of X, the mean, and the standard deviation, a problem can be converted to _____ scores.

5. A Z score value is the number of _____ _____ a value is from the mean.

6. Within a range of Z scores of ± 1 from the mean, fall _____% of the values of a normal distribution.

7. Suppose a population of values is normally distributed with a mean of 155 and a standard deviation of 12. The Z score for X = 170 is _____.

8. Suppose a population of values is normally distributed with a mean of 76 and a standard deviation of 5.2. The Z score for X = 73 is _____.

9. Suppose a population of values is normally distributed with a mean of 250 and a variance of 225. The Z score for X = 286 is _____.

10. Suppose a population of values is normally distributed with a mean of 9.8 and a standard deviation of 2.5. The probability that a value is greater than 11 in the distribution is _____.

11. A population is normally distributed with a mean of 80 and a variance of 400. The probability that X lies between 50 and 100 is _____.

12. A population is normally distributed with a mean of 115 and a standard deviation of 13. The probability that a value is less than 85 is _____.

13. A population is normally distributed with a mean of 64. The probability that a value from this population is more than 70 is .0485. The standard deviation is

_____.

14. A population is normally distributed with a mean of 90. 85.99% of the values in this population are greater than 75. The standard deviation of this population is

_____.

15. A population is normally distributed with a standard deviation of 18.5. 69.85% of the values in this population are greater than 93. The mean of the population is _____.

16. A population is normally distributed with a variance of 50. 98.17% of the values of the population are less than 27. The mean of the population is _____.

17. A population is normally distributed with a mean of 340
    and a standard deviation of 55.   10.93% of values in
    the population are less than _____.

18. In working a binomial distribution problem by using the
    normal distribution, the interval, _____, should lie
    between 0 and n.

19. A binomial distribution problem has an n of 10 and a p
    value of .20.   This problem _____ be worked
    by the normal distribution because of the size of
    n and p.

20. A binomial distribution problem has an n of 15 and a p
    value of .60.   This problem _____ be worked
    by the normal distribution because of the size of n and
    p.

21. A binomial distribution problem has an n of 30 and a p
    value of .35.   A researcher wants to determine the
    probability of X being greater than 13 and to use the
    normal distribution to work the problem.   After
    correcting for continuity, the value of X that he/she
    will be solving for is _____.

22.   A binomial distribution problem has an n of 48 and a p
      value of .80. A researcher wants to determine the
      probability of X being less than or equal to 35 and
      wants to work the problem using the normal
      distribution. After correcting for continuity, the
      value of X that he/she will be solving for is

      _____.

23.   A binomial distribution problem has an n of 60 and a p
      value of .72. A researcher wants to determine the
      probability of X being exactly 45 and use the normal
      distribution to work the problem. After correcting for
      continuity, he/she will be solving for the area between

      _____ and _____.

24.   A binomial distribution problem has an n of 27 and a p
      value of .53. If this problem were converted to a
      normal distribution problem, the mean of the
      distribution would be _____. The standard deviation
      of the distribution would be _____.

25.   A binomial distribution problem has an n of 113 and a p
      value of .29. If this problem were converted to a
      normal distribution problem, the mean of the
      distribution would be _____. The standard deviation
      of the distribution would be _____.

26. A binomial distribution problem is to determine the probability that X is less than 22 when the sample size is 40 and the value of p is .50. Using the normal distribution to work this problem produces a probability of _____.

27. A binomial distribution problem is to determine the probability that X is exactly 14 when the sample size is 20 and the value of p is .60. Using the normal distribution to work this problem produces a probability of _____.

28. A binomial distribution problem is to determine the probability that X is greater than or equal to 18 when the sample size is 30 and the value of p is .55. Using the normal distribution to work this problem produces a probability of _____.

29. A binomial distribution problem is to determine the probability that X is greater than 10 when the sample size is 20 and the value of p is .60. Using the normal distribution to work this problem produces a probability of _____. If this problem had been worked using the binomial tables, the obtained probability would have been _____. The difference in answers using these two techniques is _____.

30.   The exponential distribution is a_____
      distribution.

31.   The exponential distribution is closely related to the
      _____ distribution.

32.   The exponential distribution is skewed to the _____.

33.   Suppose random arrivals occur at a rate of 5 per
      minute. Assuming that random arrivals are Poisson
      distributed, the probability of there being at least 30
      seconds between arrivals is _____.

34.   Suppose random arrivals occur at a rate of 1 per hour.
      Assuming that random arrivals are Poisson distributed,
      the probability of there being less than 2 hours
      between arrivals is _____.

35.   Suppose random arrivals occur at a rate of 1.6 every
      five minutes. Assuming that random arrivals are
      Poisson distributed, the probability of there being
      between three minutes and six minutes between arrivals
      is _____.

36.   Suppose that the mean time between arrivals is 40
      seconds and that random arrivals are Poisson
      distributed. The probability that at least one minute
      passes between two arrivals is _____.   The
      probability that at least two minutes pass between two
      arrivals is _____.

37. Suppose that the mean time between arrivals is ten minutes and than random arrivals are Poisson distributed. The probability that no more than seven minutes pass between two arrivals is _____.

38. The mean of an exponential distribution equals

_____.

39. Suppose that random arrivals are Poisson distributed with an average arrival of 2.4 per five minutes. The associated exponential distribution would have a mean of _____ and a standard deviation of

_____.

40. An exponential distribution has an average interarrival time of 25 minutes. The standard deviation of this distribution is _____.

V.   **ANSWERS TO STUDY QUESTIONS**

1. Normal

2. Normal

3. 1

4. Z

5. Standard deviations

6. 68%

7. 1.25

8. -0.58

9. 2.40

10. .3156

11. .7745

12. .0104

13. 3.614

14. 13.89

15. 102.62

16. 12.22

17. 272.35

18. $\mu \pm 3\sigma$

19. cannot

20   can

21. $\geq$ 13.5

22. $\leq$ 35.5

23. 44.5,   45.5

24. 14.31,   2.59

25. 32.77,   4.82

26. .6808

27. .1212

28. .3557

29. .7517,   .7550,   .0033

30. Continuous

31. Poisson

32. Right

33. .0821

34. .8647

35. .2363

36. .2231,   .0498

37. .5034

38. $1 / \lambda$

39. 2.08 minutes, 2.08 minutes

40. 25 minutes

VI. SOLUTIONS TO ODD-NUMBERED PROBLEMS IN TEXT

6.1 a)   for $Z = 2.34$ $\boxed{.4904}$

b)   for $Z = 1.64$ $\boxed{.4495}$

c)   for $Z = 0.81$ $\boxed{.2910}$

d)   for $Z = -2.93$ $\boxed{.4983}$

e)   for $Z = -0.42$ $\boxed{.1628}$

6.3 a) $\mu = 100,$ $\sigma = 9,$ $X = 115$

$$Z = \frac{X - \mu}{\sigma} = \frac{115 - 100}{9} = \frac{15}{9} = \boxed{.167}$$

b) $\mu = 34,$ $\sigma = 2.16,$ $X = 35$

$$Z = \frac{X - \mu}{\sigma} = \frac{35 - 34}{2.16} = \frac{1}{2.16} = \boxed{0.46}$$

c) $\mu = 259,$ $\sigma = 30.6,$ $X = 251$

$$Z = \frac{X - \mu}{\sigma} = \frac{251 - 259}{30.6} - \frac{-8}{30.6} = \boxed{-0.26}$$

d) $\mu = 157,$ $\sigma = 3.45,$ $X = 145$

$$Z = \frac{X - \mu}{\sigma} = \frac{145 - 157}{3.45} = \frac{-12}{3.45} = \boxed{-3.48}$$

6.5 $\mu = 200,$ $\sigma = 47$ Determine X

a)   60% of the values are greater than X:

Since 50% of the values are greater than the mean, $\mu = 200$,
10% or .1000 lie between X and the mean.   From Table A.5,
the Z value associated with an area of .1000 is Z = -0.25.
The Z value is negative since X is below the mean.
Substituting Z = -0.25, $\mu = 200$, and $\sigma = 47$ into the formula
and solving for X:

$$Z = \frac{X - \mu}{\sigma}$$

$$-0.25 = \frac{X - 200}{47}$$

$$X = \boxed{188.25}$$

b)   X is less than 17% of the values.

Since X is only less than 17% of the values, 33% (.5000-
.1700) or .3300 lie between X and the mean.   Table A.5
yields a Z value of 0.95 for an area of .3300.
Using this Z = 0.95, $\mu = 200$, and $\sigma = 47$, X can be solved
for:

$$Z = \frac{X - \mu}{\sigma}$$

$$.95 = \frac{X - 200}{47}$$

$$X = \boxed{244.65}$$

c)   22% of the values are less than X.

Since 22% of the values lie below X, 28% lie between X and
the mean (.5000 - .2200).   Table A.5 yields a Z of -0.77 for
an area of .2800.   Using the Z value of -0.77, μ = 200, and
σ = 47, X can be solved for:

$$Z = \frac{X - \mu}{\sigma}$$

$$-0.77 = \frac{X - 200}{47}$$

$$X = \boxed{163.81}$$

d)   X is greater than 55% of the values.

Since X is greater than 55% of the values, 5% (.0500) lie
between X and the mean.   From Table A.5, a Z value of 0.13
is associated with an area of .05.   Using Z = 0.13, μ = 200,
and σ = 47, X can be solved for:

$$Z = \frac{X - \mu}{\sigma}$$

$$.13 = \frac{X - 200}{47}$$

$$X = \boxed{206.11}$$

6.7 μ = $788 σ = $113

a)   Prob(X > $700):

$$Z = \frac{X - \mu}{\sigma} = \frac{\$700 - \$788}{\$113} = \frac{-\$88}{\$113} = -0.78$$
The Table A.5 value for Z = -0.78 = .2823

Prob(X > $700) = .2823 + .5000 = $\boxed{.7823}$

b)   Prob(X < $500):

$$Z = \frac{X - \mu}{\sigma} = \frac{\$500 - \$788}{\$113} = \frac{-\$288}{\$113} = -2.55$$
The Table A.5 value for Z = -2.55:   .4946

Prob(X < $500) = .5000 - .4946 = $\boxed{.0053}$

c)   Prob($\$800 \leq X \leq \$1,000$):

$$Z = \underline{\frac{X - \mu}{\sigma}} = \underline{\frac{\$1,000 - \$788}{\$113}} = \underline{\frac{\$212}{\$113}} = 1.88$$

Table A.5 value for Z = 1.88:   .4699

$$Z = \underline{\frac{X - \mu}{\sigma}} = \underline{\frac{\$800 - \$788}{\$113}} = \underline{\frac{\$12}{\$113}} = 0.11$$

Table A.5 value for Z = 0.11:   .0438

Prob($\$800 \leq X \leq \$1,000$) = .4699 - .0438 = $\boxed{.4261}$

6.9 σ = $113. Since 31% of all values are less than X = $700, .1900 (.5000 - .3100) of the values fall between X and the Mean. Table A.5 gives a Z = -0.50 for an area of .1900.

$$Z = \underline{\frac{X - \mu}{\sigma}}$$

$$-0.50 = \underline{\frac{\$700 - \mu}{\$113}}$$

$$\mu = \boxed{756.5}$$

6.11 μ = 9.7 Since 22.45% are greater than 11.6, X = 11.6 is in the upper half of the distribution and .2755 (.5000 - .2245) lie between X and the mean.

Table A.5 yields a Z = 0.76 for an area of .2755.

Solving for σ:

$$Z = \underline{\frac{X - \mu}{\sigma}}$$

$$0.76 = \underline{\frac{11.6 - 9.7}{\sigma}}$$

$$\sigma = 2.5$$

The variance: $\sigma^2 = \boxed{6.25}$

6.13 $\mu = 10.1$ $\sigma = 0.4$

a)   Prob(X > 9.5):

$$Z = \frac{X - \mu}{\sigma} = \frac{9.5 - 10.1}{0.4} = -1.50$$

From Table A.5, the Z = -1.50 yields: .4332

Prob(X > 9.5) = .4332 +.5000 = $\boxed{.9332}$

b)   Prob(10 < X < 11):

$$Z = \frac{X - \mu}{\sigma} = \frac{11 - 10.1}{0.4} = 2.25$$

From Table A.5, the Z = 2.25 yields: .4878

$$Z = \frac{X - \mu}{\sigma} = \frac{10 - 10.1}{0.4} = -0.25$$

From Table A.5, the Z = -0.25 yields: .0987

Prob(10 < X < 11) = .4878 +.0987 = $\boxed{.5865}$

c)   Prob(X < 9):

$$Z = \frac{9 - 10.1}{0.4} = -2.75$$

From Table A.5, Z = -2.75 yields: .4970

Prob(X < 9) = .5000 - 4970 = $\boxed{.0030}$

d)   Prob(9.5 ≤ X ≤ 10.5):

$$Z = \frac{X - \mu}{\sigma} = \frac{10.5 - 10.1}{0.4} = 1.00$$

From Table A.5, the Z = 1.00 yields: .3413

$$Z = \frac{X - \mu}{\sigma} = \frac{9.5 - 10.1}{0.4} = -1.50$$

From Table A.5, the Z = -1.50 yields: .4332

Prob(9.5 ≤ X ≤ 10.5) = .3413 +.4332 = $\boxed{.7745}$

6.15 a) $P(X \le 16 | n = 30 \text{ and } p = .70)$

$\mu = n \cdot p = 30(.70) = 21$

$\sigma = \sqrt{n \cdot p \cdot q} = \sqrt{30(.70)(.30)} = 2.51$

$$\boxed{P(X \le 16.5 | \mu = 21 \text{ and } \sigma = 2.51)}$$

b) $P(10 < X \le 20 | n = 25 \text{ and } p = .50)$

$\mu = n \cdot p = 25(.50) = 12.5$

$\sigma = \sqrt{n \cdot p \cdot q} = \sqrt{25(.50)(.50)} = 2.5$

$$\boxed{P(10.5 \le X \le 20.5 | \mu = 12.5 \text{ and } \sigma = 2.5)}$$

c) $P(X = 22 | n = 40 \text{ and } p = .60)$

$\mu = n \cdot p = 40(.60) = 24$

$\sigma = \sqrt{n \cdot p \cdot q} = \sqrt{40(.60)(.40)} = 3.10$

$$\boxed{P(21.5 \le X \le 22.5 | \mu = 24 \text{ and } \sigma = 3.10)}$$

d) $P(X > 14 | n = 16 \text{ and } p = .45)$

$\mu = n \cdot p = 16(.45) = 7.2$

$\sigma = \sqrt{n \cdot p \cdot q} = \sqrt{16(.45)(.55)} = 1.99$

$$\boxed{P(X \ge 14.5 | \mu = 7.2 \text{ and } \sigma = 1.99)}$$

6.17 a) $P(X = 8 | n = 25$ and $p = .40)$

  $\mu = n \cdot p = 25(.40) = 10$

  $\sigma = \sqrt{n \cdot p \cdot q} = \sqrt{25(.40)(.60)} = 2.449$

  $\mu \pm 3\sigma = 10 \pm 3(2.449) = 10 \pm 7.347$

  (2.653 to 17.347) lies between 0 and 25.
  Approximation by the normal curve is sufficient.

  $P(7.5 \leq X \leq 8.5 | \mu = 10$ and $\sigma = 2.449)$:

$Z = \dfrac{7.5 - 10}{2.449} = -1.02$

From Table A.5, area = .3461

$Z = \dfrac{8.5 - 10}{2.449} = -0.61$

From Table A.5, area = .2291

$P(7.5 \leq X \leq 8.5) = .3461 - .2291 = $ $\boxed{.1170}$

From Table A.2 (binomial tables) = $\boxed{.120}$

b) $P(X \geq 13 | n = 20$ and $p = .60)$

$\mu = n \cdot p = 20(.60) = 12$

  $\sigma = \sqrt{n \cdot p \cdot q} = \sqrt{20(.60)(.40)} = 2.19$

$\mu \pm 3\sigma = 12 \pm 3(2.19) = 12 \pm 6.57$

(5.43 to 18.57) lies between 0 and 20.
Approximation by the normal curve is sufficient.

$P(X \geq 12.5 | \mu = 12$ and $\sigma = 2.19)$:

$Z = \dfrac{X - \mu}{\sigma} = \dfrac{12.5 - 12}{2.19} = \dfrac{0.5}{2.19} = 0.23$

From Table A.5, area = .0910

$P(X \geq 12.5) = .5000 - .0910 = $ $\boxed{.4090}$

From Table A.2 (binomial tables) = $\boxed{.415}$

c) $P(X = 7 | n = 15$ and $p = .50)$

$\mu = n \cdot p = 15(.50) = 7.5$

$\sigma = \sqrt{n \cdot p \cdot q} = \sqrt{15(.50)(.50)} = 1.9365$

$\mu \pm 3\sigma = 7.5 \pm 3(1.9365) = 7.5 \pm 5.81$

(1.69 to 13.31) lies between 0 and 15.
Approximation by the normal curve is sufficient.

$P(6.5 \leq X \leq 7.5 | \mu = 7.5$ and $\sigma = 1.9365)$:

$Z = \dfrac{X - \mu}{\sigma} = \dfrac{6.5 - 7.5}{1.9365} = -0.52$

From Table A.5, area = $\boxed{.1985}$

From Table A.2 (binomial tables) = $\boxed{.196}$

d) $P(X < 3 | n = 10$ and $p = .70)$:

$\mu = n \cdot p = 10(.70) = 7$

$\sigma = \sqrt{n \cdot p \cdot q} = \sqrt{10(.70)(.30)} = 1.449$

$\mu \pm 3\sigma = 7 \pm 3(1.449) = 7 \pm 4.347$

(2.653 to 11.347) does not lie between 0 and 10.
The normal curve is not a good approximation to this
problem.

6.19 n = 70 and p = .225

P(X < 15|n = 70 and p = .255)

$\mu = n \cdot p = 70(.255) = 17.85$

$\sigma = \sqrt{n \cdot p \cdot q} = \sqrt{70(.255)(.745)} = 3.647$

$\mu \pm 3\sigma = 17.85 \pm 3(3.647) = 17.85 \pm 10.941$

(6.909 to 28.791) lies between 0 and 70.
The normal curve approximation is okay.

P(X ≤ 14.5|μ = 17.85 and σ = 3.647):

$Z = \dfrac{X - \mu}{\sigma} = \dfrac{14.5 - 17.85}{3.647} = -0.92$

From Table A.5, area = $\boxed{.3212}$

P(X ≤ 14.5) = .5000 - .3212 = $\boxed{.1788}$

6.21 P(X < 5|n = 35 and p = .41)

$\mu = n \cdot p = 35(.41) = 14.35$

$\sigma = \sqrt{n \cdot p \cdot q} = \sqrt{35(.41)(.59)} = 2.91$

$\mu \pm 3\sigma = 14.35 \pm 3(2.91) = 14.35 \pm 8.73$

(5.62 to 23.08) lies between 0 and 35.
The normal curve approximation is sufficient.

P(X ≤ 4.5|μ = 14.35 and σ = 2.91):

$Z = \dfrac{X - \mu}{\sigma} = \dfrac{4.5 - 14.35}{2.91} = -3.38$

From Table A.5, area = .4996

P(X ≤ 4.5) = .5000 - .4996 = $\boxed{.0004}$

6.23 a) $P(X \leq 20 | n = 150 \text{ and } p = .29)$

$\mu = n \cdot p = 150(.29) = 43.5$

$\sigma = \sqrt{n \cdot p \cdot q} = \sqrt{150(.29)(.71)} = 5.56$

$\mu \pm 3\sigma = 43.5 \pm 3(5.56) = 43.5 \pm 16.68$

(26.82 to 60.18) lies between 0 and 150.
The normal curve approximation is sufficient.

$P(X \leq 20.5 | \mu = 43.5 \text{ and } \sigma = 5.56):$

$Z = \dfrac{X - \mu}{\sigma} = \dfrac{20.5 - 43.5}{5.56} = -4.14$

From Table A.5, area = .5000

$P(X \leq 20.5) = .5000 - .5000 = \boxed{.0000}$

b) $P(X \leq 20 | n = 150 \text{ and } p = .07)$

$\mu = n \cdot p = 150(.07) = 10.5$

$\sigma = \sqrt{n \cdot p \cdot q} = \sqrt{150(.07)(.93)} = 3.125$

$\mu \pm 3\sigma = 10.5 \pm 3(3.125) = 10.5 \pm 9.375$

(1.125 to 19.875) lies between 0 and 150.
The normal curve approximation is sufficient.

$P(X \leq 20.5 | \mu = 10.5 \text{ and } \sigma = 3.125):$

$Z = \dfrac{X - \mu}{\sigma} = \dfrac{20.5 - 10.5}{3.125} = 3.2$

From Table A.5, area = .4993

$P(X \leq 20.5) = .5000 - .4993 = \boxed{.9993}$

6.25 a) $\lambda = 3.25$

$$\mu = \frac{1}{\lambda} = 1/3.25 = \boxed{0.31}$$

$$\sigma = \frac{1}{\lambda} = \boxed{0.31}$$

b) $\lambda = 0.7$

$$\mu = \frac{1}{\lambda} = 1/.007 = \boxed{1.43}$$

$$\sigma = \frac{1}{\lambda} = \boxed{1.43}$$

c) $\lambda = 1.1$

$$\mu = \frac{1}{\lambda} = 1/1.1 = \boxed{0.91}$$

$$\sigma = \frac{1}{\lambda} = \boxed{0.91}$$

d) $\lambda = 6.0$

$$\mu = \frac{1}{\lambda} = 1/6 = \boxed{0.17}$$

$$\sigma = \frac{1}{\lambda} = \boxed{0.17}$$

6.27 $\lambda = 0.3/week$

a) $P(X \leq 1 | \lambda = 0.3) = 1 - P(X > 1 | \lambda = 0.3) =$

  for $X_0 = 1$ $Prob = 1 - e^{-\lambda X} = 1 - e^{-0.3(1)} = 1 - e^{-.3} = 1 - .7408$

  $= \boxed{.2592}$

b) $P(X > 4 | \lambda = 0.3)$

  for $X_0 = 4$ $Prob = e^{-\lambda X_0} = e^{-0.3(4)} = e^{-1.2}$

  $= \boxed{.3012}$

c) $P(X \geq 36 | \lambda = 0.3) =$

  for $X_0 = 36$ $Prob = e^{-\lambda X_0} = e^{-0.3(36)} = e^{-10.8}$

  $= \boxed{.0000}$

6.29 $\mu = 20$ years

  $\lambda = \dfrac{1}{20} = .05/year$

X_0	$Prob(X \geq X_0) = e^{-\lambda X_0}$
1	.9512
2	.9048
3	.8607

If the foundation is guaranteed for 2 years, based on past history, 90.48% of the foundations will last at least 2 years without major repair and only 9.52% will require a major repair before 2 years.

6.31 λ = 1.12 planes/hr.

a) $\mu = \dfrac{1}{\lambda} = \dfrac{1}{1.12}$ = .89 hr. = 53.4 min.

b)   P(X $\geq$ 2 hrs| λ = 1.12 planes/hr.) =

Let X_0 = 2

$e^{-\lambda X_0} = e^{-1.12(2)} = e^{-2.24}$

= $\boxed{.1065}$

c)   P(X < 10 min| λ = 1.12/hr.) =

1 - P(X $\geq$ 10 min| λ = 1.12/hr.)

Change λ to 1.12/60 = .01867/min.

1 - P(X $\geq$ 10 min| λ = .01867/min)=

Let X_0 = 10

$1 - e^{-\lambda X_0} = 1 - e^{-.01867(10)} = 1 - e^{-.1861} = 1 - .8297$

= $\boxed{.1703}$

6.33 a) P(X < 21|μ = 25 and σ = 4)

$Z = \dfrac{X - \mu}{\sigma} = \dfrac{21 - 25}{4} = \dfrac{-4}{4} = -1.00$

From Table A.5, area = .3413

P(X < 21) = .5000 −.3413 = $\boxed{.1587}$

b)   P(X $\geq$ 77|n = 50 and σ = 9)

$Z = \dfrac{X - \mu}{\sigma} = \dfrac{77 - 50}{9} = \dfrac{27}{9} = 3.00$

From Table A.5, area = .4987

P(X $\geq$ 77) = .5000 −.4987 = $\boxed{.0013}$

c) $P(X > 47 | \mu = 50 \text{ and } \sigma = 6)$

$$Z = \frac{X - \mu}{\sigma} = \frac{47 - 50}{6} = \frac{-3}{6} = -0.50$$

From Table A.5, area = .1915

$$P(X > 47) = .5000 + .1915 = \boxed{.6915}$$

d) $P(13 < X < 29 | \mu = 23 \text{ and } \sigma = 4)$

$$Z = \frac{X - \mu}{\sigma} = \frac{13 - 23}{4} = \frac{-10}{4} = -2.50$$

From Table A.5, area = .4938

$$Z = \frac{X - \mu}{\sigma} = \frac{29 - 23}{4} = \frac{6}{4} = 1.50$$

From Table A.5, area = .4332

$$P(13 < X < 29) = .4938 + .4332 = \boxed{.9270}$$

e) $P(X \geq 105 | \mu = 90 \text{ and } \sigma = 2.86)$

$$Z = \frac{X - \mu}{\sigma} = \frac{105 - 90}{2.86} = 5.24$$

From Table A.5, area = .5000

$$P(X \geq 105) = .5000 - .5000 = \boxed{.0000}$$

6.35

a) $P(X \geq 3 | \lambda = 1.3)$

let $x_0 = 3$

$P(X \geq 3 | \lambda = 1.3) = e^{-\lambda x} = e^{-1.3(3)} = e^{-3.9}$

$= \boxed{.0202}$

b) $P(X < 2 | \lambda = 2.0)$

Let $x_0 = 2$

$P(X < 2 | \lambda = 2.0) = 1 - P(X \geq 2 | \lambda = 2.0) =$

$1 - e^{-\lambda x} = 1 - e^{-2(2)} = 1 - e^{-4} = 1 - (.0183)$

$= \boxed{.9817}$

c) $P(1 \leq X \leq 3 | \lambda = 1.65)$

$P(X \geq 1 | \lambda = 1.65):$

Let $x_0 = 1$

$e^{-\lambda x} = e^{-1.65(1)} = e^{-1.65} = .1920$

$P(X \geq 3 | \lambda = 1.65):$

Let $X_0 = 3$

$e^{-\lambda x} = e^{-1.65(3)} = e^{-4.95} = .0071$

$P(1 \leq X \leq 3) = P(X \geq 1) - P(X \geq 3) = .1920 - .0071$

$= \boxed{.1849}$

d) $P(X > 2 | \lambda = 0.405)$

Let $x_0 = 2$

$e^{-\lambda x} = e^{-(.405)(2)} = e^{-.81}$

$= \boxed{.4449}$

6.37 $\mu = 3.482$

93.19% were higher than 2.50.
Therefore, 2.50 is at the lower end of the distribution and
.9319 - .5000 = .4319 of the values lie between
X = 2.50 and the mean, $\mu = 3.482$.

Table A.5 contains a Z = -1.49 for area of .4319.

Using Z = -1.49, X = 2.50 and $\mu = 3.482$, solving for σ:

$$Z = \frac{X - \mu}{\sigma}$$

$$-1.49 = \frac{2.50 - 3.482}{\sigma}$$

$$\boxed{\sigma = .659}$$

6.39 $\mu = 161$ $\sigma = 32.63$

Only 20% fewer than X.
X is located in the lower region of the distribution.

.5000 - .2000 = .3000 of the values lie between X and the
mean. Table A.5 shows a value of Z = -.84 near to an area
of .3000. Using Z = -.84, $\mu = 161$, $\sigma = 32.63$, the value of
X can be solved for:

$$Z = \frac{X - \mu}{\sigma}$$

$$-0.84 = \frac{X - 161}{32.63}$$

$$X = \boxed{133.59}$$

6.41 $\mu = 42$

60% of the values fall between 33 and 51

Since 33 and 51 are equal distance from the mean, .3000 of
the area lies between x = 51 and the mean.
Table A.5 yields a Z = 0.84 for area = .3000.
Using $\mu = 42$, X = 51, Z = 0.84, σ can be solved for:

$$Z = \frac{X - \mu}{\sigma}$$

$$0.84 = \frac{51 - 42}{\sigma}$$

$$\sigma = 10.714$$

$$\boxed{\sigma^2 = 114.8}$$

6.43 $\mu_1 = 1,750$ $\sigma_1 = 2.75$ (4-year universities)

$\mu_2 = 650$ $\sigma_2 = 215$ (2-year colleges)

Four-year universities:

Using the empirical rule, almost all values fall within
$\mu \pm 3\sigma$.
Virtually, no four-year universities would have tuition less
than $\mu - 3\sigma = 1,750 - 3(275) = 925$.

Two-year colleges:

How many two-year colleges have tuition greater than X =
$925?

$$Z = \frac{X - \mu}{\sigma} = \frac{925 - 650}{215} = 1.28$$

From Table A.5, area = .3997

$P(X > 925) = .5000 - .3997 = \boxed{.1003}$

Approximately 10% of the two-year colleges would have
tuition greater than the lowest of the four-year
universities.

6.45 $\mu = 88$ $\sigma = 6.4$

a)   p(x < 70):

Z = $\frac{70 - 88}{6.4}$ = -2.81

From Table A.5, area = .4975

P(X < 70) = .5000 - .4975 = $\boxed{.0025}$

b)   P(X > 80):

Z = $\frac{80 - 88}{6.4}$ = -1.25

From Table A.5, area = .3944

P(X > 80) = .5000 + .3944 = $\boxed{.8944}$

c)   P(90 ≤ X ≤ 100):

Z = $\frac{100 - 88}{6.4}$ = 1.88

From Table A.5, area = .4699

Z = $\frac{90 - 88}{6.4}$ = .31

From Table A.5, area = .1217

P(90 ≤ X ≤ 100) = .4699 - .1217 = $\boxed{.3482}$

6.47 $\mu = 4.03$ $\sigma = 1.3$

a) $P(X > 6)$:

   $Z = \dfrac{6 - 4.03}{1.3} = 1.52$

   From Table A.5, area = .4357

   $P(X > 6) = .5000 - .4357 = \boxed{.0643}$

b) $P(3 \le X \le 4)$:

   $Z = \dfrac{3 - 4.03}{1.3} = -0.79$

   From Table A.5, area = .2852

   $Z = \dfrac{4 - 4.03}{1.3} = \dfrac{-0.03}{1.3} = -.03$

   From Table A.5, area = .0120

   $P(3 \le X \le 4) = .2852 - .0120 = \boxed{.2732}$

c) $P(X < 1)$:

   $Z = \dfrac{1 - 4.03}{1.3} = -2.33$

   From Table A.5, area = .4901

   $P(X < 1) = .5000 - .4901 = \boxed{.0099}$

d) $\mu = 4.03$

Since 85% of the values are greater than 2.7,
X = 2.7 is in the lower tail of the distribution.
.8500 - .5000 = .3500 of the values lie between X = 2.7 and
the mean.

From Table A.5, Z = -1.04 is obtained for an area of .3500.

Solving for σ:

$$Z = \frac{X - \mu}{\sigma}$$

$$-1.04 = \frac{2.7 - 4.03}{\sigma}$$

$$\boxed{\sigma = 1.28 \text{ inches/month}}$$

6.49 Since .629 prefer Japanese brands,

P = 1 - .629 = .371 do not prefer

n = 200

P(X > 100):

$\mu = n \cdot p = 200(.371) = 74.2$

$\sigma = \sqrt{n \cdot p \cdot q} = \sqrt{200(.371)(.629)} = 6.83$

$\mu \pm 3\sigma = 74.2 \pm 3(6.83) = 74.2 \pm 20.49$

(53.71 to 94.69) lies between 0 and 200.
The normal curve approximation is sufficient.

P(X $\geq$ 100.5 | μ = 74.2 and σ = 6.83):

$$Z = \frac{100.5 - 74.2}{6.83} = \frac{26.3}{6.83} = 3.85$$

From Table A.5, area = .5000

P(X $\geq$ 100.5) = .5000 - .5000 = $\boxed{.0000}$

6.51 n = 500   P = .02

P(X = 0):

$\mu = n \cdot p = 500(.02) = 10$

$\sigma = \sqrt{n \cdot p \cdot q} = 3.13$

$\mu \pm 3\sigma = 10 \pm 3(3.13) = 10 \pm 9.39$

(0.61 to 19.39) lies between 0 and 500.

The normal curve approximation is sufficient.

$P(0 \le X \le +0.5 | \mu = 10$ and $\sigma = 3.13)$:

(Cannot correct into negatives here.
 Negatives not possible.)

$Z = \dfrac{X - \sigma}{\sigma} = \dfrac{0.5 - 10}{3.13} = -3.04$

From Table A.5, area = .4988

$Z = \dfrac{X - \mu}{\sigma} = \dfrac{0 - 10}{3.13} = -3.19$

From Table A.5, area = .4993

$P(-0.5 \le X \le +0.5) = .4993 - .4988 = \boxed{.0005}$

Expected number $= \mu = \boxed{10}$

6.53 Rhode Island: 100% - 56% = 44% = .44 had some increase in administrative costs.   n = 75

Expected value = μ = n·p = 75(.44) = $\boxed{33}$

Oregon: 100% - 66% = 34% = .34 had some increase in administrative costs.   n = 75

Expected value = μ = n·p = 75(.34) = $\boxed{25.5}$

Rhode Island: 56% = p = .56 = probability no increase in administrative costs.   n = 75

P(X ≥ 42|n = 75 and p = .56):

μ = n·p = 75(.56) = 42

$\sigma = \sqrt{n \cdot p \cdot q} = \sqrt{75(.56)(.44)} = 4.30$

$\mu \pm 3\sigma = 42 \pm 3(4.30) = 42 \pm 12.90$

(29.1 to 54.9) lies between 0 and n = 75.
The normal curve approximation is sufficient.

P(X ≥ 41.5|μ = 42 and σ = 4.30)

$Z = \dfrac{X - \mu}{\sigma} = \dfrac{41.5 - 42}{4.30} = \dfrac{-0.5}{4.30} = -0.12$

From Table A.5, area = .0478

P(X ≥ 41.5) = .0478 + .5000 = $\boxed{.5478}$

6.55 μ = 9 minutes

$\lambda = 1/\mu = .1111/\text{minute} = .1111(60)/\text{hour}$

λ = 6.67/hour

P(X $\geq$ 5 minutes $\mid$ λ = .1111/minute) =

1 - P(X $\geq$ 5 minutes$\mid$ λ =.1111/minute):

Let X_0 = 5

P(X $\geq$ 5 minutes $\mid$ λ = .1111/minute) =

$e^{-\lambda \, X_0} = e^{-.1111(5)} = e^{-.5555} = .5738$

P(X < 5 minutes) = 1 - P(X $\geq$ 5 minutes) = 1 - .5738

= $\boxed{.4262}$

6.57 $\lambda = 1$ meteor/20 minutes

P(X $\geq$ 1 hour| $\lambda = 1/$ 20 minutes):

Since Lambda and X are for different time periods,

Change Lambda to: $\lambda = 3$/hour

P(X $\geq$ 1 hour| $\lambda = 3$/hour

Let $X_0 = 1$

$$P(X \geq 1) = e^{-\lambda X_0} = e^{-3(1)} = e^{-3} = \boxed{.0498}$$

10 minutes = $\dfrac{10}{60}$ = .167 hour and

30 minutes = $\dfrac{30}{60}$ = .500 hour and

P(.167 $\leq$ X $\leq$ .500 hour| $\lambda = 3$/hour) =

P(X $\geq$ .167) - P(X $\geq$ .500)

Let $X_0 = .167$

$$P(X \geq .167) = e^{-\lambda X_0} = e^{-3(.167)} = e^{-.501} = .6059$$

Let $X_0 = .500$

$$P(X \geq .500) = e^{-\lambda X_0} = e^{-3(.5)} = e^{-1.5} = .2231$$

P(X $\geq$ .167) - P(X $\geq$ .500) = .6059 - .2231 = $\boxed{.3828}$

5 minutes = $\dfrac{5}{60}$ = $\dfrac{1}{12}$ = .0833 hour

P(X $\leq$ .0833| $\lambda = 3$/hours):

1 - P(X > .0833| $\lambda = 3$/hour) =

Let $X_0 = .0833$

$$P(X > .0833) = e^{-\lambda X_0} = e^{-3(.0833)} = e^{-.2499} = .7789$$

P(X $\leq$ .0833) = 1 - P(X > .0833) = 1 - .7789 = $\boxed{.2211}$

6.59 λ = 1.8/ 15 sec.

a) μ = $\dfrac{1}{\lambda}$ = 1/1.8 = .5556 of 15 sec. = $\boxed{\text{8.33 sec.}}$

b)   P(X $\geq$ 25 sec| λ =1.8/ 15 sec.):

X and Lambda have different intervals.

Change Lambda to seconds: λ = 1.8/15 = 0.12 per second

P(X $\geq$ 25 seconds | λ = 0.12/second):

Let X_0 = 25

$P(X \geq 25) = e^{-\lambda X_0} = e^{-0.12(25)} = e^{-3}$

= $\boxed{.0498}$

c)   P(X < 5 seconds| λ = 0.12/second) =

1 - P(X $\geq$ 5 seconds | λ = 0.12/second)

P(X $\geq$ 5 seconds):
Let X_0 = 5

$P(X \geq 5) = e^{-\lambda X_0} = e^{-0.12(5)} = e^{-0} = .5488$

P(X < 5 seconds) = 1 - P(X $\geq$ 5 seconds) = 1 - .5488

= $\boxed{.4512}$

d)   P(X $\geq$ 1 minute| λ = 1.8/ 15 seconds)

Since X and Lambda are for different intervals,
Change Lambda to 1.8(4) = 7.2/minute.

P(X $\geq$ 1 minute | λ = 7.2/ 1 minute)

Let X_0 = 1

$P(X \geq 1) = e^{-\lambda X_0} = e^{-7.2(1)} = e^{-7.2}$

= $\boxed{.0007}$

7

SAMPLING, SAMPLING DISTRIBUTIONS, AND QUALITY CONTROL

I. **CHAPTER OBJECTIVES**

The three main learning objectives for chapter seven are to give you (a) an appreciation for the proper application of sampling techniques, (b) an understanding of the sampling distributions of several statistics, and (c) the ability to apply several quality control techniques - thereby enabling you to:

1. Distinguish between random and nonrandom sampling.

2. Decide when to use various sampling techniques.

3. Use the sampling distributions of $\overline{X}$, $\hat{p}$, $\overline{X}_1 - \overline{X}_2$, and $\hat{p}_1 - \hat{p}_2$ to analyze data.

4. Use quality control terminology, and construct control charts.

170

7.6 Quality Control

      What is Quality?

      What is Quality Control?

      Total Quality Management

      Diagnostic Techniques

            Pareto Analysis

            Fishbone Diagram

            Quality Circles

            Just-in-Time Systems

      Control Charts

            $\overline{X}$ Charts

            R Charts

            P Charts

III. **KEY WORDS**

Frame	Omission Error
Random Sampling	Detail Error
Nonrandom Sampling	Central Limit Theorem
Simple Random Sampling	Finite Correction Factor
Stratified Random Sampling	Sample Proportion
Proportionate Stratified	Quality
Random Sampling	Quality Control
Disproportionate Stratified	After-Process Quality Control
Random Sampling	In-Process Quality Control
Systematic Sampling	Total Quality Management
Cluster(or Area) Sampling	Pareto Analysis
Two-Stage Sampling	Fishbone Diagram
Convenience Sampling	Quality Circle
Judgment Sampling	Just-in-Time Inventory System
Quota Sampling	Control Charts
Sampling Error	X Chart
Nonsampling Errors	R Chart
Telescoping Error	P Chart

IV. **STUDY QUESTIONS**

   1. Saving time and money are reasons to take a

      _____ rather than a census.

   2. If the research process is destructive, taking a

      _____ may be the only option in gathering

      data.

   3. A researcher may opt to take a _____ to

      eliminate the possibility that by chance randomly

      selected items are not representative of the population.

   4. The directory or map from which a sample is taken is

      called the _____.

   5. If the population list from which the researcher takes

      the sample contains fewer units than the target

      population, then the list has _____.

   6. There are two main types of sampling, _____

      sampling and _____ sampling.

   7. If every unit of the population does not have the same

      probability of being selected to the sample, then the

      researcher is probably conducting _____

      sampling.

   8. Nonrandom sampling is sometimes referred to as

      _____ sampling.

   9. The most elementary type of random sampling is

      _____ random sampling.

10. In _____ random sampling, the population is divided into nonoverlapping subpopulations called strata.

11. Whenever the proportions of the strata in the sample are different than the proportions of the strata in the population, _____ _____ random sampling occurs.

12. With _____ random sampling, there is homogeneity within a subgroup or stratum.

13. If a researcher selects every kth item from a population of N items, then he/she is likely conducting _____ random sampling.

14. When the population is divided into nonoverlapping areas and then random samples are drawn from the areas, the researcher is likely conducting _____ or _____ sampling.

15. A nonrandom sampling technique in which elements are selected for the sample based on the convenience of the researcher is called _____ sampling.

16. A nonrandom sampling technique in which elements are selected for the sample based on the judgment of the researcher is called _____ sampling.

17. A nonrandom sampling technique which is similar to stratified random sampling is called _____ sampling.

18. _____ error occurs when, by chance, the sample is not representative of the population.

19. Missing data and recording errors are examples of _____ errors.

20. When a respondent to a survey attributes an event to a wrong time period, it is called a(n) _____ error.

21. When a respondent to a survey fails to mention past events, it is called a(n) _____ error.

22. When a respondent to a survey remembers an event incorrectly, it is called a(n) _____ error.

23. The central limit theorem states that if n is large enough, the sample means are _____ distributed regardless of the shape of the population.

24. According to the central limit theorem, the mean of the sample means for a given size of sample is equal to the _____ _____.

25. According to the central limit theorem, the standard deviation of sample means for a given size of sample equals _____.

26. If samples are being drawn from a known population size, the Z formula for sample means includes a _____ _____ factor.

27. Suppose a population has a mean of 90 and a standard deviation of 27. If a random sample of size 49 is drawn from the population, the probability of drawing a sample with a mean of more than 95 is _____.

28. Suppose a population has a mean of 455 and a variance of 900. If a random sample of size 65 is drawn from the population, the probability that the sample mean is between 448 and 453 is _____.

29. Suppose .60 of the population posses a given characteristic. If a random sample of size 300 is drawn from the population, then the probability that .53 or fewer of the sample possess the characteristic is

    _____.

30. Suppose .36 of a population posses a given characteristic. If a random sample of size 1200 is drawn from the population, then the probability that less than 480 posses that characteristic in the sample is _____.

31. Suppose that there is no difference in the means of two populations. Suppose also that the variance of the first population is 28 and the variance of the second population is 32. A random sample of size 40 is drawn from the first population and a random sample of size 46 is drawn from the second population. The probability of the difference between the first sample mean and the second sample mean being greater than 3 is _____.

32. Suppose that there is no difference in the means of two populations. Suppose also that the standard deviation of the first population is 15 and the standard deviation of the second population is 13. A random sample of size 67 is drawn from the first population and a random sample of size 75 is drawn from the second population. The sample mean of the sample from the first population is 90 and the sample mean of the sample from the second population is 84. The probability of the difference between the first sample mean and the second sample mean being this great or greater is _____.

33. Suppose that .55 of each of two populations possess a given characteristic. Samples of size 500 are randomly drawn from each population. The probability that the difference between the first sample proportion which possess the given characteristic and the second sample proportion which possess the given characteristic being more than +.03 is _____.

34. Suppose that only 12% of all people in each of two populations possess a given characteristic. Suppose a random sample of size 700 is drawn from the first population resulting in a sample proportion of .14 who possess the characteristic. Suppose a random sample of size 570 is drawn from the second population resulting in 63 people who possess the characteristic. The probability of obtaining this difference in sample proportions or more from these populations is _____.

35. When a product delivers what is stipulated for it in its specifications, some people would say that the product has _____.

36. A collection of strategies, techniques, and actions taken by an organization to assure themselves that they are producing a quality product is called

    _____ _____.

37. Inspecting the attributes of a finished product to determine whether the product is acceptable, is in need of rework, or is to be rejected is called _____ quality control.

38. Measuring product attributes at various intervals throughout the manufacturing process in an effort to pinpoint problem areas is called _____ quality control.

39. When an effort at quality control is a long-term total company effort, it is sometimes referred to as

    _____ _____ _____ .

40. One type of quality control diagnostic technique which graphs the common types of defects as a vertical bar chart is called a _____ chart.

41. Another type of quality control diagnostic technique in which cause-and-effect relationships are charted with the problem depicted at the front of the diagram is called a _____ diagram.

42. A _____ _____ is a small group of workers consisting of supervisors and six to ten employees who meet regularly to consider quality issues in their department or area of business.

43. If a company has implemented an inventory system which has as its goal that no extra raw materials or inventory of parts are stored for production, then the company is probably using a _____ inventory system.

44. A graph which displays computed means for a series of small random samples over a period of time is called a(n) _____ chart.

45. A plot of the sample ranges over a period of time is called a(n) _____ chart.

46. A graph which plots the proportions of items in noncompliance for multiple samples is called a _____ chart.

V.   **ANSWERS TO STUDY QUESTIONS**

1. Sample

2. Sample

3. Census

4. Frame

5. Underregistration

6. Random, Nonrandom

7. Nonrandom

8. Nonprobability

9. Simple

10. Stratified

11. Disproportionate Stratified

12. Stratified

13. Systematic

14. Area, Cluster

15. Convenience

16. Judgment

17. Quota

18. Sampling

19. Nonsampling

20. Telescoping

21. Omission

22. Detail

23. Normally

24. Population Mean

25. $\sigma / \sqrt{n}$

26. Finite Correction

27. .0968

28. .2645

29. .0068

30. .9981

31. .0055

32. .0057

33. .1711

34. .0537

35. Quality

36. Quality Control

37. After-process

38. In-Process

39. Total Quality Management

40. Pareto

41. Fishbone

42. Quality Circle

43. Just-in-time

44. $\overline{X}$

45. R

46. P

VI. SOLUTIONS TO ODD-NUMBERED PROBLEMS IN TEXT

7.1 a) i. A union membership list for the company.
         ii. A list of all employees of the company.

     b) i. White pages of the telephone directory for Utica, New York.
         ii. Utility company list of all customers.

     c) i. Airline company list of phone and mail purchasers of tickets from the airline during the past six months.
         ii. A list of frequent flyer club members for the airline.

     d) i. List of boat manufacturer's employees.
         ii. List of members of a boat owners association.

     e) i. Cable company telephone directory.
         ii. Membership list of cable management association.

7.5 a) Under 21 years of age, 21 to 39 years of age, 40 to 55 years of age, over 55 years of age.

     b) Under $1,000,000 sales per year, $1,000,000 to $4,999,999 sales per year, $5,000,000 to $19,999,999 sales per year, $20,000,000 to $49,000,000 per year, $50,000,000 to $99,999,999 per year, over $100,000,000 per year.

     c) Less than 2,000 sq. ft., 2,000 to 4,999 sq. ft., 5,000 to 9,999 sq. ft., over 10,000 sq. ft.

     d) East, southeast, midwest, south, southwest, west, northwest.

     e) Government worker, teacher, lawyer, physician, engineer, business person, police officer, fire fighter, computer worker.

     f) Manufacturing, finance, communications, health care, retailing, chemical, transportation.

7.7 $N = n \cdot K =$ 825

7.9   a)   i.   Counties
           ii.   Metropolitan areas

      b)   i.   States (beside which the oil wells lie)
           ii.   Companies that own the wells

      c)   i.   States
           ii.   Counties

7.11 Go to a conference where some of the _Fortune_ 500 executives
      attend. Approach those executives who appear to be
      friendly and approachable.

7.13 $\mu = 50$, $\sigma = 10$ $n = 64$

a) $P(\overline{X} > 52)$:

$$Z = \frac{\overline{X} - \mu}{\dfrac{\sigma}{\sqrt{n}}} = \frac{52 - 50}{\dfrac{10}{\sqrt{64}}} = 1.6$$

from Table A.5 Prob. = .4452

Prob. $(\overline{X} > 52) = .5000 - .4452 =$ $\boxed{.0548}$

b) $P(\overline{X} < 51)$:

$$Z = \frac{\overline{X} - \mu}{\dfrac{\sigma}{\sqrt{n}}} = \frac{51 - 50}{\dfrac{10}{\sqrt{64}}} = 0.80$$

from Table A.5, prob. = .2881

Prob. $(\overline{X} < 51) = .5000 + .2881 =$ $\boxed{.7881}$

c)   Prob$(\overline{X} < 47)$:

$$Z = \frac{\overline{X} - \mu}{\dfrac{\sigma}{\sqrt{n}}} = \frac{47 - 50}{\dfrac{10}{\sqrt{64}}} = -2.40$$

from Table A.5, prob. = .4918

Prob. $(\overline{X} < 47) = .5000 - .4918 =$ $\boxed{.0082}$

d)   Prob. $(48.5 \leq \overline{X} \leq 52.4)$:

$$Z = \frac{\overline{X} - \mu}{\dfrac{\sigma}{\sqrt{n}}} = \frac{48.5 - 50}{\dfrac{10}{\sqrt{64}}} = -1.20$$

from Table A.5, prob. = .3849

$$Z = \frac{\overline{X} - \mu}{\dfrac{\sigma}{\sqrt{n}}} = \frac{52.4 - 50}{\dfrac{10}{\sqrt{64}}} = 1.92$$

from Table A.5, prob. = .4726

Prob. $(48.5 \leq \overline{X} \leq 52.4) = .3849 + .4726 =$ $\boxed{.8575}$

e)   Prob.$(50.6 \leq \overline{X} \leq 51.3)$

$$Z = \frac{\overline{X}-\mu}{\frac{\sigma}{\sqrt{n}}} = \frac{50.6 - 50}{\frac{10}{\sqrt{64}}} = 0.48$$

from Table A.5, prob. = .1844

$$Z = \frac{\overline{X}-\mu}{\frac{\sigma}{\sqrt{n}}} = \frac{51.3 - 50}{\frac{10}{\sqrt{64}}} = 1.04$$

from Table A.5, prob. = .3508

Prob.$(50.6 \leq \overline{X} \leq 51.3)$ = .3508 - .1844 = $\boxed{.1644}$

7.15   n = 36 μ = 278

P($\overline{X}$ < 280) = .86

.3600 of the area lies between $\overline{X}$ = 280 and μ = 278. This probability is associated with Z = 1.08 from Table A.5. Solving for σ:

$$Z = \frac{\overline{X}-\mu}{\frac{\sigma}{\sqrt{n}}}$$

$$1.08 = \frac{280 - 278}{\frac{\sigma}{\sqrt{36}}}$$

$$\frac{1.08\sigma}{6} = 2$$

1.08σ = 12

$\sigma = \frac{12}{1.08} = \boxed{11.11}$

7.17 a) $N = 1,000$ $n = 60$ $\mu = 75$ $\sigma = 6$

Prob$(\overline{X} < 76.5)$:

$$Z = \frac{\overline{X}-\mu}{\frac{\sigma}{\sqrt{n}}\sqrt{\frac{N-n}{N-1}}} = \frac{76.5 - 75}{\frac{6}{\sqrt{60}}\sqrt{\frac{1000-60}{1000-1}}} = 2.00$$

from Table A.5,   prob. = .4772

Prob.$(\overline{X} < 76.5)$ = .4772 + .5000 = $\boxed{.9772}$

b) $N = 90$ $n = 36$ $\mu = 108$ $\sigma = 3.46$

Prob.$(107 < \overline{X} < 107.7)$:

$$Z = \frac{\overline{X}-\mu}{\frac{\sigma}{\sqrt{n}}\sqrt{\frac{N-n}{N-1}}} = \frac{107 - 108}{\frac{3.46}{\sqrt{36}}\sqrt{\frac{90-36}{90-1}}} = -2.23$$

from Table A.5,   prob. = .4871

$$Z = \frac{\overline{X}-\mu}{\frac{\sigma}{\sqrt{n}}\sqrt{\frac{N-n}{N-1}}} = \frac{107.7 - 108}{\frac{3.46}{\sqrt{36}}\sqrt{\frac{90-36}{90-1}}} = 0.67$$

from Table A.5,   prob. = .2486

Prob.$(107 < \overline{X} < 107.7)$ = .4871 - .2486 = $\boxed{.2385}$

c) $N = 250$ $n = 100$ $\mu = 35.6$ $\sigma = 4.89$

Prob $(\overline{X} \geq 36)$:

$$Z = \frac{\overline{X}-\mu}{\frac{\sigma}{\sqrt{n}}\sqrt{\frac{N-n}{N-1}}} = \frac{36 - 35.6}{\frac{4.89}{\sqrt{100}}\sqrt{\frac{250-100}{250-1}}} = 1.05$$

from Table A.5, prob.   = .3531

Prob.$(\overline{X} \geq 36)$ = .5000 - .3531 = $\boxed{.1469}$

d) $N = 5000$ $n = 60$ $\mu = 125$ $\sigma = 13.4$

Prob. $(\bar{X} \leq 123)$:

$$Z = \frac{\bar{X} - \mu}{\frac{\sigma}{\sqrt{n}}\sqrt{\frac{N-n}{N-1}}} = \frac{123 - 125}{\frac{13.4}{\sqrt{60}}\sqrt{\frac{5000-60}{5000-1}}} = -1.16$$

from Table A.5, prob. $= .3770$

Prob. $(\bar{X} \leq 123) = .5000 - .3770 = \boxed{.1230}$

7.19 $\mu = \$65.12$ $\sigma = \$21.45$ $n = 45$

Prob. $(\bar{X} > \bar{X}_0) = .2300$

Prob. $\bar{X}$ lies between $\bar{X}_0$ and $\mu = .5000 - .2300 = .2700$

from Table A.5, $Z_{.2700} = 0.74$

Solving for $\bar{X}_0$

$$Z = \frac{\bar{X}_0 - \mu}{\frac{\sigma}{\sqrt{n}}}$$

$$0.74 = \frac{\bar{X}_0 - 65.12}{\frac{21.45}{\sqrt{45}}}$$

$$.74 \left(\frac{21.45}{\sqrt{45}}\right) = \bar{X}_0 - 65.12$$

$$2.366 = \bar{X}_0 - 65.12$$

$\bar{X}_0 = 65.12 + 2.366 = \boxed{67.486}$

7.21 $\mu = \$109,000$ $n = 42$ $\sigma = \$31,000$

a)   Prob.$(\overline{X} > \$120,000)$:

$$Z = \dfrac{\overline{X}-\mu}{\dfrac{\sigma}{\sqrt{n}}} = \dfrac{120,000 - 109,000}{\dfrac{31,000}{\sqrt{42}}} = 2.30$$

from Table A.5, prob. = .4893

Prob.$(\overline{X} > \$120,000) = .5000 - .4893 =$ $\boxed{.0107}$

b)   Prob.$(\overline{X} < \$100,000)$:

$$Z = \dfrac{\overline{X}-\mu}{\dfrac{\sigma}{\sqrt{n}}} = \dfrac{100,000 - 109,000}{\dfrac{31,000}{\sqrt{42}}} = -1.88$$

from Table A.5, prob. = .4699

Prob.$(\overline{X} < \$100,000) = .5000 - .4699 =$ $\boxed{.0301}$

c)   Prob.$(\$102,000 < \overline{X} < \$107,000)$:

$$Z = \dfrac{\overline{X}-\mu}{\dfrac{\sigma}{\sqrt{n}}} = \dfrac{102,000 - 109,000}{\dfrac{31,000}{\sqrt{42}}} = -1.46$$

from Table A.5, prob. = .4279

$$Z = \dfrac{\overline{X}-\mu}{\dfrac{\sigma}{\sqrt{n}}} = \dfrac{107,000 - 109,000}{\dfrac{31,000}{\sqrt{42}}} = -0.42$$

from Table A.5, prob. = .1628

Prob.$(\$102,000 < \overline{X} < \$107,000) = .4279 - .1628 =$ $\boxed{.2651}$

d)   Prob. ($108,000 < $\overline{X}$ < $111,000):

$$Z = \frac{\overline{X} - \mu}{\frac{\sigma}{\sqrt{n}}} = \frac{108,000 - 109,000}{\frac{31,000}{\sqrt{42}}} = -0.21$$

from Table A.5, prob. = .0832

$$Z = \frac{\overline{X} - \mu}{\frac{\sigma}{\sqrt{n}}} = \frac{111,000 - 109,000}{\frac{31,000}{\sqrt{42}}} = 0.42$$

from Table A.5, prob. = .1628

Prob. ($108,000 < $\overline{X}$ < $111,000) = .0832 + .1628 = $\boxed{.2460}$

e)   Prob ($\overline{X}$ > $106,000) = .71

Prob. (106,000 < $\overline{X}$ < 109,000) = .7100 - .5000 = .2100

from Table A.5, $Z_{.2100}$ = -0.55

Solving for σ:

$$Z = \frac{\overline{X} - \mu}{\frac{\sigma}{\sqrt{n}}}$$

$$-0.55 = \frac{106,000 - 109,000}{\frac{\sigma}{\sqrt{42}}}$$

$$-0.55 = \frac{-3,000}{\frac{\sigma}{\sqrt{45}}}$$

$$-0.55 \frac{\sigma}{\sqrt{42}} = -3,000$$

$$\sigma = \frac{-3,000\sqrt{42}}{-0.55} = \boxed{35,349.5}$$

7.23   P = .90

a)   n = 75   Prob($\hat{p}$ < .89):

$$Z = \frac{\hat{p}-P}{\sqrt{\dfrac{P \cdot Q}{n}}} = \frac{.89 - .90}{\sqrt{\dfrac{(.90)(.10)}{75}}} = -0.29$$

from Table A.5,   prob. = .1141

Prob.($\hat{p}$ < .89) = .5000 - .1141 = $\boxed{.3859}$

b)   n = 40   Prob($\hat{p}$ ≤ .89):

$$Z = \frac{\hat{p}-P}{\sqrt{\dfrac{P \cdot Q}{n}}} = \frac{.89 - .90}{\sqrt{\dfrac{(.90)(.10)}{40}}} = -0.21$$

from Table A.5,   prob. = .0832

Prob.($\hat{p}$ ≤ .89) = .5000 - .0832 = $\boxed{.4168}$

c)   n = 200   Prob($\hat{p}$ ≥ .85):

$$Z = \frac{\hat{p}-P}{\sqrt{\dfrac{P \cdot Q}{n}}} = \frac{.85 - .90}{\sqrt{\dfrac{(.90)(.10)}{200}}} = -2.36$$

from Table A.5,   prob. = .4909

Prob.($\hat{p}$ ≥ .85) = .4909 + .5000 = $\boxed{.9909}$

d)   n = 1,100 and Prob ($\hat{p}$ > .93):

$$Z = \frac{\hat{p}-P}{\sqrt{\dfrac{P \cdot Q}{n}}} = \frac{.93 - .90}{\sqrt{\dfrac{(.90)(.10)}{1,100}}} = 3.32$$

from Table A.5,   prob. = .4995

Prob.($\hat{p}$ > .93) = .5000 - .4995 = $\boxed{.0005}$

e) $n = 450$ Prob$(.80 \leq \hat{p} \leq .86)$:

$$Z = \frac{\hat{p}-P}{\sqrt{\dfrac{P \cdot Q}{n}}} = \frac{.80 - .90}{\sqrt{\dfrac{(.90)(.10)}{450}}} = -7.07$$

from Table A.5, prob. = .5000

$$Z = \frac{\hat{p}-P}{\sqrt{\dfrac{P \cdot Q}{n}}} = \frac{.86 - .90}{\sqrt{\dfrac{(.90)(.10)}{450}}} = -2.83$$

from Table A.5, prob. = .4977

Prob.$(.80 \leq \hat{p} \leq .86) = .5000 - .4977 = \boxed{.0023}$

7.25 $P = .28$ $n = 140$ Prob.$(\hat{p} < \hat{p}_0) = .3000$

Prob.$(\hat{p}_0 \leq \hat{p} \leq .28) = .5000 - .3000 = .2000$
from Table A.5, $Z_{.2000} = -0.52$

Solving for $\hat{p}_0$:

$$Z = \frac{\hat{p}_0 - P}{\sqrt{\dfrac{PQ}{n}}}$$

$$-0.52 = \frac{\hat{p}_0 - .28}{\sqrt{\dfrac{(.28)(.72)}{140}}}$$

$-.02 = \hat{p}_0 - .28$

$\hat{p}_0 = .28 - .02 = \boxed{.26}$

7.27 $n = 200$ $P(\text{Harley}) = .59$ $p = \dfrac{110}{200} = .55$

$\text{Prob}(\hat{p} < .55):$

$$Z = \frac{\hat{p} - P}{\sqrt{\dfrac{P \cdot Q}{n}}} = \frac{.55 - .59}{\sqrt{\dfrac{(.59)(.41)}{200}}} = -1.15$$

from Table A.5, prob. = .3749

$\text{Prob.}(\hat{p} < .55) = .5000 - .3749 =$ $\boxed{.1251}$

$n = 200$ $P(\text{Honda}) = .15$ $\hat{p} = \dfrac{50}{200} = .25$

$\text{Prob.}(\hat{p} > .25):$

$$Z = \frac{\hat{p} - P}{\sqrt{\dfrac{P \cdot Q}{n}}} = \frac{.25 - .15}{\sqrt{\dfrac{(.15)(.85)}{200}}} = 3.96$$

from Table A.5, prob. = .5000

$\text{Prob.}(\hat{p} > .25) = .5000 - .5000 =$ $\boxed{.0000}$

7.29 $P = .30$ $n = 100$

a) $X = 35$ $\hat{p} = \dfrac{35}{100} = .35$

Prob.$(\hat{p} > .35)$:

$$Z = \frac{\hat{p}-P}{\sqrt{\dfrac{P \cdot Q}{n}}} = \frac{.35 - .30}{\sqrt{\dfrac{(.30)(.70)}{100}}} = 1.09$$

from Table A.5, prob. $= .3621$

Prob.$(\hat{p} > .35) = .5000 - .3621 =$ $\boxed{.1379}$

b) $X = 20$ $\hat{p} = \dfrac{20}{100} = .20$

Prob.$(\hat{p} < .20)$:

$$Z = \frac{\hat{p}-P}{\sqrt{\dfrac{P \cdot Q}{n}}} = \frac{.20 - .30}{\sqrt{\dfrac{(.30)(.70)}{100}}} = -2.18$$

from Table A.5, prob. $= .4854$

Prob.$(\hat{p} < .20) = .5000 - .4854 =$ $\boxed{.0146}$

c) $X_1 = 20$ $X_2 = 40$

$\hat{p}_1 = \dfrac{20}{100} = .20$ $\hat{p}_2 = \dfrac{40}{100} = .40$

Prob.$(.20 \leq \hat{p} \leq .40)$:

$$Z = \frac{\hat{p}-P}{\sqrt{\dfrac{P \cdot Q}{n}}} = \frac{.20 - .30}{\sqrt{\dfrac{(.30)(.70)}{100}}} = -2.18$$

from Table A.5, prob. $= .4854$

$$Z = \frac{\hat{p}-P}{\sqrt{\dfrac{P \cdot Q}{n}}} = \frac{.40 - .30}{\sqrt{\dfrac{(.30)(.70)}{100}}} = +2.18$$

from Table A.5, prob. $= .4854$

Prob.$(.20 \leq \hat{p} \leq .40) = .4854 + .4854 =$ $\boxed{.9708}$

d)   X = 45 $\hat{p} = \dfrac{45}{100} = .45$

Prob. $(\hat{p} > .45)$:

$$Z = \frac{\hat{p}-P}{\sqrt{\dfrac{P \cdot Q}{n}}} = \frac{.45 - .30}{\sqrt{\dfrac{(.30)(.70)}{100}}} = 3.27$$

from Table A.5, prob. = .4995

Prob. $(\hat{p} > .45)$ = .5000 - .4995 = $\boxed{.0005}$

The reason for the low probability could be:

1)   The more than 45 high-risk mothers was just a "rare" chance occurrence.

2)   The thirty percent figure for all mothers is not true or is not true for this population. That is, this sample does not come from the same population as the one with the thirty percent figure.

7.31 $n_1 = 45$ $n_2 = 40$
        $\mu_1 = 150$ $\mu_2 = 120$ $\mu_1 - \mu_2 = 150 - 120 = 30$
        $\sigma_1 = 10$ $\sigma_2 = 20$

a)   Prob$(\overline{X}_1 - \overline{X}_2 > 50)$:

$$Z = \frac{(\overline{X}_1 - \overline{X}_2) - (\mu_1 - \mu_2)}{\sqrt{\dfrac{\sigma_1^2}{n_1} + \dfrac{\sigma_2^2}{n_2}}} = \frac{50 - 30}{\sqrt{\dfrac{10^2}{45} + \dfrac{20^2}{40}}} = 5.72$$

from Table A.5, prob. = .5000

Prob.$(\overline{X}_1 - \overline{X}_2 > 50) = .5000 - .5000 = \boxed{.0000}$

b)   Prob.$(\overline{X}_1 - \overline{X}_2 > 40)$:

$$Z = \frac{(\overline{X}_1 - \overline{X}_2) - (\mu_1 - \mu_2)}{\sqrt{\dfrac{\sigma_1^2}{n_1} + \dfrac{\sigma_2^2}{n_2}}} = \frac{40 - 30}{\sqrt{\dfrac{10^2}{45} + \dfrac{20^2}{40}}} = 2.86$$

from Table A.5, prob. = .4979

Prob.$(\overline{X}_1 - \overline{X}_2 > 40) = .5000 - .4979 = \boxed{.0021}$

c)   Prob.$(\overline{X}_1 - \overline{X}_2 > 30)$:

$$Z = \frac{(\overline{X}_1 - \overline{X}_2) - (\mu_1 - \mu_2)}{\sqrt{\dfrac{\sigma_1^2}{n_1} + \dfrac{\sigma_2^2}{n_2}}} = \frac{30 - 30}{\sqrt{\dfrac{10^2}{45} + \dfrac{20^2}{40}}} = 0$$

from Table A.5, prob. = .0000

Prob.$(\overline{X}_1 - \overline{X}_2 > 30) = .5000 - .0000 = \boxed{.5000}$

d)   Prob.$(\overline{X}_1 - \overline{X}_2 > 20)$:

$$Z = \frac{(\overline{X}_1 - \overline{X}_2) - (\mu_1 - \mu_2)}{\sqrt{\dfrac{\sigma_1^2}{n_1} + \dfrac{\sigma_2^2}{n_2}}} = \frac{20 - 30}{\sqrt{\dfrac{10^2}{45} + \dfrac{20^2}{40}}} = -2.86$$

from Table A.5, prob. = .4979

Prob.$(\overline{X}_1 - \overline{X}_2 > 20) = .4979 + .5000 = \boxed{.9979}$

7.33 $\mu_1 = \$62,000$ $\mu_2 = \$51,000$
             $\sigma_1 = \$18,600$ $\sigma_2 = \$14,700$
             $n_1 = \quad 35$ $n_2 = \quad 32$

$$\mu_1 - \mu_2 = \$62,000 - \$51,000 = \$11,000$$

Prob$(\overline{X}_1 - \overline{X}_2 > \$15,000)$:

$$Z = \frac{(\overline{X}_1 - \overline{X}_2) - (\mu_1 - \mu_2)}{\sqrt{\dfrac{\sigma_1^2}{n_1} + \dfrac{\sigma_2^2}{n_2}}} = \frac{15,000 - 11,000}{\sqrt{\dfrac{18,600^2}{35} + \dfrac{14,700^2}{32}}} = 0.98$$

from Table A.5, prob. = .3365

Prob.$(\overline{X}_1 - \overline{X}_2 > \$15,000) = .5000 - .3365 = \boxed{.1635}$

7.35 $P = .30$ $Q = .70$ Same Population: $P_1 - P_2 = 0$

a) $\hat{p}_1 = .33$ $\hat{p}_2 = .27$ $n_1 = 100$ $n_2 = 120$

$\hat{p}_1 - \hat{p}_2 = .33 - .27 = .06$

Prob. $(\hat{p}_1 - \hat{p}_2 \geq .06)$:

$$Z = \frac{(\hat{p}_1 - \hat{p}_2) - (P_1 - P_2)}{\sqrt{\dfrac{P_1 Q_1}{n_1} + \dfrac{P_2 Q_2}{n_2}}} = \frac{.06 - 0}{\sqrt{\dfrac{(.30)(.70)}{100} + \dfrac{(.30)(.70)}{120}}} = 0.97$$

from Table A.5, prob. $= .3340$

Prob. $(\hat{p}_1 - \hat{p}_2 \geq .06) = .5000 - .3340 = \boxed{.1660}$

b) $\hat{p}_1 = .35$ $\hat{p}_2 = .25$ $n_1 = 100$ $n_2 = 120$

$\hat{p}_1 - \hat{p}_2 = .35 - .25 = .10$

Prob. $(\hat{p}_1 - \hat{p}_2 \geq .10)$:

$$Z = \frac{(\hat{p}_1 - \hat{p}_2) - (P_1 - P_2)}{\sqrt{\dfrac{P_1 Q_1}{n_1} + \dfrac{P_2 Q_2}{n_2}}} = \frac{.10 - 0}{\sqrt{\dfrac{(.30)(.70)}{100} + \dfrac{(.30)(.70)}{120}}} = 1.61$$

from Table A.5, prob. $= .4463$

Prob. $(\hat{p}_1 - \hat{p}_2 \geq .10) = .5000 - .4463 = \boxed{.0537}$

c) $\hat{p}_1 = .35$ $\hat{p}_2 = .25$ $n_1 = 1,000$ $n_2 = 1,200$

$\hat{p}_1 - \hat{p}_2 = .35 - .25 = .10$

Prob. $(\hat{p}_1 - \hat{p}_2 \geq .10)$:

$$Z = \frac{(\hat{p}_1 - \hat{p}_2) - (P_1 - P_2)}{\sqrt{\dfrac{P_1 Q_1}{n_1} + \dfrac{P_2 Q_2}{n_2}}} = \frac{.10 - 0}{\sqrt{\dfrac{(.30)(.70)}{1,000} + \dfrac{(.30)(.70)}{1,200}}} = 5.10$$

from Table A.5, prob. $= .5000$

Prob. $(\hat{p}_1 - \hat{p}_2 \geq .10) = .5000 - .5000 = \boxed{.0000}$

7.37

1991	1976
$n_1 = 970$	$n_2 = 780$
$X_1 = 730$	$X_2 = 375$

$$\hat{p}_1 = \frac{730}{970} = .75 \qquad \hat{p}_2 = \frac{375}{780} = .48$$

$$P_1 = .75 \qquad\qquad P_2 = .50$$

$$\hat{p}_1 - \hat{p}_2 = .753 - .481 = .27 \qquad\qquad P_1 - P_2 = .75 - .50 = .25$$

Prob.$(\hat{p}_1 - \hat{p}_2 \geq .27)$:

$$Z = \frac{(\hat{p}_1 - \hat{p}_2) - (P_1 - P_2)}{\sqrt{\dfrac{P_1 Q_1}{n_1} + \dfrac{P_2 Q_2}{n_2}}} = \frac{.27 - .25}{\sqrt{\dfrac{(.75)(.25)}{970} + \dfrac{(.50)(.50)}{780}}} = 0.88$$

from Table A.5, prob. = .3106

Prob.$(\hat{p}_1 - \hat{p}_2 \geq .27)$ = .5000 - .3106 = $\boxed{.1894}$

7.39

$$\overline{X}_1 = 27 \qquad R_1 = 8$$
$$\overline{X}_2 = 24.286 \qquad R_2 = 8$$
$$\overline{X}_3 = 25.286 \qquad R_3 = 9$$
$$\overline{X}_4 = 27.714 \qquad R_4 = 7$$
$$\overline{X}_5 = 25.857 \qquad R_5 = 6$$

$$\overline{\overline{X}} = \frac{27 + 24.286 + 25.286 + 27.714 + 25.857}{5}$$

$\overline{\overline{X}} = 26.03$ (centerline)

$$\overline{R} = \frac{8 + 8 + 9 + 7 + 6}{5} = 7.6$$

Since n = 7, from Table A.9: $A_1 = .419$

UCL = $\overline{\overline{X}} + A_1 \ \overline{R} = 26.03 + (.419)(7.6) = 29.2$

LCL = $\overline{\overline{X}} - A_1 \ \overline{R} = 26.03 - (.419)(7.6) = 22.85$

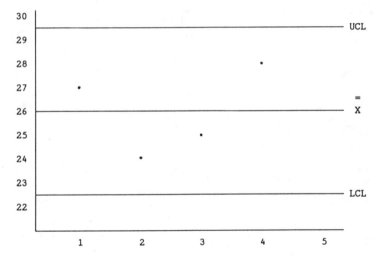

S
A
M
P
L
E
M
E
A
N
S

SAMPLE

$\overline{R}$ = 7.6 (Centerline)

n = 7, from Table A.9:

D_3 = 0.76
D_4 = 1.924

LCL = (0.76)(7.6) = .5776

UCL = (1.924)(7.6) = 14.62

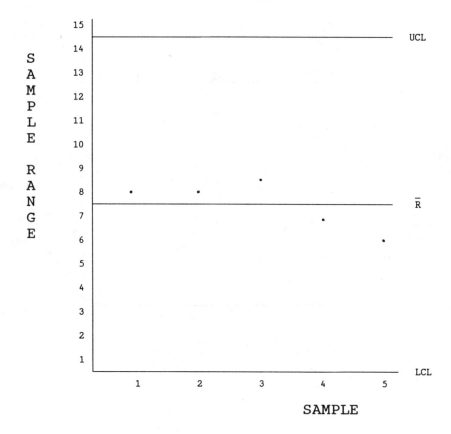

7.41 The values of $\hat{p}$:

Sample	$\hat{p}$ (out of Compliance)
1	2/100 = .02
2	7/100 = .07
3	.04
4	.03
5	.03
6	.05
7	.02
8	.00
9	.01
10	.06

$$P = \frac{.02 + .07 + .04 + .03 + .03 + .05 + .02 + .00 + .01 + .06}{10}$$

$P = .033$ (Centerline)

$$UCL = .033 + 3\sqrt{\frac{(.033)(.967)}{100}} = .087$$

$$LCL = .033 - 3\sqrt{\frac{(.033)(.967)}{100}} = -.021$$

$LCL = 0$ (cannot be negative)

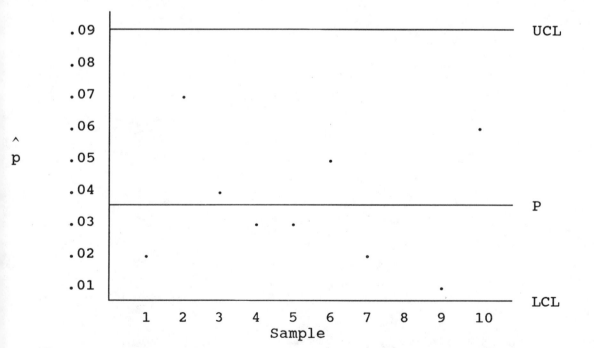

7.43 There is a limit to the amount of funding available for this project ($100,000). If a census is taken, there will be only an average of $5.00 employee for developing, administering, and reporting an attitude study. The measurements will be limited and inflexible. On the other hand, a sample of say 200 employees would allow for an average of $500 per employee. This amount of money would allow for a much greater detail of analysis including personal interviews and in-depth investigation. The greater amount of funding per unit allows for training of investigators, more time with each employee, focus groups, more detail summarization and reporting, etc.

7.47

Under 18	$250(.22) =$	55
18 - 25	$250(.18) =$	45
26 - 50	$250(.36) =$	90
51 - 65	$250(.10) =$	25
over 65	$250(.14) =$	35
	n =	250

7.49 $N = 12,080$
$n = 300$

$$K = \frac{N}{n} = \frac{12,080}{300} = 40.27$$

Select every 40th outlet to assure $n \geq 300$ outlets.

Use a table of random numbers to select a value between 0 and 40 as a starting point.

7.51
1)   The managers from some of the companies you are interested in studying do not belong to the American Managers Association.

2)   The membership list of the American Managers Association is not up-to-date.

3)   You are not interested in studying managers from some of the companies belonging to the American Management Association.

4)   The wrong questions are asked.

5)   The manager incorrectly interprets a question.

6)   The assistant accidently marks the wrong answer.

7)   The wrong statistical test is used to analyze the data.

8)   An error is made in statistical calculations.

9)   The statistical results are misinterpreted.

7.53 $\mu = \$125$ $n = 32$ $\overline{X} = \$110$ $\sigma^2 = \$525$

Prob. $(\overline{X} \geq \$110)$:

$$Z = \frac{\overline{X} - \mu}{\frac{\sigma}{\sqrt{n}}} = \frac{\$110 - \$125}{\frac{\sqrt{525}}{\sqrt{32}}} = -3.70$$

from Table A.5, Prob.= .5000

Prob. $(\overline{X} \geq \$110)$ = .5000 + .5000 = $\boxed{1.0000}$

Prob. $(\overline{X} \geq \$135)$:

$$Z = \frac{\overline{X} - \mu}{\frac{\sigma}{\sqrt{n}}} = \frac{\$135 - \$125}{\frac{\sqrt{525}}{\sqrt{32}}} = 2.47$$

from Table A.5, Prob.= .4932

Prob. $(\overline{X} \geq \$135)$ = .5000 - .4932 = $\boxed{.0068}$

Prob. $(\$120 < \overline{X} < \$130)$:

$$Z = \frac{\overline{X} - \mu}{\frac{\sigma}{\sqrt{n}}} = \frac{\$120 - \$125}{\frac{\sqrt{525}}{\sqrt{32}}} = -1.23$$

$$Z = \frac{\overline{X} - \mu}{\frac{\sigma}{\sqrt{n}}} = \frac{\$130 - \$125}{\frac{\sqrt{525}}{\sqrt{32}}} = +1.23$$

from Table A.5, Prob.= .3907

Prob. $(\$120 < \overline{X} < \$130)$ = .3907 + .3907 = $\boxed{.7814}$

7.55 $\mu=56.8$ n=51 $\sigma=12.3$

a)   Prob.$(\overline{X} > 60)$:

$$Z = \frac{\overline{X} - \mu}{\frac{\sigma}{\sqrt{n}}} = \frac{60 - 56.8}{\frac{12.3}{\sqrt{51}}} = 1.86$$

from Table A.5, Prob.= .4686

Prob.$(\overline{X} > 60) = .5000 - .4686 =$ .0314

b)   Prob.$(\overline{X} > 58)$:

$$Z = \frac{\overline{X} - \mu}{\frac{\sigma}{\sqrt{n}}} = \frac{58 - 56.8}{\frac{12.3}{\sqrt{51}}} = 0.70$$

from Table A.5, Prob.= .2580

Prob.$(\overline{X} > 58) = .5000 - .2580 =$ .2420

c)   Prob.$(56 < \overline{X} < 57)$:

$$Z = \frac{\overline{X} - \mu}{\frac{\sigma}{\sqrt{n}}} = \frac{56 - 56.8}{\frac{12.3}{\sqrt{51}}} = -0.46$$

from Table A.5, Prob.= .1772

$$Z = \frac{\overline{X} - \mu}{\frac{\sigma}{\sqrt{n}}} = \frac{57 - 56.8}{\frac{12.3}{\sqrt{51}}} = 0.12$$

from Table A.5, Prob.= .0478

Prob.$(56 < \overline{X} < 57) = .1772 + .0478 =$ .2250

d)   Prob. $(\overline{X} < 55)$:

$$Z = \frac{\overline{X} - \mu}{\frac{\sigma}{\sqrt{n}}} = \frac{55 - 56.8}{\frac{12.3}{\sqrt{51}}} = -1.05$$

from Table A.5, Prob.= .3531

Prob. $(\overline{X} < 55)$ = .5000 - .3531 = $\boxed{.1469}$

e)   Prob. $(\overline{X} < 50)$:

$$Z = \frac{\overline{X} - \mu}{\frac{\sigma}{\sqrt{n}}} = \frac{50 - 56.8}{\frac{12.3}{\sqrt{51}}} = -3.95$$

from Table A.5, Prob.= .5000

Prob. $(\overline{X} < 50)$ = .5000 - .5000 = $\boxed{.0000}$

7.57   P=.75   n=150   x=120 $\hat{p} = \frac{120}{150} = .80$

Prob. $(\hat{p} \geq .80)$:

$$Z = \frac{\hat{p} - P}{\sqrt{\frac{P \cdot Q}{n}}} = \frac{.80 - .75}{\sqrt{\frac{(.75)(.25)}{150}}} = 1.41$$

from Table A.5, Prob. = .4207

Prob. $(\hat{p} \geq .80)$ = .5000 - .4207 = $\boxed{.0793}$

7.59   n=84

a)   P=.09 child care centers

Prob. $(\hat{p} < .05)$:

$$Z = \frac{\hat{p} - P}{\sqrt{\frac{P \cdot Q}{n}}} = \frac{.05 - .09}{\sqrt{\frac{(.09)(.91)}{84}}} = -1.28$$

from Table A.5, Prob. = .3997

$$\text{Prob.}(\hat{p} < .05) = .5000 - .3997 = \boxed{.1003}$$

b)   P=.09

$$\text{Prob.}(\hat{p} > .15):$$

$$Z = \frac{\hat{p} - P}{\sqrt{\frac{P \cdot Q}{n}}} = \frac{.15 - .09}{\sqrt{\frac{(.09)(.91)}{84}}} = 1.92$$

from Table A.5, Prob. = .4726

$$\text{Prob.}(\hat{p} > .15) = .5000 - .4726 = \boxed{.0274}$$

c)   P=.89 dependent-care spending accounts

$$\text{Prob.}(\hat{p} < .70):$$

$$Z = \frac{\hat{p} - P}{\sqrt{\frac{P \cdot Q}{n}}} = \frac{.70 - .89}{\sqrt{\frac{(.89)(.91)}{84}}} = -5.57$$

from Table A.5, Prob. = .5000

$$\text{Prob.}(\hat{p} > .15) = .5000 - .5000 = \boxed{.0000}$$

d)   P=.41 resource and referral services

$$\text{Prob.}(.35 < \hat{p} < .50):$$

$$Z = \frac{\hat{p} - P}{\sqrt{\frac{P \cdot Q}{n}}} = \frac{.35 - .41}{\sqrt{\frac{(.41)(.59)}{84}}} = -1.12$$

from Table A.5, Prob. = .3686

$$Z = \frac{\hat{p} - P}{\sqrt{\frac{P \cdot Q}{n}}} = \frac{.50 - .41}{\sqrt{\frac{(.41)(.59)}{84}}} = 1.68$$

from Table A.5, Prob. = .4535

$$\text{Prob.}(.35 < \hat{p} < .50) = .3686 + .4535 = \boxed{.8221}$$

7.61

Iowa	Minnesota
$\mu_1 = \$125$	$\mu_2 = \$120$
$\sigma_1 = 525$	$\sigma_2 = 18$
$n_1 = 50$	$n_2 = 50$

$$\mu_1 - \mu_2 = \$125 - \$120 = \$5$$

$$\text{Prob}(\overline{X}_1 - \overline{X}_2) \geq \$10):$$

$$Z = \frac{(\overline{X}_1 - \overline{X}_2) - (\mu_1 - \mu_2)}{\sqrt{\dfrac{\sigma_1^2}{n_1} + \dfrac{\sigma_2^2}{n_2}}} = \frac{\$10 - \$5}{\sqrt{\dfrac{525}{50} + \dfrac{18^2}{50}}} = 1.21$$

from Table A.5, Prob. = .3869

$$\text{Prob}(\overline{X}_1 - \overline{X}_2 \geq \$10) = .5000 - .3869 = \boxed{.1131}$$

7.63

Finance, etc.	Service
$n_1 = 47$	$n_2 = 55$
$\overline{X}_1 = \$39,000$	$\overline{X}_2 = \$33,000$
$\sigma_1 = \$10,090$	$\sigma_2 = \$9,850$

$$\mu_1 = \mu_2 = \mu$$

$$\mu_1 - \mu_2 = 0$$

$$\text{Prob}(\overline{X}_1 - \overline{X}_2 \geq \$6,000):$$

$$Z = \frac{(\overline{X}_1 - \overline{X}_2) - (\mu_1 - \mu_2)}{\sqrt{\dfrac{\sigma_1^2}{n_1} + \dfrac{\sigma_2^2}{n_2}}} = \frac{\$6,000 - 0}{\sqrt{\dfrac{10,090^2}{47} + \dfrac{9,850^2}{55}}} = 3.03$$

from Table A.5, Prob. = .4988

$$\text{Prob}(\overline{X}_1 - \overline{X}_2 \geq \$6,000) = .5000 - .4988 = \boxed{.0012}$$

7.65 $\underline{1977}$ $\underline{1987}$

$P_1 = .41$ $P_2 = .36$

$n_1 = 200$ $n_2 = 245$

$P_1 - P_2 = .41 - .36 = .05$

Prob.$(\hat{p}_1 - \hat{p}_2 > .12)$:

$$Z = \frac{(\hat{p}_1 - \hat{p}_2) - (P_1 - P_2)}{\sqrt{\dfrac{P_1 Q_1}{n_1} + \dfrac{P_2 Q_2}{n_2}}} = \frac{.12 - .05}{\sqrt{\dfrac{(.41)(.59)}{200} + \dfrac{(.36)(.64)}{245}}} = 1.51$$

from Table A.5, Prob. = .4345

Prob$(\hat{p}_1 - \hat{p}_2 > .12) = .5000 - .4345 = \boxed{.0655}$

7.67 $\underline{West}$ $\underline{Midwest}$

$n_1 = 400$ $n_2 = 500$

$x_1 = 176$ $x_2 = 200$

$\hat{p}_1 = \dfrac{176}{400} = .44$ $\hat{p}_2 = \dfrac{200}{500} = .40$

$P_1 = P_2 = P = .42$ $P_1 - P_2 = 0$

Prob$(\hat{p}_1 - \hat{p}_2) \geq .04)$:

$$Z = \frac{(\hat{p}_1 - \hat{p}_2) - (P_1 - P_2)}{\sqrt{\dfrac{P_1 Q_1}{n_1} + \dfrac{P_2 Q_2}{n_2}}} = \frac{.04 - 0}{\sqrt{\dfrac{(.42)(.58)}{400} + \dfrac{(.42)(.58)}{500}}} = 1.21$$

from Table A.5, Prob. = .3869

Prob$(\hat{p}_1 - \hat{p}_2 \geq .04) = .5000 - .3869 = \boxed{.1131}$

7.69   <u>Los Angeles</u>   <u>Las Vegas</u>

$P_1 = .60$ $P_2 = .584$ $P_1 - P_2 = .60 - .584 = .016$

$n_1 = 565$ $n_2 = 381$

$x_1 = 344$ $x_2 = 217$

$\hat{p}_1 = .61$ $\hat{p}_2 = .57$ $\hat{p}_1 - \hat{p}_2 = .61 - .57 = .04$

$Prob(\hat{p}_1 - \hat{p}_2) \geq .04$:

$$Z = \frac{(\hat{p}_1 - \hat{p}_2) - (P_1 - P_2)}{\sqrt{\dfrac{P_1 Q_1}{n_1} + \dfrac{P_2 Q_2}{n_2}}} = \frac{.04 - .016}{\sqrt{\dfrac{(.60)(.40)}{565} + \dfrac{(.584)(.416)}{381}}} = 0.74$$

from Table A.5, Prob. = .2704

$Prob(\hat{p}_1 - \hat{p}_2 \geq .04) = .5000 - .2704 = \boxed{.2296}$

7.71   The values of $\hat{p}$:

Sample	$\hat{p}$ (out of compliance)
1	.06
2	.22
3	.14
4	.04
5	.10
6	.16
7	.00
8	.18
9	.02
10	.12

$$P = \frac{(.06+.22+.14+.04+.10+.16+.00+.18+.02+.12)}{10} = .104$$

$P = .104$ Centerline

$$UCL = .104 + 3\sqrt{\frac{(.104)(.896)}{50}} = .234$$

$$LCL = .104 - 3\sqrt{\frac{(.104)(.896)}{50}} = -.026$$

$LCL = 0$ (cannot be negative)

P Chart:

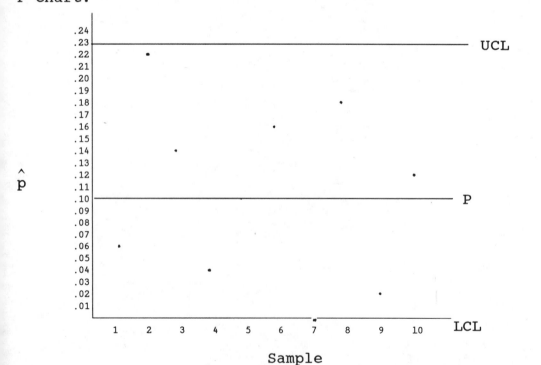

8

CONFIDENCE INTERVALS: LARGE SAMPLES

I. CHAPTER OBJECTIVES

The overall objective of chapter eight is to help you understand estimating parameters for situations in which the sample size is large and the formulas are derived from the central limit theorem, thereby enabling you to:

1. Estimate a population mean from a sample mean.

2. Estimate a population proportion from a sample proportion.

3. Estimate the difference in two population means from the difference in two sample means.

4. Estimate the difference in two population proportions from the difference in two sample proportions.

5. Estimate the minimum sample size necessary to achieve given statistical goals.

CHAPTER OUTLINE

8.1 Estimating the Population Mean

Finite Correction Factor

Confidence Interval to Estimate μ When σ is Unknown

8.2 Estimating the Population Proportion

8.3 Estimating the Difference in Two Population Means

8.4 Estimating the Difference in Two Population Proportions

8.5 Estimating Sample Size

Sample Size When Estimating μ

Determing Sample Size When Estimating P

Determining Sample Size When Estimating $\mu_1 - \mu_2$

III. **KEY WORDS**

Point Estimate   Sample Size Estimation
Interval Estimate   Error of Estimation

IV.   **STUDY QUESTIONS**

1. When a statistic taken from the sample is used to estimate a population parameter, it is called a(n) _____ estimate.

2. When a range of values is used to estimate a population parameter, it is called a(n) _____ estimate.

3. The Z value associated with a two-sided 90% confidence interval is _____.

4. The Z value associated with a two-sided 95% confidence interval is _____.

5. The Z value associated with a two-sided 80% confidence interval is _____.

6. Suppose a random sample of 40 is selected from a population with a standard deviation of 13. If the sample mean is 118, the 98% confidence interval to estimate the population mean is _____.

7. Suppose a random sample of size 75 is selected from a population. The sample yields a mean of 26 and a standard deviation of 6.4. From this information, the 90% confidence interval to estimate the population mean can be computed as _____.

8. The following random sample of numbers are drawn from a
population: 45, 61, 55, 43, 49, 60, 62, 53, 57, 44, 39,
48, 57, 40, 61, 62, 45, 39, 38, 56, 55, 59, 63, 50, 41,
39, 45, 47, 56, 51, 61, 39, 36, 57.   From this data, a
99% confidence interval to estimate the population mean
can be computed as _____.

9. A random sample of 63 items is selected from a
population of 400 items.   The sample mean is 211 and the
sample standard deviation is 48.   From this data, a 95%
confidence interval to estimate the population mean can
be computed as _____.

10. A researcher wants to estimate the proportion of the
population which possesses a given characteristic.   A
random sample of size 800 is taken resulting in 380
items which possess the characteristic. The point
estimate for this population proportion is

_____.

11. A researcher wants to estimate the proportion of a
population which possesses a given characteristic.   A
random sample of size 1250 is taken and .67 of the
sample possess the characteristic.   The 90% confidence
interval to estimate the population proportion is

_____.

12. A random sample of 255 items from a population results in 44% possessing a given characteristic. Using this information, the researcher constructs a 99% confidence interval to estimate the population proportion. The resulting confidence interval is _____.

13. What proportion of a population possesses a given characteristic? To estimate this, a random sample of 1700 people are interviewed from the population. Seven hundred and fourteen of the people sampled posses the characteristic. Using this information, the researcher computes an 88% confidence interval to estimate the proportion of the population who posses the given characteristic. The resulting confidence interval is

    _____.

14. A researcher wants to estimate the difference in the means of two populations. A random sample of 40 items from the first population results in a sample mean of 433 with a sample standard deviation of 112. A random sample of 50 items from the second population results in a sample mean of 467 with a sample standard deviation of 120. From this information, a point estimate of the difference of population means can be computed as

    _____.

15. Using the information from question 14, the researcher can compute a 95% confidence interval to estimate the difference in population means. The resulting confidence interval is _____.

16. A random sample of 32 items is taken from a population which has a population variance of 93. The resulting sample mean is 45.6. A random sample of 37 items is taken from a population which has a population variance of 88. The resulting sample mean is 49.4. Using this information, a 98% confidence interval can be computed to estimate the difference in means of these two populations. The resulting interval is

_____.

17. A researcher desires to estimate the difference in means of two populations. To accomplish this, he/she takes a random sample of 85 items from the first population. The sample yields a mean of 168 with a variance of 783. A random sample of 70 items is taken from the second population yielding a mean of 161 with a variance of 780. A 94% confidence interval is computed to estimate the difference in population means. The resulting confidence interval is _____.

18. A researcher is interested in estimating the difference in two populations proportions. A sample of 1000 from each population results in sample proportions of .61 and .64. The point estimate of the difference in the population proportions is _____.

19. Using the data from question 18, the researcher computes a 90% confidence interval to estimate the difference in population proportions. The resulting confidence interval is _____.

20. A random sample of 400 items from a population shows that 110 of the sample items possess a given characteristic. A random sample of 550 items from a second population resulted in 154 of the sample items possessing the characteristic. Using this data, a 99% confidence interval is constructed to estimate the difference in population proportions which possess the given characteristic. The resulting confidence interval is _____.

21. A researcher desires to estimate the difference in
    proportions of two populations. To accomplish this,
    he/she samples 338 and 332 items respectively from each
    population. The resulting sample proportions are .71
    and .68 respectively. Using this data, a 90% confidence
    interval can be computed to estimate the difference in
    population proportions. The resulting confidence
    interval is _____.

22. In estimating the sample size necessary to estimate μ,
    the error of estimation, E, is equal to _____.

23. In estimating sample size, if the population standard
    deviation is unknown, it can be estimated by using

    _____.

24. Suppose a researcher wants to conduct a study to
    estimate the population mean. He/she plans to use a 95%
    level of confidence to estimate the mean and the
    population standard deviation is approximately 34. The
    researcher wants the error to be no more than 4. The
    sample size should be at least _____.

25. A researcher wants to determine the sample size
    necessary to adequately conduct a study to estimate the
    population mean to within 5 points. The range of
    population values is 80 and the researcher plans to use
    a 90% level of confidence. The sample size should be at
    least _____.

26. A study is going to be conducted in which a population mean will be estimated using a 92% confidence interval. The estimate needs to be within 12 of the actual population mean. The population variance is estimated to be around 2200. The necessary sample size should be at least _____.

27. In estimating the sample size necessary to estimate P, if there is no good approximation for the value of P available, the value of _____ should be used as an estimate of P in the formula.

28. A researcher wants to estimate the population proportion with a 95% level of confidence. He/she estimates from previous studies that the population proportion is no more than .30. The researcher wants the estimate to have an error of no more than .02. The necessary sample size is at least _____.

29. A study will be conducted to estimate the population proportion. A level of confidence of 99% will be used and an error of no more than .05 is desired. There is no knowledge as to what the population proportion will be. The size of sample should be at least

_____.

30. A researcher conducts a study to determine what the population proportion is for a given characteristic. Is it believed from previous studies that the proportion of the population will be at least .65. The researcher wants to use a 98% level of confidence. He/she also wants the error to be no more than .03. The sample size should be at least _____.

31. In determining the sample size necessary to estimate the difference in two population means, it is assumed in the formula that the sample sizes taken from each population are _____.

32. In determining the sample size necessary to estimate the difference in two population means, it is assumed in the formula that the population variances are

    _____.

33. The formula used to determine the necessary sample size to estimate the difference in two population means is the same as the formula used to determine the necessary sample size to estimate a population mean except that it produces n values _____ as large, all other things being the same.

34. A researcher wants to determine the necessary sample size to estimate the difference in two population means. He/she assumes that the variances of the two populations are about the same with a value of 380. The researcher wants to be 90% confidence of the results and within 4 of the true difference. The size of sample necessary from each population is _____.

35. A study is being undertaken to estimate the difference in two population means. It is desired that the estimation be within 9 of the actual difference with a 95% level of confidence. It is estimated that the standard deviation of each population is about 42. The size of sample necessary from each population is _____.

V.   **ANSWERS TO STUDY QUESTIONS**

1. Point

2. Interval

3. 1.645

4. 1.96

5. 1.28

6. $113.2 \leq \mu \leq 122.8$

7. $24.8 \leq \mu \leq 27.2$

8. $46.6 \leq \mu \leq 54.2$

9. $200.1 \leq \mu \leq 221.9$

10. .475

11. $.648 \leq P \leq .692$

12. $.36 \leq P \leq .52$

13. $.401 \leq P \leq .439$

14. -34

15. $-82.07 \leq \mu_1 - \mu_2 \leq 14.07$

16. $-9.16 \leq \mu_1 - \mu_2 \leq 1.56$

17. $-1.48 \leq \mu_1 - \mu_2 \leq 15.48$

18. -.03

19. $-.066 \leq P_1 - P_2 \leq .006$

20. $-.081 \leq P_1 - P_2 \leq .071$

21. $-.0285 \leq P_1 - P_2 \leq .0885$

22. $\overline{X} - \mu$

23. 1/4 Range

24. 278

25. 44

26. 47

27. .50

28. 2,017

29. 664

30. 1,373

31. Equal

32. Equal

33. Twice

34. 129

35. 168

VI. **SOLUTIONS TO ODD-NUMBERED PROBLEMS IN TEXT**

8.1 $n=36$ $\overline{X}=211$ $\sigma=23$

95% C.I. $Z_{.025} = 1.96$

$$\overline{X} \pm Z\frac{\sigma}{\sqrt{n}}$$

$$211 \pm 1.96 \ \frac{23}{\sqrt{36}}$$

$$211 \pm 7.51$$

$$\boxed{203.49 \leq \mu \leq 218.51}$$

8.3 $n=15$ $\overline{X}=8.67$ $\sigma^2=6.12$

80% C.I. $Z_{.10}=1.28$

$$\overline{X} \pm Z\frac{\sigma}{\sqrt{n}}$$

$$8.67 \pm (1.28) \ \frac{\sqrt{6.12}}{\sqrt{15}}$$

$$8.67 \pm .82$$

$$\boxed{7.85 \leq \mu \leq 9.49}$$

8.5   n=39   N=200 $\overline{X}$=66   S=11

96% C.I. = $Z_{.02}$ = 2.06

$$\overline{X} \pm Z\frac{S}{\sqrt{n}}\sqrt{\frac{N-n}{N-1}}$$

$$66 \pm 2.06 \ \frac{11}{\sqrt{39}}\sqrt{\frac{200-39}{200-1}}$$

$$66 \pm 3.26$$

$$\boxed{62.74 \le \mu \le 69.26}$$

$$\boxed{\overline{X} = 66 \qquad \text{Point Estimate}}$$

8.7   N=1500   n=187 $\overline{X}$=5.3 years   S=1.28 years

95% C.I. $Z_{.025}$ = 1.96

$$\boxed{\overline{X} = 5.3 \text{ years} \quad \text{Point Estimate}}$$

$$\overline{X} \pm Z\frac{S}{\sqrt{n}}\sqrt{\frac{N-n}{N-1}}$$

$$5.3 \pm 1.96 \ \frac{1.28}{\sqrt{187}}\sqrt{\frac{1500-187}{1500-1}}$$

$$5.3 \pm .17$$

$$\boxed{5.13 \le \mu \le 5.47}$$

8.9   n=36 $\overline{X}$=3.306   S=1.167
      98% C.I. $Z_{.01}$ = 2.33

$$\overline{X} \pm Z\frac{S}{\sqrt{n}}$$

3.306 ± 2.33 $\dfrac{1.167}{\sqrt{36}}$

3.306 ± .453

$$\boxed{2.853 \leq \mu \leq 3.759}$$

8.11 n=36 $\overline{X}$=2.139   S=.113

$$\boxed{\overline{X} = 2.139 \qquad \text{Point Estimate}}$$

90% C.I. $Z_{.05}$ = 1.645

$$\overline{X} \pm Z\frac{S}{\sqrt{n}}$$

2.139 ± 1.645 $\dfrac{(.113)}{\sqrt{36}}$

2.139 ± .03

$$\boxed{2.109 \leq \mu \leq 2.169}$$

8.13 a) n=116   x=57   99% C.I. $Z_{.005} = 2.33$

$$\hat{p} = \frac{x}{n} = \frac{57}{116} = .49$$

$$\hat{p} \pm Z\sqrt{\frac{\hat{p}\cdot\hat{q}}{n}}$$

$$.49 \pm 2.33\sqrt{\frac{(.49)(.51)}{116}}$$

$$.49 \pm .11$$

$$\boxed{.38 \ \le \ P \ \le \ .60}$$

b)   n=800   x=479   97% C.I. $Z_{.015} = 2.17$

$$\hat{p} = \frac{x}{n} = \frac{479}{800} = .60$$

$$\hat{p} \pm Z\sqrt{\frac{\hat{p}\cdot\hat{q}}{n}}$$

$$.60 \pm 2.17\sqrt{\frac{(.60)(.40)}{800}}$$

$$.60 \pm .038$$

$$\boxed{.562 \le P \le .638}$$

c)   n=240   x=106   85% C.I. $Z_{.075} = 1.44$

$$\hat{p} = \frac{x}{n} = \frac{106}{240} = .44$$

$$\hat{p} \pm Z\sqrt{\frac{\hat{p}\cdot\hat{q}}{n}}$$

$$.44 \pm 1.44\sqrt{\frac{(.44)(.56)}{240}}$$

$$.44 \pm .046$$

$$\boxed{.394 \le P \le .486}$$

d) $n=60$ $x=21$ 90% C.I. $Z_{.05} = 1.645$

$\hat{p} = \dfrac{21}{60} = .35$

$\hat{p} \pm Z\sqrt{\dfrac{\hat{p}\cdot\hat{q}}{n}}$

$.35 \pm 1.645\sqrt{\dfrac{(.35)(.65)}{60}}$

$.35 \pm .10$

$$\boxed{.25 \ \le\ P \le\ .45}$$

8.15 n=75   x=29

$\hat{p} = \dfrac{29}{75} = .39$

$$\boxed{\hat{p} = .39 \qquad \text{Point Estimate}}$$

99% C.I. $Z_{.005} = 2.575$

$\hat{p} \pm Z\sqrt{\dfrac{\hat{p} \cdot \hat{q}}{n}}$

$.39 \pm 2.575\sqrt{\dfrac{(.39)(.61)}{75}}$

$.39 \pm .145$

$$\boxed{.245 \le P \le .535}$$

n=750 $\hat{p}=.39$

$\hat{p} \pm Z\sqrt{\dfrac{\hat{p} \cdot \hat{q}}{n}}$

$.39 \pm 2.575\sqrt{\dfrac{(.39)(.61)}{750}}$

$.39 \pm .046$

$$\boxed{.344 \le P \le .436}$$

All things being constant, increasing the sample size reduces the width of the interval.

8.17 n=1250   x=997   98% C.I. $Z_{.01} = 2.33$

$$\hat{p} = \frac{x}{n} = \frac{997}{1250} = .80$$

$$\hat{p} \pm Z\sqrt{\frac{\hat{p}\cdot\hat{q}}{n}}$$

$$.80 \pm 2.33\sqrt{\frac{(.80)(.20)}{1250}}$$

$$.80 \pm .026$$

$$\boxed{.774 \ \leq \ P \ \leq \ .826}$$

8.19 n=89   x=48   85% C.I. $Z_{.075} = 1.44$

$$\hat{p} = \frac{x}{n} = \frac{48}{89} = .54$$

$$\hat{p} \pm Z\sqrt{\frac{\hat{p}\cdot\hat{q}}{n}}$$

$$.54 \pm 1.44\sqrt{\frac{(.54)(.46)}{89}}$$

$$.54 \pm .076$$

$$\boxed{.464 \ \leq \ P \ \leq \ .616}$$

8.21   <u>Sample 1</u>   <u>Sample 2</u>
$n_1 = 32$ $n_2 = 31$

$\overline{X}_1 = 70.4$ $\overline{X}_2 = 68.7$

$S_1 = 5.76$ $S_2 = 6.1$

90% C.I. $Z_{.05} = 1.645$

$$(\overline{X}_1 - \overline{X}_2) \pm Z \sqrt{\frac{S_1^{\,2}}{n_1} + \frac{S_1^{\,2}}{n_2}}$$

$$(70.4 - 68.7) \pm 1.645 \sqrt{\frac{5.76^2}{32} + \frac{6.1^2}{31}}$$

1.7 ± 2.465

$$\boxed{-0.76 \leq \mu_1 - \mu_2 \leq 4.16}$$

8.23

A.L.	N.L.
$n_1 = 50$	$n_2 = 60$
$\overline{X}_1 = 3.82$	$\overline{X}_2 = 3.62$
$S_1 = 1.46$	$S_2 = 1.29$

98% C.I. $Z_{.01} = 2.33$

$$(\overline{X}_1 - \overline{X}_2) \pm Z \sqrt{\frac{S_1^2}{n_1} + \frac{S_1^2}{n_2}}$$

$$(3.82 - 3.62) \pm 2.33 \sqrt{\frac{1.46^2}{50} + \frac{1.29^2}{60}}$$

$$0.20 \pm .62$$

$$\boxed{-0.42 \leq \mu_1 - \mu_2 \leq 0.82}$$

$$\boxed{\mu_1 - \mu_2 = 0.20 \quad \text{Point Estimate}}$$

Since the interval is bounded by positive and negative values and zero lies in the interval, it is possible that there is no difference in runs scored between the two leagues, on average.

8.25   <u>Partner</u>   <u>No Partner</u>
$n_1 = 37$ $n_2 = 44$

$\overline{X}_1 = \$62,000$ $\overline{X}_2 = \$39,000$

$S_1 = \$5,590$ $S_2 = \$8,025$

90% C.I. $Z_{.05} = 1.645$

$$(\overline{X}_1 - \overline{X}_2) \pm Z\sqrt{\frac{S_1^2}{n_1} + \frac{S_1^2}{n_2}}$$

$$(\$62,000 - \$39,000) \pm 1.645\sqrt{\frac{5,590^2}{37} + \frac{8,025^2}{44}}$$

$\$23,000 \pm \$2,499$

$\boxed{\$20,501 \le \mu_1 - \mu_2 \le \$25,499}$

$\boxed{\$23,000 = \text{Point Estimate}}$

8.27 a) $n_1 = 200$ $n_2 = 300$ $x_1 = 174$ $x_2 = 189$

$\hat{p}_1 = \dfrac{174}{200} = .87$ $\hat{p}_2 = \dfrac{189}{300} = .63$

86% C.I. $Z_{.07} = 1.48$

$$(\hat{p}_1 - \hat{p}_2) \pm Z \sqrt{\dfrac{\hat{p}_1 \cdot \hat{q}_1}{n_1} + \dfrac{\hat{p}_2 \cdot \hat{q}_2}{n_2}}$$

$$(.87 - .63) \pm 1.48 \sqrt{\dfrac{(.87)(.13)}{200} + \dfrac{(.63)(.37)}{300}}$$

$.24 \pm .054$

$$\boxed{.186 \leq P_1 - P_2 \leq .294}$$

b) $n_1 = 430$ $n_2 = 399$ $x_1 = 275$ $x_2 = 275$

$\hat{p}_1 = \dfrac{275}{430} = .64$ $\hat{p}_2 = \dfrac{275}{399} = .69$

85% C.I. $Z_{.075} = 1.44$

$$(\hat{p}_1 - \hat{p}_2) \pm Z \sqrt{\dfrac{\hat{p}_1 \cdot \hat{q}_1}{n_1} + \dfrac{\hat{p}_2 \cdot \hat{q}_2}{n_2}}$$

$$(.64 - .69) \pm 1.44 \sqrt{\dfrac{(.64)(.36)}{430} + \dfrac{(.69)(.31)}{399}}$$

$.05 \pm .047$

$$\boxed{-.097 \leq P_1 - P_2 \leq -.003}$$

c) $n_1 = 49$ $n_2 = 64$ $x_1 = 25$ $x_2 = 35$

$\hat{p}_1 = \dfrac{25}{49} = .51$ $\hat{p}_2 = \dfrac{35}{64} = .547$

95% C.I. $Z_{.025} = 1.96$

$$(\hat{p}_1 - \hat{p}_2) \pm Z \sqrt{\dfrac{\hat{p}_1 \cdot \hat{q}_1}{n_1} + \dfrac{\hat{p}_2 \cdot \hat{q}_2}{n_2}}$$

$$(.51 - .547) \pm 1.96 \sqrt{\dfrac{(.51)(.49)}{49} + \dfrac{(.547)(.453)}{64}}$$

$-.037 \pm .186$ •

$$\boxed{-.223 \le P_1 - P_2 \le .149}$$

d) $n_1 = 1500$ $n_2 = 1500$ $x_1 = 1050$ $x_2 = 1100$

$\hat{p}_1 = \dfrac{1050}{1500} = .70$ $\hat{p}_2 = \dfrac{1100}{1500} = .733$

80% C.I. $Z_{.10} = 1.28$

$$(\hat{p}_1 - \hat{p}_2) \pm Z \sqrt{\dfrac{\hat{p}_1 \cdot \hat{q}_1}{n_1} + \dfrac{\hat{p}_2 \cdot \hat{q}_2}{n_2}}$$

$$(.70 - .733) \pm 1.28 \sqrt{\dfrac{(.70)(.30)}{1500} + \dfrac{(.733)(.267)}{1500}}$$

$-.033 \pm .02$

$$\boxed{-.053 \le P_1 - P_2 \le -.013}$$

8.29

Governor	Lieutenant Governor
$n_1 = 650$	$n_2 = 650$
$x_1 = 330$	$x_2 = 300$
$\hat{p}_1 = \dfrac{330}{650} = .508$	$\hat{p}_2 = \dfrac{300}{650} = .462$

95% C.I. $Z_{.025} = 1.96$

$$(\hat{p}_1 - \hat{p}_2) \pm Z \sqrt{\frac{\hat{p}_1 \cdot \hat{q}_1}{n_1} + \frac{\hat{p}_2 \cdot \hat{q}_2}{n_2}}$$

$$(.508 - .462) \pm 1.96 \sqrt{\frac{(.508)(.492)}{650} + \frac{(.462)(.538)}{650}}$$

$.046 \pm .054$

$$\boxed{-.008 \leq P_1 - P_2 \leq .100}$$

8.31

July	January
$n_1 = 900$	$n_2 = 900$
$x_1 = 647$	$x_2 = 380$
$\hat{p}_1 = \dfrac{647}{900} = .72$	$\hat{p}_2 = \dfrac{380}{900} = .42$

80% C.I. $Z_{.10} = 1.28$

$$(\hat{p}_1 - \hat{p}_2) \pm Z \sqrt{\frac{\hat{p}_1 \cdot \hat{q}_1}{n_1} + \frac{\hat{p}_2 \cdot \hat{q}_2}{n_2}}$$

$$(.72 - .42) \pm 1.28 \sqrt{\frac{(.72)(.28)}{900} + \frac{(.42)(.58)}{900}}$$

$.30 \pm .028$

$$\boxed{.272 \leq P_1 - P_2 \leq .328}$$

8.33 a) $\sigma=15$ E=4   99% confidence $Z_{.005} = 2.575$

$$n = \frac{Z^2\sigma^2}{E^2} = \frac{(2.575)^2(15)^2}{4^2} = 93.24$$

SAMPLE 94

b) $\sigma=4.25$ E=1   85% confidence $Z_{.075} = 1.44$

$$n = \frac{Z^2\sigma^2}{E^2} = \frac{(1.44)^2(4.25)^2}{1^2} = 37.45$$

SAMPLE 38

c) $\sigma^2=900$ E=5   80% confidence $Z_{.10} = 1.28$

$$n = \frac{Z^2\sigma^2}{E^2} = \frac{(1.28)^2(900)}{5^2} = 58.98$$

SAMPLE 59

8.35 a) $\sigma=20.4$ E=7.3   98% confidence $Z_{.01} = 2.33$

$n = \dfrac{2Z^2\sigma^2}{E^2} = \dfrac{2(2.33)^2(20.4)^2}{(7.3)^2} = 84.79$

Sample 85 in each group

b) $\sigma^2=2000$ E=15   88% confidence $Z_{.06} = 1.555$

$n = \dfrac{2Z^2\sigma^2}{E^2} = \dfrac{2(1.555)^2(2000)^2}{(15)^2} = 42.99$

Sample 43 in each group

c) $\sigma^2=140$ E=3   92% confidence $Z_{.04} = 1.75$

$n = \dfrac{2Z^2\sigma^2}{E^2} = \dfrac{2(1.75)^2(140)^2}{3^2} = 95.28$

Sample 96 in each group

8.37   E=$2 σ=$12.50   90% Confidence $Z_{.05} = 1.645$

$$n = \frac{Z^2\sigma^2}{E^2} = \frac{(1.645)^2(12.50)^2}{(\$2)^2} = 105.7$$

SAMPLE 106

8.39   P=.20   Q=.80   E=.02

90% Confidence, $Z_{.05} = 1.645$

$$n = \frac{Z^2 \cdot P \cdot Q}{E^2} = \frac{(1.645)^2(.20)(.80)}{(.02)^2} = 1082.41$$

SAMPLE 1083

8.41   E=.10   P=.50   Q=.50

95% Confidence, $Z_{.025} = 1.96$

$$n = \frac{Z^2 \cdot P \cdot Q}{E^2} = \frac{(1.96)^2(.50)(.50)}{(.10)^2} = 96.04$$

SAMPLE 97

8.43 E=10 σ=75

99% Confidence $Z_{.005} = 2.575$

$$n = \frac{2Z^2\sigma^2}{E^2} = \frac{2(2.575)^2(75)^2}{(10)^2} = 745.95$$

Sample 746 in each group

8.45 a) $\bar{X}=25$ $\sigma=3.5$ $n=60$

95% Confidence $Z_{.025} = 1.96$

$$\bar{X} \pm Z \frac{\sigma}{\sqrt{n}}$$

$$25 \pm 1.96 \frac{3.5}{\sqrt{60}}$$

$25 \pm .89$

24.11 $\leq \mu \leq$ 25.89

b) $\bar{X}=119.6$ $S=23.89$ $n=75$

98% Confidence $Z_{.01} = 2.33$

$$\bar{X} \pm Z \frac{S}{\sqrt{n}}$$

$$119.6 \pm 2.33 \frac{23.89}{\sqrt{75}}$$

119.6 ± 6.43

113.17 $\leq \mu \leq$ 126.03

c) $\bar{X}=3.419$ $S=0.974$ $n=32$

90% C.I. $Z_{.05} = 1.645$

$$\bar{X} \pm Z \frac{S}{\sqrt{n}}$$

$$3.419 \pm 1.645 \frac{0.974}{\sqrt{32}}$$

$3.419 \pm .283$

3.136 $\leq \mu \leq$ 3.702

d) $\overline{X}=56.7$ $\sigma=12.1$ N=500   n=47

80% C.I. $Z_{.10} = 1.28$

$$\overline{X} \pm Z \frac{\sigma}{\sqrt{n}} \sqrt{\frac{N-n}{N-1}}$$

$$56.7 \pm 1.28 \frac{12.1}{\sqrt{47}} \sqrt{\frac{500-47}{500-1}}$$

56.7 ± 2.15

$$\boxed{54.55 \leq \mu \leq 58.85}$$

8.47 a) $n_1=39$ $\overline{X}_1=50$ $S_1=6.79$

$n_2=45$ $\overline{X}_2=55$ $S_2=8.0$

98% Confidence $Z_{.01}=2.33$

$$(\overline{X}_1 - \overline{X}_2) \pm Z\sqrt{\frac{S_1^2}{n_1} + \frac{S_2^2}{n_2}}$$

$$(50-55) \pm 2.33\sqrt{\frac{6.79^2}{39} + \frac{8^2}{45}}$$

-5 ± 3.76

$$\boxed{-8.76 \leq \mu_1-\mu_2 \leq -1.24}$$

b) $n_1=87$ $\overline{X}_1=1157$ $\sigma_1=200$

$n_2=101$ $\overline{X}_2=1203$ $\sigma_2=210$

92% Confidence $Z_{.04}=1.75$

$$(\overline{X}_1 - \overline{X}_2) \pm Z\sqrt{\frac{\sigma_1^2}{n_1} + \frac{\sigma_2^2}{n_2}}$$

$$(1157-1203) \pm 1.75\sqrt{\frac{200^2}{87} + \frac{210^2}{101}}$$

-46 ± 52.4

$$\boxed{-98.4 \leq \mu_1-\mu_2 \leq 6.4}$$

8.49 a) $\sigma=36$ $E=5$ 95% Confidence $Z_{.025} = 1.96$

$$n = \frac{Z^2\sigma^2}{E^2} = \frac{(1.96)^2(36)^2}{(5)^2} = 199.15$$

> Sample 200

b) $\sigma=4.13$ $E=1$ 99% Confidence $Z_{.005} = 2.575$

$$n = \frac{Z^2\sigma^2}{E^2} = \frac{(2.575)^2(4.13)^2}{(1)^2} = 113.1$$

> Sample 114

c) $E=10$ Range $= 500 - 80 = 420$

$\sigma \approx 1/4$ Range $= 1/4(420) = 105$

90% Confidence $Z_{.05} = 1.645$

$$n = \frac{Z^2\sigma^2}{E^2} = \frac{(1.645)^2(105)^2}{(10)^2} = 298.3$$

> Sample 299

d) $E=3$ Range $= 108 - 50 = 58$

$\sigma \approx 1/4$ Range $= 1/4(58) = 14.5$

88% Confidence $Z_{.06} = 1.555$

$$n = \frac{Z^2\sigma^2}{E^2} = \frac{(1.555)^2(14.5)^2}{(3)^2} = 56.5$$

> Sample 57

8.51 a)   E=12 σ=48   98% Confidence $Z_{.01} = 2.33$

$$n = \frac{2Z^2\sigma^2}{E^2} = \frac{2(2.33)^2(48)^2}{(12)^2} = 173.7$$

Sample 174

b)   E=1.28 σ=11.6   88% Confidence $Z_{.06} = 1.555$

$$n = \frac{2Z^2\sigma^2}{E^2} = \frac{2(1.555)^2(11.6)^2}{(1.28)^2} = 397.2$$

Sample 398

c)   E=3.3 σ=15   90% Confidence $Z_{.05} = 1.645$

$$n = \frac{2Z^2\sigma^2}{E^2} = \frac{2(1.645)^2(15)^2}{(3.3)^2} = 111.8$$

Sample 112

d)   E=40 σ=300   95% Confidence $Z_{.025} = 1.96$

$$n = \frac{2Z^2\sigma^2}{E^2} = \frac{2(1.96)^2(300)^2}{(40)^2} = 432.2$$

Sample 433

8.53 n=60 $\overline{X}$=4.717   S=3.059   N=300

98% Confidence $Z_{.01}$ = 2.33

$$\overline{X} \pm Z \frac{S}{\sqrt{n}} \sqrt{\frac{N-n}{N-1}}$$

$$4.717 \pm 2.33 \frac{3.059}{\sqrt{60}} \sqrt{\frac{300-60}{300-1}}$$

$$4.717 \pm 0.824$$

$$\boxed{3.89 \leq \mu \leq 5.54}$$

8.55 n=45 $\overline{X}$=213   S=48

98% Confidence $Z_{.01}$ = 2.33

$$\overline{X} \pm Z \frac{S}{\sqrt{n}}$$

$$213 \pm 2.33 \frac{48}{\sqrt{45}}$$

$$213 \pm 16.67$$

$$\boxed{196.33 \leq \mu \leq 229.67}$$

8.57 n=90   x=30 $\hat{p}=\dfrac{30}{90}=.33$

95% Confidence $Z_{.025} = 1.96$

$$\hat{p} \pm Z\sqrt{\dfrac{\hat{p}\cdot\hat{q}}{n}}$$

$$.33 \pm 1.96\sqrt{\dfrac{(.33)(.67)}{90}}$$

$.33 \pm .097$

$$\boxed{.233 \le P \le .427}$$

8.59 n=245   x=189 $\hat{p} = \dfrac{x}{n} = \dfrac{189}{245} = .77$

90% Confidence $Z_{.05}= 1.645$

$$\hat{p} \pm Z\sqrt{\dfrac{\hat{p}\cdot\hat{q}}{n}}$$

$$.77 \pm (1.645)\sqrt{\dfrac{(.77)(.23)}{245}}$$

$.77 \pm .044$

$$\boxed{.726 \le P \le .814}$$

8.61   n=1,255   x=714 $\hat{p} = \dfrac{x}{n} = \dfrac{714}{1,255} = .569$

95% Confidence $Z_{.025} = 1.96$

$$\hat{p} \pm Z\sqrt{\frac{\hat{p} \cdot \hat{q}}{n}}$$

$$.569 \pm 1.96\sqrt{\frac{(.569)(.431)}{1,255}}$$

$.569 \pm .027$

$$\boxed{.542 \le P \le .596}$$

$$\boxed{P = .569 \quad \text{Point Estimate}}$$

8.63 $n_1 = 800$ $n_2 = 840$

         $\overline{X}_1 = 4.47$ $\overline{X}_2 = 3.08$

         $S_1 = 0.28$ $S_2 = 0.49$

96% Confidence $Z_{.02} = 2.06$

$$(\overline{X}_1 - \overline{X}_2) \pm Z\sqrt{\frac{S_1^2}{n_1} + \frac{S_2^2}{n_2}}$$

$$(4.47 - 3.08) \pm 2.06\sqrt{\frac{(.28)^2}{800} + \frac{(.49)^2}{840}}$$

$1.39 \pm .04$

$$\boxed{1.35 \le \mu_1 - \mu_2 \le 1.43}$$

8.65

Aerospace	Automobile
$n_1 = 33$	$n_2 = 35$
$\overline{X}_1 = 12.4$	$\overline{X}_2 = 4.6$
$S_1 = 2.9$	$S_2 = 1.8$

99% Confidence $Z_{.005} = 2.575$

$$(\overline{X}_1 - \overline{X}_2) \pm Z \sqrt{\frac{S_1^2}{n_1} + \frac{S_2^2}{n_2}}$$

$$(12.4 - 4.6) \pm 2.575 \sqrt{\frac{(2.9)^2}{33} + \frac{(1.8)^2}{35}}$$

7.8 ± 1.52

$$\boxed{6.28 \leq \mu_1 - \mu_2 \leq 9.32}$$

8.67

Specialty	Discount
$n_1 = 350$	$n_2 = 500$
$\hat{p}_1 = .75$	$\hat{p}_2 = .52$

90% Confidence $Z_{.05} = 1.645$

$$(\hat{p}_1 - \hat{p}_2) \pm Z \sqrt{\frac{\hat{p}_1 \cdot \hat{q}_1}{n_1} + \frac{\hat{p}_2 \cdot \hat{q}_2}{n_2}}$$

$$(.75 - .52) \pm 1.645 \sqrt{\frac{(.75)(.25)}{350} + \frac{(.52)(.48)}{500}}$$

$.23 \pm .053$

$$\boxed{.177 \leq P_1 - P_2 \leq .283}$$

8.69 $\underline{\text{Steak}}$ $\underline{\text{Italian}}$

$n_1 = 236$ $n_2 = 165$

$x_1 = 200$ $x_2 = 113$

$\hat{p}_1 = \dfrac{x_1}{n_1} = \dfrac{200}{236} = .847$ $\hat{p}_2 = \dfrac{x_2}{n_2} = \dfrac{113}{165} = .685$

98% Confidence $Z_{.01} = 2.33$

$$(\hat{p}_1 - \hat{p}_2) \pm Z \sqrt{\frac{\hat{p}_1 \cdot \hat{q}_1}{n_1} + \frac{\hat{p}_2 \cdot \hat{q}_2}{n_2}}$$

$$(.847 - .685) \pm 2.33 \sqrt{\frac{(.847)(.153)}{236} + \frac{(.685)(.315)}{165}}$$

$.162 \pm .10$

$$\boxed{.062 \le P_1 - P_2 \le .262}$$

8.71 $\underline{1980}$ $\underline{1990}$

$n_1 = 546$ $n_2 = 483$

$x_1 = 421$ $x_2 = 218$

$\hat{p}_1 = \dfrac{x_1}{n_1} = .771$ $\hat{p}_2 = \dfrac{x_2}{n_2} = \dfrac{218}{483} = .451$

95% Confidence $Z_{.025} = 1.96$

$$\hat{p}_1 - \hat{p}_2 \pm Z \sqrt{\frac{\hat{p}_1 \cdot \hat{q}_1}{n_1} + \frac{\hat{p}_2 \cdot \hat{q}_2}{n_2}}$$

$$(.771 - .451) \pm 1.96 \sqrt{\frac{(.771)(.229)}{546} + \frac{(.451)(.549)}{483}}$$

$.32 \pm .057$

$$\boxed{.263 \le P_1 - P_2 \le .377}$$

8.73 E=$20   Range = $600 - $30 = $570

$\sigma \approx 1/4$ Range = 1/4($570) = $142.50

95% Confidence $Z_{.025} = 1.96$

$n = \dfrac{Z^2\sigma^2}{E^2} = \dfrac{(1.96)^2\,(142.50)^2}{(20)^2} = 195.02$

Sample 196

8.75 P=.40   E=.03

90% Confidence $Z_{.05} = 1.645$

$n = \dfrac{Z^2 \cdot P \cdot Q}{E^2} = \dfrac{(1.645)^2\,(.40)\,.60)}{(.03)^2} = 721.61$

Sample 722

8.77 E=$100 $\sigma= \$4.50$

90% Confidence $Z_{.05} = 1.645$

$n = \dfrac{2Z^2 \cdot \sigma^2}{E^2} = \dfrac{2(1.645)^2\,(\$4.50)^2}{(\$1.00)^2} = 109.59$

Sample 110

HYPOTHESIS TESTING: LARGE SAMPLES

I. **CHAPTER OBJECTIVES**

The main objective of chapter nine is to help you to learn how to test hypotheses by using statistics for large samples, specifically enabling you to:

1. Understand the logic of hypothesis testing, and know how to establish null and alternate hypotheses.

2. Understand Type I and Type II errors, and know how to solve for Type II errors.

3. Use large samples to test hypotheses about a single population mean and a single population proportion.

4. Use large samples to test hypotheses about the differences in two population means and in two population proportions.

II. **CHAPTER OUTLINE**

III. **KEY WORDS**

Hypothesis Testing
Indirect Proof
Null Hypothesis
Alternative Hypothesis
Rejection Region
Critical Value
Acceptance Region
Type I Error
Alpha

Level of Significance
Type II Error
Beta
Power
One-Tailed Test
Two-Tailed Test
Critical Value Method
Probability Method

IV. **STUDY QUESTIONS**

1. Hypothesis testing is derived from the mathematical notion of _____ _____.

2. The first step in testing a hypothesis is to establish a(n) _____ hypothesis and a(n) _____ hypothesis.

3. In testing hypotheses, the researcher initially assumes that the _____ hypothesis is true.

4. The region of the distribution in hypothesis testing in which the null hypothesis is rejected is called the _____ region.

5. The rejection and acceptance regions are divided by a point called the _____ value.

6. The portion of the distribution which is not in the rejection region is called the _____ region.

7. The probability of committing a Type I error is called _____.

8. Another name for alpha is _____ _____ _____.

9. When a true null hypothesis is rejected, the researcher has committed a _____ error.

10. When a researcher fails to reject a false null hypothesis, a _____ error has been committed.

11. The probability of committing a Type II error is represented by _____.

12. Power is equal to _____.

13. Whenever hypotheses are established such that the alternative hypothesis is directional, then the researcher is conducting a _____-tailed test.

14. A _____-tailed test is nondirectional.

15. If in testing hypotheses, the researcher uses a method in which the probability of the calculated statistic is compared to alpha to reach a decision, the researcher is using the _____ method.

16. Suppose H_o: μ = 95 and H_a: $\mu \neq$ 95. If the sample size is 50 and α = .05, the critical value of z is _____.

17. Suppose H_o: $\mu \geq$ 2.36 and H_a: $\mu <$ 2.36. If the sample size is 64 and α = .01, the critical value of z is _____.

18. Suppose H_o: μ = 24.8 and H_a: $\mu \neq$ 24.8. If the sample size is 49 and α = .10, the critical value of z is _____.

19. Suppose a researcher is testing a null hypothesis that μ = 61. A random sample of n = 38 is taken resulting in $\overline{X}$ = 63 and S = 8.76. The calculated Z value is _____.

20. Suppose a researcher is testing a null hypothesis that $\mu \geq 413$. A random sample of n = 70 is taken resulting in $\overline{X} = 405$. The population standard deviation is 34. The calculated Z value is _____ .

21. A researcher is testing a hypothesis of a single mean. The critical Z value for $\alpha = .05$ and a one-tailed test is 1.645. The calculated Z value from sample data is 1.13. The decision made by the researcher based on this information is to _____ the null hypothesis.

22. A researcher is testing a hypothesis of a single mean. The critical Z value for $\alpha = .05$ and a two-tailed test is $\pm$ 1.96. The calculated Z value from sample data is -1.85. The decision made by the researcher based on this information is to _____ the null hypothesis.

23. A researcher is testing a hypothesis of a single mean. The critical Z value for $\alpha = .01$ and a one-tailed test is -2.33. The calculated Z value from sample data is -2.45. The decision made by the researcher based on this information is to _____ the null hypothesis.

24. A researcher has a theory that the average age of
     managers in a particular industry is over 35-years-old.
     The null hypothesis to conduct a statistical test on
     this theory would be _____.

25. A company produces, among other things, a metal plate
     that is supposed to have a six inch hole punched in the
     center. A quality control inspector is concerned that
     the machine which punches the hole is "out-of-control".
     In an effort to test this, the inspector is going to
     gather a sample of metal plates punched by the machine
     and measure the diameter of the hole. The alternative
     hypothesis used to statistical test to determine if the
     machine is out-of-control is _____.

26. A political scientist want to statistically test the
     null hypothesis that her candidate for governor is
     currently carrying at least 57% of the vote in the
     state. She has her assistants randomly sample 550
     eligible voters in the state by telephone and only 300
     declare that they support her candidate. The
     calculated Z value for this problem is _____.

27. Problem 26 is a _____-tailed test.

28. Suppose that the value of alpha for problem 26 is .05.
     After comparing the calculated value to the critical
     value, the political scientist decided to
     _____ the null hypothesis.

29. A company believes that it controls .27 of the total market share in the South for one of its products. To test this belief, a random sample of 1150 purchases of this product in the South are contracted. 385 of the 1150 purchased this company's brand of the product. If a researcher wants to conduct a statistical test for this problem, the alternative hypothesis would be

_____.

30. The calculated value of Z for problem 29 is

_____.

31. Problem 29 would result in a _____-tailed test.

32. Suppose that a .01 value of alpha were used in problem 29. The critical value of Z for the problem is

_____.

33. Upon comparing the calculated value of Z to the critical value of Z, it is determined to _____ the null hypothesis in problem 29.

34. Is there a difference in the average number years of experience of assembly line employees between company A and company B? A researcher wants to conduct a statistical test to answer this question. He is likely to be conducting a _____-tailed test.

35. The researcher who is conducting the test to determine if there is a difference in the average number of years of experience of assembly line workers between companies A and B is using an alpha of .10. The critical value of Z for this problem is _____.

36. Suppose the researcher conducting an experiment to test the question raised in question 34 randomly samples forty-five assembly-line workers from company A and discovers that the sample average is 7.1 years with a sample standard deviation of 2.3. Fifty-two assembly-line workers from company B are randomly selected resulting in a sample average of 6.2 years and a sample standard deviation of 2.7. The calculated Z value for this problem is _____.

37. Using an alpha of .10 and the critical values determined in questions 35 and 36, the decision is to _____ the null hypothesis.

38. A researcher has a theory that the mean for population A is less than the mean for population B. To test this, she randomly samples thirty-eight items from population A and determines that the sample average is 38.4 with a variance of 50.5 She randomly samples thirty-two items from population B and determines that the sample average is 44.3 with a variance of 48.6 Alpha is .05. She is going to conduct a _____-tailed test.

39. Using the information from question 38, the critical Z value is _____.

40. Using the information from question 38, the calculated value of Z is _____.

41. Using the results determined in question 39 and 40, the decision is to _____ the null hypothesis.

42. A statistician is being asked to test a new theory that the proportion of population A possessing a given characteristic is greater than the proportion of population B possessing the characteristic. A random sample of 625 from population A has been taken and it is determined that 463 possess the characteristic. A random sample of 704 taken from population B results in 428 possessing the characteristic. The alternative hypothesis for this problem is _____.

43. The calculated value of Z for question 42 is _____.

44. Suppose alpha is .10. The critical value of Z for question 42 is _____.

45. Based on the results of question 43 and 44, the decision for the problem in question 42 is to _____ the null hypothesis.

V.   **ANSWERS TO STUDY QUESTIONS**

1.   Indirect proof

2.   Null, alternative

3.   Null

4.   Rejection

5.   Critical

6.   Acceptance

7.   Alpha

8.   Level of significance

9.   Type I

10.   Type II

11.   Beta

12. $1 - \beta$

13.   One

14.   Two

15.   Probability

16.   1.96

17.   2.33

18.   1.645

19.   1.41

20.   -1.97

21.   Fail to reject

22.   Fail to reject

23.   Reject

24. $\mu \leq 35$

25. $\mu \neq 6''$

26. -1.16

27. One

28. Fail to reject

29. P = .27

30. 4.95

31. Two

32. ±1.645

33. Reject

34. Two

35. ±1.645

36. 1.77

37. Reject

38. One

39. -1.645

40. -3.50

41. Reject

42. $P_A - P_B > 0$

43. 5.15

44. 1.28

45. Reject

VI. SOLUTIONS TO ODD-NUMBERED PROBLEMS IN TEXT

9.1   a) H_o: $\mu = 25$

         H_a: $\mu \neq 25$

$\overline{X} = 28.1$ $n = 57$ $S = 8.46$ $\alpha = .01$

For two-tail, $\alpha/2 = .005$

$Z_c = 2.575$

$$Z = \frac{(\overline{X}_c - \mu)}{\frac{S}{\sqrt{n}}} = \frac{28.1 - 25}{\frac{8.46}{\sqrt{57}}} = \boxed{2.77}$$

calculated $Z = 2.77 > Z_c = 2.575$

$$\boxed{\text{Reject the null hypothesis}}$$

b)   critical mean values:

$$Z_c = \frac{(\overline{X}_c - \mu)}{\frac{S}{\sqrt{n}}}$$

$$\pm\, 2.575 = \frac{(\overline{X}_c - 25)}{\frac{8.46}{\sqrt{57}}}$$

$\overline{X}_c = 25 \pm 2.885$

$$\boxed{\overline{X}_c = 27.885 \quad \text{(upper value)}}$$

$$\boxed{\overline{X}_c = 22.115 \quad \text{(lower value)}}$$

9.3   a) H_o: $\mu \leq 1,200$
              H_a: $\mu > 1,200$

$\overline{X}=1,215$ n=113   S=100 $\alpha=.10$

For one-tail, $\alpha = .10$

$Z_c = 1.28$

$$Z = \frac{(\overline{X}_c - \mu)}{\frac{S}{\sqrt{n}}} = \frac{1,215 - 1,200}{\frac{100}{\sqrt{113}}} = \boxed{1.59}$$

calculated Z = 1.59 > Z_c = 1.28

$$\boxed{\text{Reject the null hypothesis}}$$

b)   Probability $\geq$ calculated Z = 1.59 is .0559 which is less than α = .10.   Reject the null hypothesis.

c)   Critical mean value:

$$Z_c = \frac{(\overline{X}_c - \mu)}{\frac{S}{\sqrt{n}}}$$

$$1.28 = \frac{(\overline{X}_c - 1,200)}{\frac{100}{\sqrt{113}}}$$

$\overline{X}_c = 1,200 + 12.04$

$$\boxed{\overline{X}_c = 1212.04}$$

Since calculated $\overline{X}$ = 1215 which is greater than the critical $\overline{X}$ = 1212.04, reject the null hypothesis.

9.5 H_o: $\mu \geq \$4.70$
       H_a: $\mu < \$4.70$

$\overline{X}=\$4.58$ $n=54$ $S=\$0.86$ $\alpha=.05$

For one-tail, $\alpha = .05$

$Z_c = -1.645$

Solving for $\overline{X}_c$:

$$Z_c = \frac{(\overline{X}_c-\mu)}{\dfrac{S}{\sqrt{n}}}$$

$$-1.645 = \frac{(\overline{X}_c-\$4.70)}{\dfrac{\$0.86}{\sqrt{54}}}$$

$\overline{X}_c = \$4.70 - .193 = \$4.507$

$\overline{X} = \$4.58 > \overline{X}_c = \$4.507$

$$\boxed{\text{Fail to reject the null hypothesis}}$$

9.7 H_o: $\mu \geq \$35,500$
       H_a: $\mu < \$35,500$

$\overline{X}=\$33,900$ $n=48$ $S=\$6,570$ $\alpha=.10$

For one-tail, $\alpha = .10$

$Z_c = -1.28$

$$Z = \frac{(\overline{X}-\mu)}{\dfrac{S}{\sqrt{n}}} = \frac{\$33,900-\$35,500}{\dfrac{\$6,570}{\sqrt{48}}} = \boxed{-1.69}$$

calculated $Z = -1.69 < Z_c = -1.28$

$$\boxed{\text{Reject the null hypothesis}}$$

9.9 H_0: $\mu \geq \$4,292$
         H_a: $\mu < \$4,292$

$\overline{X}=\$4,008$ $n=55$ $S=\$386$ $\alpha=.01$

For one-tail, $\alpha = .01$

$Z_c = -2.33$

$$Z = \frac{(\overline{X}-\mu)}{\frac{S}{\sqrt{n}}} = \frac{\$4,008-\$4,292}{\frac{\$386}{\sqrt{55}}} = \boxed{-5.46}$$

calculated $Z = -5.46 < Z_c = -2.33$

$\boxed{\text{Reject the null hypothesis}}$

9.11 H_0: $P \geq 0.63$
          H_a: $P < 0.63$

$n=100$ $x=55$ $\hat{p} = \dfrac{x}{n} = \dfrac{55}{100} = .55$

For one-tail, $\alpha = .01$

$Z_c = -2.33$

$$Z = \frac{\hat{p}-P}{\sqrt{\frac{P \cdot Q}{n}}} = \frac{.55-.63}{\sqrt{\frac{(.63)(.37)}{100}}} = \boxed{-1.66}$$

calculated $Z = -1.66 < Z_c = -2.33$

$\boxed{\text{Fail to reject the null hypothesis}}$

9.13 H_o: P $\leq$ 0.20
        H_a: P $>$ 0.20

n=380   x=87 $\hat{p} = \dfrac{x}{n} = \dfrac{87}{380} = .229$

For one-tail, α = .10

Z_c = +1.28

$$Z = \dfrac{\hat{p}-P}{\sqrt{\dfrac{P \cdot Q}{n}}} = \dfrac{.229-.20}{\sqrt{\dfrac{(.20)(.80)}{380}}} = \boxed{1.41}$$

calculated Z = 1.41 > Z_c = 1.28

$\boxed{\text{Reject the null hypothesis}}$

9.15 H_o: P = .10

        H_a: P $\neq$ .10

n=165   x=12 $\hat{p} = \dfrac{x}{n} = \dfrac{12}{165} = .073$

For two-tail, $\alpha/2$ = .05

Z_c = ±1.645

$$Z = \dfrac{\hat{p}-P}{\sqrt{\dfrac{P \cdot Q}{n}}} = \dfrac{.073-.10}{\sqrt{\dfrac{(.10)(.90)}{165}}} = \boxed{-1.16}$$

calculated Z = -1.16 < Z_c = -1.645

$\boxed{\text{Fail to reject the null hypothesis}}$

9.17 $\quad$ H_o: $\quad$ P $\geq$ .39
$\qquad$ H_a: $\quad$ P < .39

n=1,150 $\qquad$ x=414 $\qquad$ $\hat{p} = \dfrac{x}{n} = \dfrac{414}{1,150} = .36$

For one-tail, α = .05

Z_c = -1.645

$$Z = \frac{\hat{p}-P}{\sqrt{\dfrac{P \cdot Q}{n}}} = \frac{.36-.39}{\sqrt{\dfrac{(.39)(.61)}{1,150}}} = \boxed{-2.09}$$

calculated Z = -2.09 > Z_c = -1.645

$\boxed{\text{Reject the null hypothesis}}$

critical proportion:

$$Z_c = \frac{\hat{p}_c-P}{\sqrt{\dfrac{P \cdot Q}{n}}}$$

$$-1.645 = \frac{\hat{p}_c-.39}{\sqrt{\dfrac{(.39)(.61)}{1,150}}}$$

$\hat{p}_c$ = .39 - .024 = $\boxed{.366}$

9.19 H_o: $P \leq .12$
            H_a: $P > .12$

$n=378$ $x=71$ $\hat{p} = \dfrac{x}{n} = \dfrac{71}{378} = .188$

For one-tail, $\alpha = .01$

$Z_c = 2.33$

$Z = \dfrac{\hat{p}-P}{\sqrt{\dfrac{P \cdot Q}{n}}} = \dfrac{.188-.12}{\sqrt{\dfrac{(.12)(.88)}{378}}} = \boxed{4.07}$

calculated $Z = 4.07 > Z_c = 2.33$

$$\boxed{\text{Reject the null hypothesis}}$$

9.21   <u>Sample 1</u>   <u>Sample 2</u>

                        $\overline{X}_1 = 88.23$ $\overline{X}_2 = 81.2$

                        $S_1^2 = 22.74$ $S_2^2 = 26.65$

                        $n_1 = 30$ $n_2 = 30$

H_o: $\mu_1 - \mu_2 \leq 0$
H_a: $\mu_1 - \mu_2 > 0$

For one-tail test, $\alpha = .02$

$Z_c = +2.06$

$Z = \dfrac{(\overline{X}_1-\overline{X}_2) - (\mu_1-\mu_2)}{\sqrt{\dfrac{S_1^2}{n_1} + \dfrac{S_2^2}{n_2}}} = \dfrac{(88.23-81.2)-(0)}{\sqrt{\dfrac{22.74}{30}+\dfrac{26.65}{30}}} = \boxed{5.48}$

Calculated $Z = 5.48 > Z_c = 2.06$

$$\boxed{\text{Reject the null hypothesis}}$$

9.23   **Computers/electronics**   **Sample 2**

$$\overline{X}_1 = 2.2 \qquad\qquad \overline{X}_2 = 3.1$$

$$S_1^2 = 1 \qquad\qquad S_2^2 = 1$$

$$n_1 = 50 \qquad\qquad n_2 = 50$$

H_o: $\mu_1 - \mu_2 = 0$

H_a: $\mu_1 - \mu_2 \neq 0$

For two-tail test, $\alpha/2 = .005$
$Z_c = \pm 2.575$

$$Z = \frac{(\overline{X}_1-\overline{X}_2) - (\mu_1-\mu_2)}{\sqrt{\dfrac{S_1^2}{n_1} + \dfrac{S_1^2}{n_2}}} = \frac{(2.2-3.1)-(0)}{\sqrt{\dfrac{1}{50}+\dfrac{1}{50}}} = \boxed{-4.50}$$

Calculated $Z = -4.50 < Z_c = -2.575$

$$\boxed{\text{Reject the null hypothesis}}$$

9.25   **Burlington**   **Springfield**

$$\overline{X}_1 = \$95 \qquad\qquad \overline{X}_2 = \$92$$
$$S_1 = \$14 \qquad\qquad S_2 = \$12$$
$$n_1 = 31 \qquad\qquad n_2 = 34$$

H_o: $\mu_1 - \mu_2 \leq 0$
H_a: $\mu_1 - \mu_2 > 0$

For one-tail test, $\alpha = .10$
$Z_c = -1.28$

$$Z = \frac{(\overline{X}_1-\overline{X}_2) - (\mu_1-\mu_2)}{\sqrt{\dfrac{S_1^2}{n_1} + \dfrac{S_2^2}{n_2}}} = \frac{(\$95-\$92)-(0)}{\sqrt{\dfrac{(\$14)^2}{31}+\dfrac{(\$12)^2}{34}}} = \boxed{0.92}$$

Calculated $Z = 0.92 < Z_c = 1.28$

$$\boxed{\text{Fail to reject the null hypothesis}}$$

9.27   <u>Canon</u>   <u>Pioneer</u>

$$\overline{X}_1 = 5.8 \qquad \overline{X}_2 = 5.0$$
$$S_1 = 1.7 \qquad S_2 = 1.4$$
$$n_1 = 36 \qquad n_2 = 45$$

$H_o:$ $\mu_1 - \mu_2 = 0$

$H_a:$ $\mu_1 - \mu_2 \neq 0$

For two-tail test, $\alpha/2 = .025$
$Z_c = \pm 1.96$

$$Z = \frac{(\overline{X}_1 - \overline{X}_2) - (\mu_1 - \mu_2)}{\sqrt{\dfrac{S_1^2}{n_1} + \dfrac{S_2^2}{n_2}}} = \frac{(5.8 - 5.0) - (0)}{\sqrt{\dfrac{(1.7)^2}{36} + \dfrac{(1.4)^2}{45}}} = \boxed{2.27}$$

Calculated $Z = 2.27 > Z_c = 1.96$

$\boxed{\text{Reject the null hypothesis}}$

9.29

Sample 1	Sample 2

$n_1 = 368$ $n_2 = 405$

$x_1 = 175$ $x_2 = 182$

$$\hat{p}_1 = \frac{X_1}{n_1} = \frac{175}{368} = .476 \qquad \hat{p}_2 = \frac{X_2}{n_2} = \frac{182}{405} = .449$$

$$\overline{P} = \frac{X_1 + X_2}{n_1 + n_2} = \frac{175 + 182}{368 + 405} = \frac{357}{773} = .462$$

H_o: $P_1 - P_2 = 0$

H_a: $P_1 - P_2 \neq 0$

For two-tail, $\alpha/2 = .025$

$Z_c = \pm 1.96$

$$Z = \frac{(\hat{p}_1 - \hat{p}_2) - (P_1 - P_2)}{\sqrt{\overline{P} \cdot \overline{Q} \left(\frac{1}{n_1} + \frac{1}{n_2} \right)}} = \frac{(.476 - .449) - (0)}{\sqrt{(.462)(.538) \left(\frac{1}{368} + \frac{1}{405} \right)}} = \boxed{0.75}$$

Calculated $Z = 0.75 < Z_c = 1.96$

> Fail to reject the null hypothesis

9.31

<u>Sample 1</u>	<u>Sample 2</u>
$x_1 = 568$	$x_2 = 703$
$n_1 = 1,250$	$n_2 = 1,352$

$$\hat{p}_1 = \frac{x_1}{n_1} = \frac{568}{1,250} = .454 \qquad \hat{p}_2 = \frac{x_2}{n_2} = \frac{703}{1,352} = .520$$

$$\bar{P} = \frac{x_1 + x_2}{n_1 + n_2} = \frac{568 + 703}{1,250 + 1,352} = .488$$

$H_o:$ $P_1 - P_2 \geq 0$
$H_a:$ $P_1 - P_2 < 0$

For one-tail test, $\alpha = .01$

$Z_c = -2.33$

$$Z = \frac{(\hat{p}_1 - \hat{p}_2) - (P_1 - P_2)}{\sqrt{\bar{P} \cdot \bar{Q} \left(\frac{1}{n_1} + \frac{1}{n_2} \right)}} = \frac{(.454 - .520) - (0)}{\sqrt{(.488)(.512)\left(\frac{1}{1,250} + \frac{1}{1,352} \right)}} = \boxed{-3.37}$$

Calculated $Z = -3.37 < Z_c = -2.33$

$\boxed{\text{Reject the null hypothesis}}$

9.33

| Agricultural   Retail |

$$\hat{p}_1 = .18 \qquad\qquad \hat{p}_2 = .16$$

$$n_1 = 128 \qquad\qquad n_2 = 157$$

$$\bar{P} = \frac{n_1 \hat{p}_1 + n_2 \hat{p}_2}{n_1 + n_2} = \frac{128(.18) + 157(.16)}{128 + 157} = .169$$

$H_o: \quad P_1 - P_2 \leq 0$
$H_a: \quad P_1 - P_2 > 0$

For one-tail test, $\alpha = .10$

$Z_c = 1.28$

$$Z = \frac{(\hat{p}_1 - \hat{p}_2) - (P_1 - P_2)}{\sqrt{\bar{P} \cdot \bar{Q} \left(\frac{1}{n_1} + \frac{1}{n_2}\right)}} = \frac{(.18 - .16) - (0)}{\sqrt{(.169)(.831)\left(\frac{1}{128} + \frac{1}{157}\right)}} = \boxed{0.45}$$

Calculated $Z = 0.45 < Z_c = 1.28$

$$\boxed{\text{Fail to reject the null hypothesis}}$$

9.35

1970	1990
$\hat{p}_1 = .32$	$\hat{p}_2 = .42$
$n_1 = 349$	$n_2 = 268$

$$\bar{P} = \frac{n_1\hat{p}_1 + n_2\hat{p}_2}{n_1 + n_2} = \frac{349(.32) + 268(.42)}{349 + 268} = .363$$

H_o: $P_1 - P_2 \geq 0$
H_a: $P_1 - P_2 < 0$

For one-tail test, $\alpha = .05$

$Z_c = -1.645$

$$Z = \frac{(\hat{p}_1 - \hat{p}_2) - (P_1 - P_2)}{\sqrt{\bar{P}\cdot\bar{Q}\left(\frac{1}{n_1} + \frac{1}{n_2}\right)}} = \frac{(.32 - .42) - (0)}{\sqrt{(.363)(.637)\left(\frac{1}{349} + \frac{1}{268}\right)}} = \boxed{-2.56}$$

Calculated $Z = -2.56 < Z_c = -1.645$

$\boxed{\text{Reject the null hypothesis}}$

9.37

$$\underline{\text{Nielsen}} \qquad\qquad \underline{\text{Information Resources}}$$

$$\hat{p}_1 = .214 \qquad\qquad \hat{p}_2 = .220$$

$$n_1 = 1,500 \qquad\qquad n_2 = 1,500$$

$$\bar{P} = \frac{n_1\hat{p}_1 + n_2\hat{p}_2}{n_1 + n_2} = \frac{(1,500)(.214) + (1,500)(.220)}{1,500 + 1,500} = .217$$

H_o: $P_1 - P_2 = 0$

H_a: $P_1 - P_2 \neq 0$

For two-tail test, $\alpha/2 = .005$

$Z_c = \pm 2.575$

$$Z = \frac{(\hat{p}_1 - \hat{p}_2) - (P_1 - P_2)}{\sqrt{\bar{P}\cdot\bar{Q}(\frac{1}{n_1} + \frac{1}{n_2})}} = \frac{(.214 - .220) - (0)}{\sqrt{(.217)(.783)(\frac{1}{1,500} + \frac{1}{1,500})}}$$

$Z = \boxed{-0.40}$

Calculated $Z = -0.40 > Z_c = -2.575$

$$\boxed{\text{Fail to reject the null hypothesis}}$$

9.39 $\alpha = .05$ $\mu = 100$ $n = 48$ $S = 14$

a) $\mu_a = 98.5$
      $Z_c = -1.645$

$$Z_c = \frac{(\overline{X}_c - \mu)}{\dfrac{S}{\sqrt{n}}}$$

$$-1.645 = \frac{(\overline{X}_c - 100)}{\dfrac{14}{\sqrt{48}}}$$

$\overline{X}_c = 96.68$

$$Z = \frac{(\overline{X}_c - \mu)}{\dfrac{S}{\sqrt{n}}} = \frac{96.68 - 98.5}{\dfrac{14}{\sqrt{48}}} = -0.90$$

from Table A.5, area = .3159

$\beta = .3159 + .5000 = \boxed{.8159}$

b) $\mu_a = 98$
      $Z_c = -1.645$

$\overline{X}_c = 96.68$

$$Z = \frac{(\overline{X}_c - \mu)}{\dfrac{S}{\sqrt{n}}} = \frac{96.68 - 98}{\dfrac{14}{\sqrt{48}}} = -0.65$$

from Table A.5, area = .2422

$\beta = .2422 + .5000 = \boxed{.7422}$

c) $\mu_a = 97$

    $Z_c = -1.645$

    $\overline{X}_c = 96.68$

$$Z = \frac{(\overline{X}_c - \mu)}{\dfrac{S}{\sqrt{n}}} = \frac{96.68 - 97}{\dfrac{14}{\sqrt{48}}} = -0.16$$

from Table A.5, area = .0636

β = .0636 + .5000 = $\boxed{.5636}$

d) $\mu_a = 96$
    $Z_c = -1.645$

    $\overline{X}_c = 96.68$

$$Z = \frac{(\overline{X}_c - \mu)}{\dfrac{S}{\sqrt{n}}} = \frac{96.68 - 96}{\dfrac{14}{\sqrt{48}}} = 0.34$$

from Table A.5, area = .1331

β = .5000 + .1331 = $\boxed{.3669}$

e)   As the alternative value get farther from the null
hypothesized value, the probability of committing a Type II
error reduces. (All other variables being held constant).

9.41   a) H_0: $P \geq .65$
                   H_a: $P < .65$

$n=360$ $\alpha=.05$ $P_a=.60$

$Z_c = -1.645$

$$Z_c = \frac{\hat{P}_c - P}{\sqrt{\dfrac{P \cdot Q}{n}}}$$

$$-1.645 = \frac{\hat{P}_c - 65}{\sqrt{\dfrac{(.65)(.35)}{360}}}$$

$\hat{P}_c = .65 - .041 = .609$

$$Z = \frac{\hat{p}-P}{\sqrt{\dfrac{P \cdot Q}{n}}} = \frac{.609-.60}{\sqrt{\dfrac{(.60)(.40)}{360}}} = -0.35$$

from Table A.5, area = .1368

$\beta = .5000 - .1368 = \boxed{.3632}$

b) $P_a = .55$
       $Z_c = -1.645$
       $\hat{P}_c = .609$

$$Z = \frac{\hat{p}-P}{\sqrt{\dfrac{P \cdot Q}{n}}} = \frac{.609-.55}{\sqrt{\dfrac{(.55)(.45)}{360}}} = -2.25$$

from Table A.5 area = .4878

$\beta = .5000 - .4878 = \boxed{.0122}$

c) $P_a = .50$
       $Z_c = -1.645$
       $\hat{P}_c = .609$

$$Z = \frac{\hat{p}-P}{\sqrt{\dfrac{P \cdot Q}{n}}} = \frac{.609-.55}{\sqrt{\dfrac{(.50)(.50)}{360}}} = -4.14$$

from Table A.5 area = .5000

$\beta = .5000 - .5000 = \boxed{.0000}$

9.43 $H_o:$ $\mu = 44$

$H_a:$ $\mu \neq 44$

$\overline{X}=45.1$ $S=8.7$ $n = 58$ $\alpha =.05$

For a two-tailed test, $\alpha/2 = .025$

$Z = \pm 1.96$

$$Z = \frac{(\overline{X}-\mu)}{\frac{S}{\sqrt{n}}} = \frac{45.1 - 44}{\frac{8.7}{\sqrt{58}}} = \boxed{0.96}$$

Calculated $Z = 0.96 < Z_c = 1.96$

$$\boxed{\text{Fail to reject the null hypothesis}}$$

$\mu_a = 46$
$Z_c = \pm 1.96$

$$Z_c = \frac{(\overline{X}-\mu)}{\frac{S}{\sqrt{n}}}$$

$$\pm 1.96 = \frac{\overline{X}_c-44}{\frac{8.7}{\sqrt{58}}}$$

$\overline{X}_c = 44 \pm 2.24$

41.76   and   46.24

$$Z = \frac{(\overline{X}-\mu)}{\frac{S}{\sqrt{n}}} = \frac{46.24 - 46}{\frac{8.7}{\sqrt{58}}} = 0.21$$

from Table A.5, area $= .0832$

$$Z = \frac{(\overline{X}-\mu)}{\frac{S}{\sqrt{n}}} = \frac{41.76 - 46}{\frac{8.7}{\sqrt{58}}} = -3.71$$

from Table A.5, area = .5000

β = .5000 + .0832 = $\boxed{.5832}$

Z_c = ±1.96

$\overline{X}_c$ = 41.76 and 46.24

$$Z = \frac{(\overline{X}-\mu)}{\frac{S}{\sqrt{n}}} = \frac{46.24 - 47}{\frac{8.7}{\sqrt{58}}} = -0.67$$

from Table A.5, area = .2486

β = .5000 - .2486 = $\boxed{.2514}$

9.45 a) H_o: μ = 33

 H_a: $\mu \neq$ 33

$\overline{X}$=31.2   S=5.6   n=50 α =.05

For a two-tailed test, $\alpha/2$ = .025

Z = ±1.96

$$Z = \frac{(\overline{X}-\mu)}{\frac{S}{\sqrt{n}}} = \frac{31.2 - 33}{\frac{5.6}{\sqrt{50}}} = \boxed{-2.27}$$

Calculated Z = -2.27 < Z_c = -1.96

$\boxed{\text{Reject the null hypothesis}}$

b)

$$H_o: \quad \mu \leq 164$$
$$H_a: \quad \mu > 164$$

$\overline{X}=169$ $\qquad$ $S=24.3$ $\qquad$ $n=31$ $\qquad$ $\alpha=.10$

For a one-tail test, $\alpha = .10$

$Z_c = 1.28$

$$Z = \frac{(\overline{X}-\mu)}{\dfrac{S}{\sqrt{n}}} = \frac{169 - 164}{\dfrac{24.3}{\sqrt{31}}} = \boxed{1.15}$$

Calculated $Z = 1.15 < Z_c = 1.28$

$$\boxed{\text{Fail to reject the null hypothesis}}$$

c)

$$H_o: \quad \mu = 5.83$$
$$H_a: \quad \mu \neq 5.83$$

$\overline{X}=6.71$ $\qquad$ $S^2=4.20$ $\qquad$ $n=64$ $\qquad$ $\alpha = .01$

For a two-tailed test, $\alpha/2 = .005$

$Z_c = \pm 2.575$

$$Z = \frac{(\overline{X}-\mu)}{\dfrac{S}{\sqrt{n}}} = \frac{6.71 - 5.83}{\dfrac{\sqrt{4.20}}{\sqrt{64}}} = \boxed{3.44}$$

Calculated $Z = 3.44 > Z_c = 2.575$

$$\boxed{\text{Reject the null hypothesis}}$$

d) H_o: $\mu \geq 27$
       H_a: $\mu < 27$

$\overline{X}=26.4$ $S^2=1.5$ n=31 $\alpha =.01$

For a one-tail test, $\alpha = .01$

$Z_c = -2.33$

$$Z = \frac{(\overline{X}-\mu)}{\dfrac{S}{\sqrt{n}}} = \frac{26.4 - 27}{\dfrac{\sqrt{1.5}}{\sqrt{31}}} = \boxed{-2.73}$$

Calculated Z = -2.73 < Z_c = -2.33

$$\boxed{\text{Reject the null hypothesis}}$$

e) H_o: $\mu \leq 121$
       H_a: $\mu > 121$

$\overline{X}=123.4$ $\sigma^2=6.3$ n=14 $\alpha=.05$

For a one-tail test, $\alpha = .05$

$Z_c = 1.645$

$$Z = \frac{(\overline{X}-\mu)}{\dfrac{\sigma}{\sqrt{n}}} = \frac{123.4 - 121}{\dfrac{\sqrt{6.3}}{\sqrt{14}}} = \boxed{3.58}$$

Calculated Z = 3.58 < Z_c = 1.645

$$\boxed{\text{Reject the null hypothesis}}$$

9.47 a) H_o: $\mu_1 - \mu_2 = 0$ $\alpha = .05$

               H_a: $\mu_1 - \mu_2 \neq 0$

Sample 1	Sample 2
$n_1 = 120$	$n_2 = 125$
$\overline{X}_1 = 56.26$	$\overline{X}_2 = 58.4$
$S_1^2 = 210$	$S_2^2 = 195$

For two-tail, $\alpha/2 = .025$
$Z_c = \pm 1.96$

$$Z = \frac{(\overline{X}_1 - \overline{X}_2) - (\mu_1 - \mu_2)}{\sqrt{\dfrac{S_1^2}{n_1} + \dfrac{S_2^2}{n_2}}} = \frac{(56.26 - 58.4) - (0)}{\sqrt{\dfrac{210}{120} + \dfrac{195}{125}}} = -1.18$$

Calculated $Z = -1.18 > Z_c = -1.96$

> Fail to reject the null hypothesis

b) H_o: $\mu_1 - \mu_2 \geq 0$ $\alpha = .05$
          H_a: $\mu_1 - \mu_2 < 0$

Sample 1	Sample 2
$n_1 = 40$	$n_2 = 40$
$\overline{X}_1 = 131.3$	$\overline{X}_2 = 135.2$
$S_1^2 = 858$	$S_2^2 = 861$

For one-tail, $\alpha = .05$
$Z_c = -1.645$

$$Z = \frac{(\overline{X}_1 - \overline{X}_2) - (\mu_1 - \mu_2)}{\sqrt{\dfrac{S_1^2}{n_1} + \dfrac{S_2^2}{n_2}}} = \frac{(131.3 - 135.2) - (0)}{\sqrt{\dfrac{858}{40} + \dfrac{861}{40}}} = \boxed{-0.59}$$

Calculated $Z = -0.59 > Z_c = -1.645$

> Fail to reject the null hypothesis

c) H_o: $\mu_1-\mu_2 = 0$ $\alpha = .01$

          H_a: $\mu_1-\mu_2 \neq 0$

	Sample 1	Sample 2
	$n_1 = 84$	$n_2 = 90$
	$\overline{X}_1 = 9.64$	$\overline{X}_2 = 8.01$
	$S_1 = 1.245$	$S_2 = 1.304$

For two-tail, $\alpha/2 = .005$
$Z_c = \pm 2.575$

$$Z = \frac{(\overline{X}_1-\overline{X}_2) - (\mu_1-\mu_2)}{\sqrt{\dfrac{S_1^2}{n_1} + \dfrac{S_2^2}{n_2}}} = \frac{(9.64 - 8.01)-(0)}{\sqrt{\dfrac{(1.245)^2}{84} + \dfrac{(1.304)^2}{90}}} = 8.43$$

Calculated $Z = 8.43 > Z_c = 2.575$

$$\boxed{\text{Reject the null hypothesis}}$$

d) H_o: $\mu_1-\mu_2 \geq 0$ $\alpha = .01$
          H_a: $\mu_1-\mu_2 < 0$

	Sample 1	Sample 2
	$n_1 = 35$	$n_2 = 32$
	$\overline{X}_1 = 458.64$	$\overline{X}_2 = 479.1$
	$S_1 = 104.1$	$S_2 = 106.7$

For one-tail, $\alpha = .01$
$Z_c = -2.33$

$$Z = \frac{(\overline{X}_1-\overline{X}_2) - (\mu_1-\mu_2)}{\sqrt{\dfrac{S_1^2}{n_1} + \dfrac{S_2^2}{n_2}}} = \frac{(458.6 - 479.6)-(0)}{\sqrt{\dfrac{(104.1)^2}{35} + \dfrac{(106.7)^2}{32}}} = \boxed{-0.79}$$

Calculated $Z = -0.79 > Z_c = -2.33$

$$\boxed{\text{Fail to reject the null hypothesis}}$$

9.49 H_0: $\mu \leq \$15$
            H_a: $\mu > \$15$

$\overline{X}=\$19.34$ $n=35$ $S=\$4.52$ $\alpha=.10$

For one-tail, $\alpha = .10$

$Z_c = 1.28$

$$Z = \frac{(\overline{X}-\mu)}{\frac{S}{\sqrt{n}}} = \frac{\$19.34-\$15}{\frac{\$4.52}{\sqrt{35}}} = \boxed{5.68}$$

Calculated Z = 5.68 > Z_c = 1.28

$\boxed{\text{Reject the null hypothesis}}$

9.51 $\overline{X}=8.12$ $n=41$ $S=1.39$

a) H_0: $\mu = 8.5$
            H_a: $\mu \neq 8.5$ $\alpha = .01$

For two-tail, $\alpha/2 = .005$

$Z_c = \pm 2.575$

$$Z = \frac{(\overline{X}-\mu)}{\frac{S}{\sqrt{n}}} = \frac{8.12-8.5}{\frac{1.39}{\sqrt{41}}} = \boxed{-1.75}$$

Calculated Z = -1.75 > Z_c = -2.575

$\boxed{\text{Fail to reject the null hypothesis}}$

b) $\mu = 8.3$
$Z_c = \pm 2.575$

Solving for $\overline{X}_c$

$$Z_c = \frac{(\overline{X}_c - \mu)}{\frac{S}{\sqrt{n}}}$$

$$\pm 2.575 = \frac{(\overline{X}_c - 8.5)}{\frac{1.39}{\sqrt{41}}}$$

$\overline{X}_c = 8.5 \pm .56$

7.94   and   9.06

$$Z = \frac{(\overline{X} - \mu)}{\frac{S}{\sqrt{n}}} = \frac{7.94 - 8.3}{\frac{1.39}{\sqrt{41}}} = \boxed{-1.66}$$

from Table A.5, area = .4515

$\beta = .4515 + .5000 = \boxed{.9515}$

9.53 $\overline{X}=3.45$ $n=64$ $\sigma^2=1.31$

H_o: $\mu = 3.3$

H_a: $\mu \neq 3.3$ $\alpha = .05$

For two-tail, $\alpha/2 = .025$

$Z_c = \pm 1.96$

$$Z = \frac{(\overline{X}-\mu)}{\frac{\sigma}{\sqrt{n}}} = \frac{3.45-3.3}{\frac{\sqrt{1.31}}{\sqrt{64}}} = \boxed{1.05}$$

Calculated $Z = 1.05 < Z_c = 1.96$

$\boxed{\text{Fail to reject the null hypothesis}}$

9.55 a) H_o: $P = .12$

H_a: $P \neq .12$

$n=168$ $x = 28$ $\alpha=.05$ $\hat{p} = \dfrac{x}{n} = \dfrac{28}{168} = .167$

For two-tail, $\alpha/2 = .05$
$Z_c = \pm 1.96$

$$Z = \frac{\hat{p}-P}{\sqrt{\frac{P \cdot Q}{n}}} = \frac{.167-.12}{\sqrt{\frac{(.12)(.88)}{168}}} = \boxed{1.87}$$

Calculated $Z = 1.87 < Z_c = 1.96$

$\boxed{\text{Fail to reject the null hypothesis}}$

b) P_a = .17 Z_c = ±1.96

Solving for $\hat{p}_c$:

$$Z_c = \frac{\hat{p}_c - P}{\sqrt{\dfrac{P \cdot Q}{n}}}$$

$$\pm 1.96 = \frac{\hat{p}_c - .12}{\sqrt{\dfrac{(.12)(.88)}{168}}}$$

$\hat{p}_c$ = .12 ± .049

.071   and .169

$$Z = \frac{\hat{p}_c - P}{\sqrt{\dfrac{P \cdot Q}{n}}} = \frac{.169 - .17}{\sqrt{\dfrac{(.17)(.83)}{168}}} = \boxed{-.03}$$

from Table A.5, area = .0120

β = .5000 - .0120 = $\boxed{.4880}$

9.57   n=80   x=10 $\hat{p} = \dfrac{x}{n} = \dfrac{10}{80}$ = .125

a) H_o: P = .14 α=.01

            H_a: P ≠ .14

For two-tail, $\alpha/2$ = .005
Z_c = ±2.575

$$Z = \frac{\hat{p} - P}{\sqrt{\dfrac{P \cdot Q}{n}}} = \frac{.125 - .14}{\sqrt{\dfrac{(.14)(.86)}{80}}} = \boxed{-0.39}$$

Calculated Z = -0.39 > Z_c = -2.575

$\boxed{\text{Fail to reject the null hypothesis}}$

9.59
	Newer	Older
	$\overline{X}_1 = \$69$	$\overline{X}_2 = \$59$
	$S_1 = \$8.50$	$S_2 = \$8.10$
	$n_1 = 45$	$n_2 = 50$

H_o: $\mu_1 - \mu_2 \le 0$
H_a: $\mu_1 - \mu_2 > 0$

For one-tail test, $\alpha = .05$
$Z_c = 1.645$

$$Z = \frac{(\overline{X}_1 - \overline{X}_2) - (\mu_1 - \mu_2)}{\sqrt{\dfrac{S_1^2}{n_1} + \dfrac{S_2^2}{n_2}}} = \frac{(\$69 - \$59) - (0)}{\sqrt{\dfrac{(\$8.50)^2}{45} + \dfrac{(\$8.10)^2}{50}}} = \boxed{5.85}$$

Calculated Z = 5.85 > Z_c = 1.645

$\boxed{\text{Reject the null hypothesis}}$

9.61
	Chicago	Houston
	$\overline{X}_C = \$30.77$	$\overline{X}_H = \$15.00$
	$S_C = \$5.98$	$S_H = \$3.90$
	$n_C = 35$	$n_H = 35$

H_o: $\mu_1 - \mu_2 \le 0$ $\alpha = .05$
H_a: $\mu_1 - \mu_2 > 0$

For one-tail test, $\alpha = .05$
$Z_c = 1.645$

$$Z = \frac{(\overline{X}_C - \overline{X}_H) - (\mu_C - \mu_H)}{\sqrt{\dfrac{S_C^2}{n_C} + \dfrac{S_H^2}{n_H}}} = \frac{(\$30.77 - \$15.00) - (0)}{\sqrt{\dfrac{(\$5.98)^2}{35} + \dfrac{(\$3.90)^2}{35}}} = \boxed{13.07}$$

Calculated Z = 13.07 > Z_c = 1.645

$\boxed{\text{Reject the null hypothesis}}$

9.63   <u>With Fertilizer</u>   <u>Without Fertilizer</u>

$\overline{X}_1 = 38.4$ $\overline{X}_2 = 23.1$
$S_1 = 9.8$ $S_2 = 7.4$
$n_1 = 35$ $n_2 = 35$

H_o: $\mu_1 - \mu_2 \leq 0$ $\alpha = .01$
H_a: $\mu_1 - \mu_2 > 0$

For one-tail test, $\alpha = .01$
$Z_c = 2.33$

$$Z = \frac{(\overline{X}_1 - \overline{X}_2) - (\mu_1 - \mu_2)}{\sqrt{\dfrac{S_1^2}{n_1} + \dfrac{S_2^2}{n_2}}} = \frac{(38.4 - 23.1) - (0)}{\sqrt{\dfrac{(9.8)^2}{35} + \dfrac{(7.4)^2}{35}}} = \boxed{7.37}$$

Calculated $Z = 7.37 > Z_c = 2.33$

$\boxed{\text{Reject the null hypothesis}}$

9.65 H_o: $P_1 + P_2 = 0$ $\alpha = .10$

H_a: $P_1 + P_2 \neq 0$

Baltimore	Washington, D.C.
$X_1 = 34$	$X_2 = 34$
$n_1 = 235$	$n_2 = 215$
$\hat{p}_1 = \frac{x_1}{n_1} = \frac{35}{235} = .149$	$\hat{p}_2 = \frac{x_2}{n_1} = \frac{34}{215} = .158$

$$\bar{p} = \frac{x_1 + x_2}{n_1 + n_2} = \frac{35 + 34}{235 + 215} = .153$$

For two-tail, $\alpha/2 = .05$

$Z_c = \pm 1.645$

$$Z = \frac{(\hat{p}_1 - \hat{p}_2) - (P_1 - P_2)}{\sqrt{\bar{P} \cdot \bar{Q}\left(\frac{1}{n_1} + \frac{1}{n_2}\right)}} = \frac{(.149 - .158) - (0)}{\sqrt{(.153)(.847)\left(\frac{1}{235} + \frac{1}{215}\right)}} = \boxed{-0.26}$$

Calculated $Z = -0.26 > Z_c = -1.645$

Fail to reject the null hypothesis

9.67 H_o: $P_1 - P_2 \geq 0$ $\alpha = .01$

                H_a: $P_1 - P_2 < 0$

<u>Des Moines</u>   <u>Anaheim</u>

$\hat{p}_1 = .54$ $\hat{p}_2 = .71$

$n_1 = 390$ $n_2 = 526$

$$\bar{p} = \frac{n_1\hat{p}_1 + n_2\hat{p}_2}{n_1 + n_2} = \frac{(390)(.54) + (526)(.71)}{390 + 526} = .638$$

For one-tail, $\alpha = .01$

$Z_c = -2.33$

$$Z = \frac{(\hat{p}_1 - \hat{p}_2) - (P_1 - P_2)}{\sqrt{\bar{P} \cdot \bar{Q}\left(\frac{1}{n_1} + \frac{1}{n_2}\right)}} = \frac{(.54 - .71) - (0)}{\sqrt{(.638)(.362)\left(\frac{1}{390} + \frac{1}{526}\right)}} = \boxed{-5.29}$$

Calculated $Z = -5.29 < Z_c = -2.33$

$\boxed{\text{Reject the null hypothesis}}$

9.69   n=123   x=88 $\hat{p} = \dfrac{x}{n} = \dfrac{88}{123} = .715$

a) H_o: $P \leq .68$ $\alpha = .05$
      H_a: $P > .68$

For one-tail, $\alpha = .05$
$Z_c = 1.645$

$$Z = \dfrac{\hat{p}-P}{\sqrt{\dfrac{P \cdot Q}{n}}} = \dfrac{.715-.68}{\sqrt{\dfrac{(.68)(.32)}{123}}} = \boxed{0.83}$$

Calculated $Z = 0.83 < Z_c = 1.645$

$$\boxed{\text{Fail to reject the null hypothesis}}$$

$P_a = .75$ $Z_c = 1.645$

Solving for P_c:

$$Z_c = \dfrac{\hat{P}_c - P}{\sqrt{\dfrac{P \cdot Q}{n}}}$$

$$1.645 = \dfrac{\hat{P}_c - .68}{\sqrt{\dfrac{(.68).32)}{123}}}$$

$$\hat{P}_c = .68 + .069 = .749$$

$$Z = \dfrac{\hat{P}_c - P_a}{\sqrt{\dfrac{P_a \cdot Q_a}{n}}} = \dfrac{.749-.75}{\sqrt{\dfrac{(.75)(.25)}{123}}} = \boxed{-.03}$$

from Table A.5, area = .0120

$$\beta = .5000 - .0120 = \boxed{.4880}$$

$$P_a = .80 \qquad\qquad Z_c = 1.645 \qquad\qquad \hat{p}_c = .749$$

$$Z = \frac{\hat{p}_c - P_a}{\sqrt{\dfrac{P_a \cdot Q_a}{n}}} = \frac{.749 - .80}{\sqrt{\dfrac{(.80)(.20)}{123}}} = \boxed{-1.41}$$

from Table A.5, area = .4207

$$\beta = .5000 - .4207 = \boxed{.0793}$$

10

SMALL SAMPLE STATISTICS: HYPOTHESIS TESTS AND CONFIDENCE INTERVALS

I.   CHAPTER OBJECTIVES

The overall learning objective of Chapter ten is to help you learn to apply statistical techniques with small sample sizes, specifically enabling you to:

1.   Understand the difference between the t distribution and the Z distribution.

2.   Test hypotheses and establish confidence intervals for single means when sample size is small and the standard deviation or variance is unknown.

3.   Test hypotheses and establish confidence intervals for two sample means when sample sizes are small and the standard deviations or variances are unknown.

4.   Test hypotheses and establish confidence intervals for the mean difference in two related measures.

5.   Test hypotheses about the difference of the means for more than two samples.

II.   **CHAPTER OUTLINE**

10.1 Introduction to Small Sample Analysis

   The t Test

   Characteristics of the t Distribution

   Reading the t distribution Table

10.2 Small Sample Statistics About μ

   Hypothesis Testing

   Confidence Intervals

10.3 Small Sample Statistics About $\mu_1 - \mu_2$

   Hypothesis Testing

   Confidence Intervals

10.4 Small Sample Statistics for Two Related Samples

   Hypothesis Testing

   Confidence Intervals

10.5 Hypothesis Tests About More Than Two Means: One-Way
   Analysis of Variance

   One-Way Analysis of Variance

   Reading the F Distribution Table

   Comparison of F and t Values

   Multiple Comparisons

III. **KEY WORDS**

t Distribution	Independent Variable
Degrees of Freedom	Treatment Levels
Independent Samples	Total Variance
Related Samples	Treatment Variance
Matched-Pairs Test	Error Variance
Analysis of Variance	F Distribution
Completely Randomized Design	Multiple Comparisons

IV.   **STUDY QUESTIONS**

1.   Generally, _____ is considered the lower
     limit for large sample size.

2.   The t test was developed by _____.

3.   In order to find values in the t distribution table,
     you must convert the sample size or sizes to

     _____.

4.   The table t value associated with $\alpha = .05$ and 12
     degrees of freedom is _____.

5.   The table t value associated with $\alpha = .01$ and 27
     degrees of freedom is _____.

6.   The table t value associated with 10 degrees of
     freedom and used to compute a 95% confidence interval
     is _____.

7.   The table t value associated with 18 degrees of
     freedom and used to compute a 99% confidence interval
     is _____.

8.   The following hypotheses are being tested:

H_o: $\mu = 4.6$

H_a: $\mu \neq 4.6$

The value of alpha is .05.   To test these hypotheses, a random sample of 22 items is selected resulting in a sample mean of 4.1 with a sample standard deviation of 1.8.   It can be assumed that this measurement is normally distributed in the population.   The degrees of freedom associated with the t test used in this problem are _____.

9.   The critical t value for the problem presented in question 8 is _____.

10.   The problem presented in question 8 contains hypotheses which lead to a _____-tailed test.

11.   The calculated value of t for the problem presented in question 8 is _____.

12.   Based on the results of the calculated t value and the critical table t value, the researcher should _____ the null hypothesis in the problem presented in question 8.

13.   A researcher is interested in estimating the mean
       value for a population. She takes a random sample of
       17 items and computes a sample mean of 224 and a
       sample standard deviation of 32. She decides to
       construct a 98% confidence interval to estimate the
       mean. The degrees of freedom associated with this
       problem are _____. It can be assumed that
       these values are normally distributed in the
       population.

14.   The table t value used to construct the confidence
       interval in question 13 is _____.

15.   The confidence interval resulting from the data in
       question 13 is _____.

16.   A researcher is interested in testing to determine if
       the mean of population one is greater than the mean of
       population two. He uses the following hypotheses to
       test this theory:

$$H_o: \quad \mu_1 - \mu_2 \leq 0$$
$$H_a: \quad \mu_1 - \mu_2 > 0$$

He randomly selects a sample of 8 items from
population one resulting in a mean of 14.7 and a
standard deviation of 3.4. He randomly selects a
sample of 12 items from population two resulting in a
mean of 11.5 and a standard deviation 2.9. He is
using an alpha value of .10 to conduct this test. The

degrees of freedom for this problem are _____.
It is assumed that these values are normally
distributed in both populations.

17. The critical table t value used to conduct the
    hypothesis test in question 16 is _____.

18. The t value calculated from the sample data is _____.

19. Based on the calculated t value obtained in question
    18 and the critical table t value in question 17, the
    researcher should _____ the null hypothesis.

20. What is the difference in the means of two
    populations? A researcher wishes to determine this by
    taking random samples of size 14 from each population
    and computing a 90% confidence interval. The sample
    from the first population produces a mean of 780 with
    a standard deviation of 245. The sample from the
    second population produces a mean of 890 with a
    standard deviation of 256. The point estimate for the
    difference in the means of these two populations is
    _____. Assume that the values are normally
    distributed in each population.

21. The table t value used to construct the confidence
    interval for the problem in question 20 is _____.

22. The confidence interval constructed for the problem in
    question 20 is _____.

23. The matched-pairs t test deals with _____ samples.

24. A researcher wants to conduct a before/after study on 13 subjects to determine if a treatment results in higher scores. The hypotheses are:

$$H_o: \quad D \geq 0$$

$$H_a: \quad D < 0$$

Scores are obtained on the subjects both before and after the treatment. After subtracting the after scores from the before scores, the resulting value of $\bar{d}$ is -2.85 with a S_d of 1.01. The degrees of freedom for this test are _____. Assume that the data are normally distributed in the population.

25. The critical table t value for the problem in question 24 is _____ if $\alpha = .01$.

26. The calculated t value for the problem in question 24 is _____.

27. For the problem in question 24 based on the critical table t value obtained in question 25 and the calculated t value obtained in question 26, the decision should be to _____ the null hypothesis.

28.   A researcher is conducting a matched-pairs study. She gathers data on each pair in the study resulting in:

Pair	Group 1	Group 2
1	10	12
2	13	14
3	11	15
4	14	14
5	12	11
6	12	15
7	10	16
8	8	10

Assuming that the data are normally distributed in the population, the computed value of $\bar{d}$ is _____.

29.   The value of S_d for the problem in question 28 is _____.

30.   The degrees of freedom for the problem in question 28 is _____.

31.   The calculated value of t for the problem in question 28 is _____.

32. A researcher desires to estimate the difference between two related populations. He gathers pairs of data from the populations. The data are below:

Pair	Group 1	Group 2
1	360	280
2	345	290
3	355	300
4	325	270
5	340	300
6	365	310

It is assumed that the data are normally distributed in the population. Using this data, the value of $\bar{d}$ is

_____.

33. For the problem in 32, the value of S_d is _____.

34. The point estimate for the population difference for the problem in question 32 is _____.

35. The researcher conducting the study for the problem in question 32 wants to use a 95% level of confidence. The table t value for this confidence interval is

_____.

36. The confidence interval computed for the problem in question 32 is _____.

37. If a researcher wants to conduct test the differences in the means for more than two independent populations, he/she can use _____.

38. Analysis of variance uses the _____ test.

39. Determining the table value for the F distribution is different from finding values in the t distribution tables because the F table requires _____ values for degrees of freedom.

40. Suppose the mean squares for treatment in an ANOVA are 27.5 and the mean squares for error are 11.4. The calculated value of F is _____.

41. Suppose a researcher sets up a design in which there are four different treatments and a total of 32 measurements in the study. The degrees of freedom treatment are _____. The degrees of freedom error are _____. The total degrees of freedom are _____.

42. For α = .05, the critical table F value is _____.

43. When the numerator degrees of freedom are _____, the value of F is the same as t^2.

44. If a significant value of F is obtained in an ANOVA problem, _____ can be used to determine which means, if any, are significantly different from the others.

V.   ANSWERS TO STUDY QUESTIONS

1. $n \geq 30$

2.   William S. Gosset

3.   Degrees of freedom

4.   1.782

5.   2.473

6.   2.228

7.   2.878

8.   21

9. ± 2.08

10.   Two

11.   −1.30

12.   Fail to reject

13.   16

14.   2.583

15. $203.95 \leq \mu \leq 244.05$

16.   18

17.   1.33

18.   2.26

19.   Reject

20.   −110

21.   1.706

22. $-271.56 \leq \mu_1 - \mu_2 \leq 51.56$

23.   Related

24.   12

25. -2.681

26. -10.17

27. Reject

28. -2.125

29. 2.232

30. 7

31. -2.69

32. 56.67

33. 12.91

34. 56.67

35. 2.571

36. $43.12 \leq D \leq 70.22$

37. Analysis of Variance

38. F

39. Two

40. 2.41

41. 3, 28, 31

42. 2.95

43. 1

44. Multiple Comparisons

VI   SOLUTIONS TO ODD-NUMBERED PROBLEMS IN TEXT

10.1   n=20 $\overline{X}$=16.45   S=3.59   df = 20 − 1 = 19
           α=.05

H$_o$: $\mu = 16$

H$_a$: $\mu \neq 16$

For two-tail test, $\alpha/2 = .025$

critical $t_{.025,19} = \pm 2.093$

$$t = \frac{(\overline{X}-\mu)}{\frac{S}{\sqrt{n}}} = \frac{16.45 - 16}{\frac{3.59}{\sqrt{20}}} = \boxed{0.56}$$

Calculate $t = 0.56 < t_{.025,19} = 2.093$

Fail to reject the null hypothesis

10.3   n=11 $\overline{X}$=1,235.36   S=103.81   df=11−1=10
           α=.05

H$_o$: $\mu \leq 1,160$
H$_a$: $\mu > 1,160$
For one-tail test, $\alpha = .05$

critical $t_{.05,10} = 1.812$

$$t = \frac{(\overline{X}-\mu)}{\frac{S}{\sqrt{n}}} = \frac{1,235.36 - 1,160}{\frac{103.81}{\sqrt{11}}} = \boxed{2.44}$$

Calculate $t = 2.44 > t_{.05,10} = 1.812$

Reject the null hypothesis

10.5   n=13 $\overline{X}$=45.62   S=5.694   df=13-1=12

95% Confidence Interval
$\alpha/2$=.025

$t_{.025,12}$ = 2.179

$$\overline{X} \pm t \ \frac{S}{\sqrt{n}}$$

$45.62 \pm 2.179 \ \dfrac{5.694}{\sqrt{13}}$

45.62 ± 3.44

$$\boxed{42.18 \leq \mu \leq 49.06}$$

10.7   n=15 $\overline{X}$=2.364 S^2=0.81   df=15-1=14

90% Confidence interval
$\alpha/2$=.05

$t_{.05,14}$ = 1.76

$$\overline{X} \pm t \ \frac{S}{\sqrt{n}}$$

$2.364 \pm 1.76 \ \dfrac{\sqrt{0.81}}{\sqrt{15}}$

$2.364 \pm .409$

$$\boxed{1.955 \leq \mu \leq 2.773}$$

10.9   n=22 $\overline{X}=\$140,000$ S=$39,000   df=22-1=21
        $\alpha=.01$

        H_o: $\mu \geq \$158,000$
        H_a: $\mu < \$158,000$

        For one-tail test, $\alpha = .01$

        Critical $t_{.01,21} = -2.518$

        $$t = \frac{(\overline{X}-\mu)}{\frac{S}{\sqrt{n}}} = \frac{\$140,000 - \$158,000}{\frac{\$39,000}{\sqrt{22}}} = \boxed{-2.16}$$

        Calculate $t = -2.16 > t_{.01,21} = -2.518$

        $\boxed{\text{Fail to reject the null hypothesis}}$

10.11   n=5 $\overline{X}=20.2$ S=6.14   df=5-1=4

        95% Confidence Interval
        $\alpha/2=.025$

        $t_{.025,4} = 2.776$

        $$\overline{X} \pm t \frac{S}{\sqrt{n}}$$

        $$20.2 \pm 2.776 \frac{6.14}{\sqrt{5}}$$

        20.2 ± 7.62

        $\boxed{12.58 \leq \mu \leq 27.82}$

10.13   n=28 $\bar{X}$=5.335   S=2.016   df=28-1=27

90% Confidence Interval
$\alpha/2$=.05

$t_{.05,27}$ = 1.703

$$\bar{X} \pm t \frac{S}{\sqrt{n}}$$

$$5.335 \pm 1.703 \frac{2.016}{\sqrt{28}}$$

$$5.335 \pm .649$$

$$\boxed{4.686 \leq \mu \leq 5.984}$$

10.15   n=19 $\bar{X}$=23.263   S=4.817   df=19-1=18
α=.10

H_o: $\mu \geq 24$
H_a: $\mu < 24$

For one-tail test, α = .10

Critical $t_{.10,18}$ = -1.330

$$t = \frac{(\bar{X}-\mu)}{\frac{S}{\sqrt{n}}} = \frac{23.263 - 24}{\frac{4.817}{\sqrt{19}}} = \boxed{-0.67}$$

Calculate t = -0.67 > $t_{.10,18}$ = -1.330

$$\boxed{\text{Fail to reject the null hypothesis}}$$

10.17   n=14 $\overline{X}$=108.286   S=17.665   df=14-1=13
         $\alpha/2$=.01
         98% Confidence Interval

$$t_{.01,13} = 2.650$$

$$\overline{X} \pm t \frac{S}{\sqrt{n}}$$

$$108.286 \pm 2.650 \frac{17.665}{\sqrt{14}}$$

$$108.286 \pm 12.511$$

$$\boxed{95.775 \leq \mu \leq 120.797}$$

10.19 H_o: $\mu_1 - \mu_2 = 0$ α=.10

         H_a: $\mu_1 - \mu_2 \neq 0$ df = 20 + 20 - 2 = 38

Sample 1	Sample 2
$n_1 = 20$	$n_2 = 20$
$\overline{X}_1 = 118$	$\overline{X}_2 = 113$
$S_1 = 23.9$	$S_2 = 21.6$

For two-tail test, $\alpha/2 = .05$

Critical $t_{.05,38} = 1.697$ (used df=30)

$$t = \frac{(\overline{X}_1 - \overline{X}_2) - (\mu_1 - \mu_2)}{\sqrt{\frac{S_1^2(n_1-1) + S_2^2(n_2-1)}{n_1 + n_2 - 2}}\sqrt{\frac{1}{n_1} + \frac{1}{n_2}}} =$$

$$t = \frac{(118 - 113) - (0)}{\sqrt{\frac{(23.9)^2(19) + (21.6)^2(19)}{20 + 20 - 2}}\sqrt{\frac{1}{20} + \frac{1}{20}}} =$$

$$t = \frac{5}{(22.779)(.3162)} = \boxed{0.69}$$

Calculated t = 0.69 < $t_{.05,38}$ = 1.697

$$\boxed{\text{Fail to reject the null hypothesis}}$$

10.21 H_o: $\mu_1 - \mu_2 = 0$ $\alpha = .10$

$\quad\quad$ H_a: $\mu_1 - \mu_2 \neq 0$ $df = 18 + 18 - 2 = 34$

$\quad\quad\quad\quad$ <u>Sample 1</u>   <u>Sample 2</u>
$\quad\quad\quad\quad$ $n_1 = 18$ $n_2 = 18$

$\quad\quad\quad\quad$ $\bar{X}_1 = 5.333$ $\bar{X}_2 = 9.444$

$\quad\quad\quad\quad$ $S_1^2 = 12$ $S_2^2 = 2.026$

For two-tail test, $\alpha/2 = .05$

Critical $t_{.05,34} = \pm 1.697$ (used df=30)

$$t = \frac{(\bar{X}_1 - \bar{X}_2) - (\mu_1 - \mu_2)}{\sqrt{\dfrac{S_1^2(n_1-1) + S_2^2(n_2-1)}{n_1 + n_2 - 2}}\sqrt{\dfrac{1}{n_1} + \dfrac{1}{n_2}}} =$$

$$t = \frac{(5.333 - 9.444) - (0)}{\sqrt{\dfrac{12(17) + (2.026)17}{18 + 18 - 2}}\sqrt{\dfrac{1}{18} + \dfrac{1}{18}}} =$$

$$t = \frac{-4.111}{(2.648)(.333)} = \boxed{-4.66}$$

Calculated $t = -4.66 < t_{.05,34} = -1.697$

$\boxed{\text{Reject the null hypothesis}}$

10.23   <u>Sample 1</u>   <u>Sample 2</u>
              $n_1 = 12$ $n_2 = 11$

              $\bar{X}_1 = 1.829$ $\bar{X}_2 = 1.322$

              $S_1^2 = .236$ $S_2^2 = .099$

       $df = n_1 + n_2 - 2 = 12 + 11 - 2 = 21$

       99% Confidence Interval

       $\alpha/2 = .005$

       $t_{.005,21} = 2.831$

$$(\bar{X}_1 - \bar{X}_2) \pm t \sqrt{\frac{S_1^2(n_1-1) + S_2^2(n_2-1)}{n_1 + n_2 - 2}} \sqrt{\frac{1}{n_1} + \frac{1}{n_2}}$$

$$(1.829 - 1.322) \pm 2.831 \sqrt{\frac{(.236)(11) + (.099)(10)}{12 + 11 - 2}} \sqrt{\frac{1}{12} + \frac{1}{11}}$$

       $.507 \pm 2.831(.4132)(.4174)$

       $.507 \pm .488$

       $$\boxed{.019 \leq \mu_1 - \mu_2 \leq .995}$$

10.25

Sample 1	Sample 2

$n_1 = 25$ $\qquad\qquad\qquad$ $n_2 = 28$

$\bar{X}_1 = 563$ $\qquad\qquad\quad$ $\bar{X}_2 = 674$

$S_1^2 = 99.3$ $\qquad\qquad\;$ $S_2^2 = 103.6$

$df = n_1 + n_2 - 2 = 25 + 28 - 2 = 51$

99% Confidence Interval

$\alpha/2 = .005$

$t_{.005,51} = 2.704$ (used df=40)

$$(\bar{X}_1 - \bar{X}_2) \pm t \sqrt{\frac{S_1^2(n_1-1) + S_2^2(n_2-1)}{n_1 + n_2 - 2}} \sqrt{\frac{1}{n_1} + \frac{1}{n_2}}$$

$$(563 - 674) \pm 2.704 \sqrt{\frac{(99.3)(24) + (103.6)(27)}{25 + 28 - 2}} \sqrt{\frac{1}{25} + \frac{1}{28}}$$

$-111 \pm 2.704(10.0785)(.2752)$

-111 ± 7.50

$$\boxed{-118.5 \leq \mu_1 - \mu_2 \leq -103.5}$$

10.27 H_o: $\mu_1 - \mu_2 = 0$ $\alpha = .05$

    H_a: $\mu_1 - \mu_2 \neq 0$ df $= 21 + 26 - 2 = 45$

<u>Peoria</u>	<u>Evansville</u>
$n_1 = 21$	$n_2 = 26$
$\bar{X}_1 = \$66,900$	$\bar{X}_2 = \$64,000$
$S_1^2 = \$2,300$	$S_2^2 = \$1,750$

For two-tail test, $\alpha/2 = .025$

Critical $t_{.025,45} = \pm 2.021$ (used df=40)

$$ t = \frac{(\bar{X}_1 - \bar{X}_2) - (\mu_1 - \mu_2)}{\sqrt{\dfrac{S_1^2(n_1-1) + S_2^2(n_2-1)}{n_1 + n_2 - 2}}\sqrt{\dfrac{1}{n_1} + \dfrac{1}{n_2}}} = $$

$$ t = \frac{(\$66,900 - \$64,000) - (0)}{\sqrt{\dfrac{(2,300)^2(20) + (1,750)^2(25)}{21 + 26 - 2}}\sqrt{\dfrac{1}{21} + \dfrac{1}{26}}} = $$

$$ t = \frac{2,900 - 0}{(2,013.082)(.2934)} = \boxed{4.91} $$

Calculated $t = 4.91 > t_{.025,45} = 2.021$

$\boxed{\text{Reject the null hypothesis}}$

10.29

1987	1992

$n_1 = 17$ $n_2 = 20$

$\bar{X}_1 = 25.7$ $\bar{X}_2 = 26.1$

$S_1^2 = 22.2$ $S_2^2 = 23$

$df = n_1 + n_2 - 2 = 17 + 20 - 2 = 35$

98% Confidence Interval

$\alpha/2 = .01$

$t_{.01,35} = 2.457$ (used df=30)

$$(\bar{X}_1 - \bar{X}_2) \pm t \sqrt{\frac{S_1^2(n_1-1) + S_2^2(n_2-1)}{n_1 + n_2 - 2}} \sqrt{\frac{1}{n_1} + \frac{1}{n_2}}$$

$$(25.7 - 26.1) \pm 2.457 \sqrt{\frac{22.2(16) + 23(19)}{17 + 20 - 2}} \sqrt{\frac{1}{17} + \frac{1}{20}}$$

$-0.4 \pm 2.457(4.7576)(.3299)$

-0.4 ± 3.856

$-4.256 \leq \mu_1 - \mu_2 \leq 3.456$

10.31

<u>Toronto</u>
$n_1 = 11$

$\bar{X}_1 = \$67,381.82$

$S_1 = \$2,067.28$

<u>Mexico City</u>
$n_2 = 11$

$\bar{X}_2 = \$63,481.82$

$S_2 = \$1,594.25$

$df = n_1 + n_2 - 2 = 11 + 11 - 2 = 20$

95% Confidence Interval

$\alpha/2 = .025$

$t_{.025,20} = 2.086$

$$(\bar{X}_1 - \bar{X}_2) \pm t \sqrt{\frac{S_1^2(n_1-1) + S_2^2(n_2-1)}{n_1 + n_2 - 2}} \sqrt{\frac{1}{n_1} + \frac{1}{n_2}}$$

$(\$67,381.82 - \$63,481.82)$

$$\pm(2,086) \sqrt{\frac{(2,067.28)^2(11)+(1,594.25)^2(11)}{11 + 11 - 2}} \sqrt{\frac{1}{11}+\frac{1}{11}}$$

$3,900 \pm 2.086(1,845.98)(.4264)$

$3,900 \pm 1,641.9$

$2,258.1 \le \mu_1 - \mu_2 \le 5,541.9$

10.33

High School	Adult
$n_1 = 12$	$n_2 = 12$
$\bar{X}_1 = 13.83$	$\bar{X}_2 = 8.083$
$S_1^2 = 15.606$	$S_2^2 = 6.083$

$df = n_1 + n_2 - 2 = 12 + 12 - 2 = 22$

90% Confidence Interval

$\alpha/2 = .05$

$t_{.05,22} = 1.717$

$$(\bar{X}_1 - \bar{X}_2) \pm t \sqrt{\frac{S_1^2(n_1-1) + S_2^2(n_2-1)}{n_1 + n_2 - 2}} \sqrt{\frac{1}{n_1} + \frac{1}{n_2}}$$

$$(13.83-8.083) \pm (1.717) \sqrt{\frac{(15.606)(11)+(6.083)(11)}{12 + 12 - 2}} \sqrt{\frac{1}{12}+\frac{1}{12}}$$

$5.747 \pm 1.717(3.2931)(.4082)$

5.747 ± 2.308

$3.439 \leq \mu_1 - \mu_2 \leq 8.055$

10.35 H_o: D ≥ 0
             H_a: D < 0

n=29 $\overline{d}$=-1.053 S_d=7.621   α=.10

df = n - 1 = 29 - 1 = 28

For one-tail test, α = .10

Critical $t_{.10,28}$ = -1.313

$$t = \frac{\overline{d}-D}{\frac{S_d}{\sqrt{n}}} = \frac{-1.053-0}{\frac{7.621}{\sqrt{29}}} = -0.74$$

Calculated t = -0.74 > $t_{.10,28}$ = -1.313

Fail to reject the null hypothesis

10.37 H_o: D = 0

             H_a: D ≠ 0

Before	After	d
107	102	5
99	98	1
110	100	10
113	108	5
96	89	7
98	101	-3
100	99	1
102	102	0
107	105	2
109	110	-1
104	102	2
99	96	3
101	100	1

n=13 $\bar{d}$=2.5385 S_d=3.4789   α=.01

df = n - 1 = 13 - 1 = 12

For two-tail test, α/2 = .005

Critical $t_{.005,12}$ = ±3.055

$$t = \frac{\bar{d}-D}{\frac{S_d}{\sqrt{n}}} = \frac{2.5385-0}{\frac{3.4789}{\sqrt{13}}} = \boxed{2.63}$$

Calculated t = 2.63 < $t_{.005,12}$ = 3.055

Fail to reject the null hypothesis

10.39   n=8 $\bar{d}$=-10.43 S_d=13.97

    90% confidence interval
    $\alpha/2$=.05
    df = n - 1 = 8 - 1 = 7

    $t_{.05,7}$ = 1.895

$$\bar{d} \pm t \; \frac{S_d}{\sqrt{n}}$$

    $$-10.43 \pm (1.895) \; \frac{13.97}{\sqrt{8}}$$

    -10.43 ± 9.36

$$\boxed{-19.79 \le D \le -1.07}$$

10.41	1991	1992	d
	983	968	15
	701	723	-22
	1003	996	7
	678	721	-43
	899	930	-31
	602	578	24
	752	765	-13

$n=7$ $\bar{d}=-9$ $S_d=24.99$

$df = n - 1 = 7 - 1 = 6$

80% confidence interval
$\alpha/2=.10$

$t_{.10,6} = 1.44$

$$\bar{d} \pm t \frac{S_d}{\sqrt{n}}$$

$$-9 \pm (1.44) \frac{24.99}{\sqrt{7}}$$

-9 ± 13.6

$$\boxed{-22.6 \leq D \leq 4.6}$$

10.43 H_o: $D \leq 0$
           H_a: $D > 0$

$n=8$ $\bar{d}=20$ $S_d=8.5$ $\alpha=.05$

$df = n - 1 = 8 - 1 = 7$

For one-tail test, $\alpha = .05$

Critical $t_{.05,7} = 1.895$

$$t = \frac{\bar{d}-D}{\frac{S_d}{\sqrt{n}}} = \frac{20-0}{\frac{8.5}{\sqrt{8}}} = \boxed{6.66}$$

calculated $t = 6.66 > t_{.05,7} = 1.895$

$$\boxed{\text{Reject the null hypothesis}}$$

10.45 H_o: $D \geq 0$
            H_a: $D < 0$

Before	After	d
2	4	-2
4	5	-1
1	3	-2
3	3	0
4	3	1
2	5	-3
2	6	-4
3	4	-1
1	5	-4

$n=9$ $\bar{d}=-1.778$ $S_d=1.716$ $\alpha=.05$
$df = n - 1 = 9 - 1 = 8$

For one-tail test, $\alpha = .05$
Critical $t_{.05,8} = -1.86$

$$t = \frac{\bar{d}-D}{\frac{S_d}{\sqrt{n}}} = \frac{-1.778-0}{\frac{1.716}{\sqrt{9}}} = \boxed{-3.11}$$

calculated $t = -3.11 < t_{.05,8} = -1.86$

$$\boxed{\text{Reject the null hypothesis}}$$

10.47   n=21 $\overline{d}$=75 S_d=30

df = n - 1 = 21 - 1 = 20

90% confidence interval
α/2=.05
$t_{.05,20}$ = 1.725

$$\overline{d} \pm t \ \frac{S_d}{\sqrt{n}}$$

$$75 \pm 1.725 \ \frac{30}{\sqrt{21}}$$

$$75 \pm 11.29$$

$$\boxed{63.71 \leq D \leq 86.29}$$

10.49 H_o: D $\geq$ 0
           H_a: D < 0

n=15 $\overline{d}$=-2.85 S_d=1.9 α=.01

df = n - 1 = 15 - 1 = 14

For one-tail test, α = .01

Critical $t_{.01,14}$ = -2.624

$$t = \frac{\overline{d}-D}{\frac{S_d}{\sqrt{n}}} = \frac{-2.85-0}{\frac{1.9}{\sqrt{15}}} = \boxed{-5.81}$$

calculated t = -5.81 < $t_{.01,14}$ = -2.624

$$\boxed{\text{Reject the null hypothesis}}$$

10.51

Source	Df	SS	MS	F
Treatment	4	93.77	23.44	15.82
Error	18	26.67	1.48	
Total	22	120.43		

$\alpha = .01$

Critical $F_{.01, 4, 18} = 4.58$

Calculated $F = 15.82 > F_{.01, 4, 18} = 4.58$

Reject the null hypothesis

10.53

Source	Df	SS	MS	F
Treatment	1	64.29	64.29	17.76
Error	12	43.43	3.62	
Total	13	107.71		

$\alpha = .05$

Critical $F_{.05,1,12} = 4.75$

Calculated $F = 17.76 > F_{.05,1,12} = 4.75$

$\boxed{\text{Reject the null hypothesis}}$

Calculated t from t test =

$$\frac{1}{n_1} = 7 \qquad \frac{2}{n_2} = 7$$

$$\overline{X}_1 = 29 \qquad \overline{X}_2 = 24.71$$

$$S_1^2 = 3 \qquad S_2^2 = 4.238$$

$$t = \frac{(29-24.71-(0)}{\sqrt{\dfrac{3(6)+4.238(6)}{7+7-2}}\sqrt{\dfrac{1}{7}+\dfrac{1}{7}}}$$

$$= \frac{4.29 - 0}{(1.9024)(.5345)} = 4.22$$

$$t = \boxed{4.22} \qquad \text{(calculated t)}$$

Also, $t = \sqrt{F} = \sqrt{17.76} = 4.214$

10.55

Source	SS	df	MS	F
Treatment	29.64	2	14.82	3.03
Error	68.42	14	4.887	
Total	98.06	16		

10.57

Source	Df	SS	MS	F
Treatment	2	181562496	90781248	76.76
Error	13	15374999	1182692	
Total	15	196937504		

$\alpha = .01$

Critical $F_{.01,2,13} = 6.70$

Calculated $F = 76.76 > F_{.01,2,13} = 6.70$

Reject the null hypothesis

10.59

Source	Df	SS	MS	F
Treatment	3	550475	183492	13.46
Error	18	245384	13631	
Total	21	795859		

$\alpha = .05$

Critical $F_{.05,3,18} = 3.16$

Calculated $F = 13.46 > F_{.05,3,18} = 3.16$

| Reject the null hypothesis |

10.61

    n=12 $\bar{X}=319.17$ S=9.104   df = 12 - 1 = 11

90% confidence interval

$\alpha/2 = .05$

$t_{.05,11} = 1.796$

$$\bar{X} \pm t \frac{S}{\sqrt{n}}$$

$$319.17 \pm (1.796) \frac{9.104}{\sqrt{12}}$$

319.17 ± 4.72

| $314.45 \leq \mu \leq 323.89$ |

10.63 H_o: $\mu \leq 0$
             H_a: $\mu > 0$

n=11 $\overline{X}$=1.182   S=3.842   df = 11 - 1 = 10

For one-tail test, α = .01

Critical $t_{.01,10}$ = 2.764

$$t = \frac{\overline{X} - \mu}{\frac{S}{\sqrt{n}}} = \frac{1.182 - 0}{\frac{3.842}{\sqrt{11}}} = \boxed{1.02}$$

Calculated t = 1.02 < $t_{.01,10}$ = 2.764

$\boxed{\text{Fail to reject the null hypothesis}}$

10.65 H_o: $\mu = 45$

             H_a: $\mu \neq 45$

n=15 $\overline{X}$=43.1   S=12.5   df = 15 - 1 = 14 α=.01

For two-tail test, $\alpha/2$ = .005

Critical $t_{.005,14}$ = ± 2.977

$$t = \frac{\overline{X} - \mu}{\frac{S}{\sqrt{n}}} = \frac{43.1 - 45}{\frac{12.5}{\sqrt{15}}} = \boxed{-0.59}$$

Calculated t = -0.59 > $t_{.005,14}$ = -2.977

$\boxed{\text{Fail to reject the null hypothesis}}$

10.67

$n=27$ $\overline{X}=2.10$ $S=0.86$ $df = 27 - 1 = 26$

98% confidence interval

$\alpha/2 = .01$

$t_{.01,26} = 2.479$

$$\overline{X} \pm t \ \frac{S}{\sqrt{n}}$$

$$2.10 \pm (2.479) \ \frac{0.86}{\sqrt{27}}$$

2.10 ± 0.41

$$\boxed{1.69 \ \leq \mu \leq \ 2.51}$$

10.69

$n=17$ $\overline{X}=10.765$ $S=2.223$ $df = 17 - 1 = 16$

99% confidence interval

$\alpha/2 = .005$

$t_{.005,16} = 2.921$

$$\overline{X} \pm t \ \frac{S}{\sqrt{n}}$$

$$10.765 \pm (2.921) \ \frac{2.223}{\sqrt{17}}$$

10.765 ± 1.575

$$\boxed{9.19 \leq \mu \leq 12.34}$$

10.71 $\underline{\text{Sample 1}}$ $\underline{\text{Sample 2}}$

$\quad\quad\quad n_1 \quad = \quad 8 \quad\quad\quad\quad\quad n_2 \quad = \; 8$

$\quad\quad\quad \bar{X}_1 \quad = \; 10.875 \quad\quad\quad \bar{X}_2 \quad = \; 9.125$

$\quad\quad\quad S_1^2 \quad = \quad 1.5536 \quad\quad\quad S_2^2 \quad = \; 1.8393$

$\text{df} = 8 + 8 - 2 = 14$

99% Confidence Interval

$\alpha/2 = .005$

$t_{.005,14} = 2.977$

$$(\bar{X}_1 - \bar{X}_2) \pm t \sqrt{\frac{S_1^2(n_1-1) \; + \; S_2^2(n_2-1)}{n_1 + n_2 - 2}} \sqrt{\frac{1}{n_1} + \frac{1}{n_2}}$$

$$(10.875 - 9.125) \pm (2.977) \sqrt{\frac{1.5536(7) + 1.8393(7)}{8 + 8 - 2}} \sqrt{\frac{1}{8} + \frac{1}{8}}$$

$1.75 \pm (2.977)(1.3025)(.50)$

1.75 ± 1.94

$$\boxed{-0.19 \le \mu_1 - \mu_2 \le 3.69}$$

10.73

Sample 1		Sample 2	
n_1	= 17	n_2	= 18
$\bar{X}_1$	= 474.6	$\bar{X}_2$	= 485.4
S_1	= 29.4	S_2	= 27.6

df = 17 + 18 - 2 = 33

95% Confidence Interval

$\alpha/2$ = .025

$t_{.025,33}$ = 2.042 (used df=30)

$$(\bar{X}_1 - \bar{X}_2) \pm t \sqrt{\frac{S_1^2(n_1-1) + S_2^2(n_2-1)}{n_1 + n_2 - 2}} \sqrt{\frac{1}{n_1} + \frac{1}{n_2}}$$

$$(474.6 - 485.4) \pm (2.042) \sqrt{\frac{(29.4)^2(16) + (27.6)^2(17)}{17 + 18 - 2}} \sqrt{\frac{1}{17} + \frac{1}{18}}$$

-10.8 ± (2.042)(28.487)(.3382)

-10.8 ± 19.673

$$\boxed{-30.473 \le \mu_1 - \mu_2 \le 8.873}$$

10.75 $\underline{10 - 20}$

$n_1 \;\; = \;\; 8$

$\bar{X}_1 \;\; = \;\; 10.375$

$S_1^2 \;\; = \;\; 13.982$

$\underline{21 - 40}$

$n_2 \;\; = \;\; 6$

$\bar{X}_2 \;\; = \;\; 5.667$

$S_2^2 \;\; = \;\; 5.867$

df = 8 + 6 - 2 = 12

98% Confidence Interval

$\alpha/2 \;=\; .01$

$t_{.01, 12} \;=\; 2.681$

$$(\bar{X}_1 - \bar{X}_2) \;\pm\; t \; \sqrt{\frac{S_1^2(n_1-1) \;+\; S_2^2(n_2-1)}{n_1 + n_2 - 2}} \; \sqrt{\frac{1}{n_1} + \frac{1}{n_2}}$$

$$(10.375 - 5.667) \;\pm(2.681) \; \sqrt{\frac{13.982(7) + 5.867(5)}{8 + 6 - 2}} \; \sqrt{\frac{1}{8} + \frac{1}{6}}$$

$4.708 \;\pm\; (2.681)(3.2559)(.54006)$

$4.708 \;\pm\; 4.714$

$$\boxed{-.006 \;\le\; \mu_1 - \mu_2 \;\le\; 9.422}$$

10.77 H_o: $\mu_1 - \mu_2 = 0$ $\alpha = .01$

H_a: $\mu_1 - \mu_2 \neq 0$ $df = 10 + 6 - 2 = 14$

A		B	
n_1	= 10	n_2	= 6
$\overline{X}_1$	= 18.3	$\overline{X}_2$	= 9.667
S_1^2	= 17.122	S_2^2	= 7.467

For two-tail test, $\alpha/2 = .005$

Critical $t_{.005,14} = \pm 2.977$

$$t = \frac{(\overline{X}_1 - \overline{X}_2) - (\mu_1 - \mu_2)}{\sqrt{\frac{S_1^2(n_1-1) + S_2^2(n_2-1)}{n_1 + n_2 - 2}}\sqrt{\frac{1}{n_1} + \frac{1}{n_2}}} =$$

$$t = \frac{(18.3 - 9.667) - (0)}{\sqrt{\frac{17.122(9) + 7.467(5)}{10 + 6 - 2}}\sqrt{\frac{1}{10} + \frac{1}{6}}} =$$

$$t = \frac{8.633}{(3.6978)(.5164)} = \boxed{4.52}$$

Calculated $t = 4.52 > t_{.005,14} = 2.977$

$\boxed{\text{Reject the null hypothesis}}$

10.79 $\underline{\text{Term}}$ $\underline{\text{Whole Life}}$

$\overline{X}_t$ = \$75,000 $\overline{X}_w$ = \$45,000

S_t = \$22,000 S_w = \$15,500

n_t = 27 n_w = 29

df = 27 + 29 - 2 = 54

95% confidence interval

$\alpha/2$ = .025

$t_{.025,54}$ = 2.021 (used df=40)

$$(\overline{X}_1 - \overline{X}_2) \pm t \sqrt{\frac{S_1^2(n_1-1) + S_2^2(n_2-1)}{n_1 + n_2 - 2}} \sqrt{\frac{1}{n_1} + \frac{1}{n_2}}$$

$$(75,000-45,000) \pm (2.021) \sqrt{\frac{(22,000)^2(26) + (15,500)^2(28)}{27 + 29 - 2}} \sqrt{\frac{1}{27} + \frac{1}{29}}$$

30,000 ± (2.021)(18,910.61)(.26743)

30,000 ± 10,220.73

$$\boxed{19,779.27 \leq \mu_1 - \mu_2 \leq 40,220.73}$$

10.81

Before	After	d
1147	1130	17
1125	1110	15
1119	1118	1
1129	1107	22
1143	1125	18
1126	1100	26
1119	1111	8

$n=7$ $\bar{d}=15.286$ $S_d=8.44$ $df = 7 - 1 = 6$

90% confidence interval

$\alpha/2 = .05$

$t_{.05,6} = 1.943$

$$\bar{d} \pm t \frac{S_d}{\sqrt{n}}$$

$$15.286 \pm 1.943 \frac{8.44}{\sqrt{7}}$$

$$15.286 \pm 6.198$$

$$\boxed{9.088 \le D \le 21.484}$$

10.83 H_o: D = 0

   H_a: D ≠ 0

$\bar{d}$=5.37 S_d=11.12   n=21   df = 21 - 1 = 20
α = .10

For two-tail test, α/2 = .05

Critical $t_{.05,20}$ = ±1.725

$$t = \dfrac{\bar{d}-D}{\dfrac{S_d}{\sqrt{n}}} = \dfrac{5.37-0}{\dfrac{11.12}{\sqrt{21}}} = \boxed{2.21}$$

Calculated t = 2.21 > $t_{.05,20}$ = 1.725

$$\boxed{\text{Reject the null hypothesis}}$$

10.85

Wednesday	Friday	d
71	53	18
56	47	9
75	52	23
68	55	13
74	58	16

n=5 $\bar{d}$=15.8 S_d=5.263   df = 5 - 1 = 4

H_o: D ≤ 0   α = .05
H_a: D > 0

For one-tail test, α = .05
Critical $t_{.05,4}$ = 2.132

$$t = \dfrac{\bar{d}-D}{\dfrac{S_d}{\sqrt{n}}} = \dfrac{15.8-0}{\dfrac{5.263}{\sqrt{5}}} = \boxed{6.71}$$

Calculated t = 6.71 > $t_{.05,4}$ = 2.132

$$\boxed{\text{Reject the null hypothesis}}$$

10.87

Before	After	d
12	8	4
7	3	4
10	8	2
16	0	16
8	5	3

$n=5$ $\bar{d}=5.8$ $S_d=5.762$ $df = 5 - 1 = 4$

H_o: $D \leq 0$ $\alpha = .01$
H_a: $D > 0$

For one-tail test, $\alpha = .01$

Critical $t_{.01,4} = 3.747$

$$t = \frac{\bar{d}-D}{\frac{S_d}{\sqrt{n}}} = \frac{5.8-0}{\frac{5.762}{\sqrt{5}}} = \boxed{2.25}$$

Calculated $t = 2.25 < t_{.01,4} = 3.747$

$$\boxed{\text{Fail to reject the null hypothesis}}$$

10.89

Source	Df	SS	MS	F
Treatment	3	66.69	22.23	8.82
Error	12	30.25	2.52	
Total	15	96.94		

Critical $F_{.05,3,12} = 3.49$

Calculated $F = 8.82 > F_{.05,3,12} = 3.49$

Reject the null hypothesis

10.91

Source	Df	SS	MS	F
Treatment	2	10.69	5.35	2.28
Error	18	42.26	2.35	
Total	20	52.95		

Critical $F_{.01,2,18} = 6.01$

Calculated $F = 2.28 < F_{.01,2,18} = 6.01$

Fail to reject the null hypothesis

10.93

Source	Df	SS	MS	F
Treatment	3	90,477,696	30,159,232	7.38
Error	20	81,761,904	4,088,095	
Total	23	172,239,600		

Critical $F_{.05,3,20} = 3.10$

Calculated $F = 7.38 > F_{.05,3,20}$

Reject the null hypothesis

REGRESSION AND CORRELATION ANALYSIS

11

I. CHAPTER OBJECTIVES

The overall objective of this chapter is to give you an understanding of regression and correlation analysis, specifically enabling you to:

1. Compute simple regression analysis.

2. Compute correlation coefficients.

3. Comprehend multiple regression and how it can be used.

4. Appreciate the use of regression in forecasting.

II. **CHAPTER OUTLINE**

Testing the Multiple Regression Model

Dummy Variables

Curvilinear Models

Regression in Time-Series Data

III. **KEY WORDS**

Correlation   Coefficient of Determination
Regression   Pearson Product-Moment
Simple Regression   Correlation Coefficient
Dependent Variable   Covariance
Independent Variable   Multiple Regression
Scatter Plot   Qualitative Variable
Least Squares Analysis   Quantitative Variable
Slope of the Regression Line   Dummy Variable
Residual   Forecasting
Outliers   Time-Series Data
Homoscedasticity   Trend
Heteroscedasticity   Business Cycle
Sum of Squares of Error   Seasonality
Standard Error of the Estimate   Irregular Fluctuations

IV. STUDY QUESTIONS

1. _____ is a measure of the degree of relatedness of two variables.

2. The process of constructing a mathematical model or function that can be used to predict or determine one variable by another variable is _____.

3. Bivariate linear regression is often termed _____ regression.

4. In regression, the variable being predicted is usually referred to as the _____ variable.

5. In regression, the predictor is called the _____ variable.

6. The first step in simple regression analysis often is to graph or construct a _____.

7. In regression analysis, β_1 represents the population _____.

8. In regression analysis, b_0 represents the sample _____.

9. A researcher wants to develop a regression model to predict the price of gold by the prime interest rate. The dependent variable is _____.

10. In an effort to develop a regression model, the following data were gathered:

   X: 2,   9, 11, 19, 21, 25

   Y: 26, 17, 18, 15, 15,   8

   The slope of the regression line determined from these data is _____.   The Y intercept is _____.

11. A researcher wants to develop a regression line from the data given below:

   X: 12, 11,   5,   6,   9

   Y: 31, 25, 14, 12, 16

   The equation of the regression line is

   _____.

12. In regression, the value of $Y - \hat{Y}$ is called the

   _____.

13. Data points that lie apart from the rest of the points are called _____.

14. The regression assumption of constant error variance is called _____.   If the error variances are not constant, it is called _____.

15. Suppose the graph of residuals looks like:

   This is an indication that the error terms are

   _____.

16.   Suppose the graph of the residuals looks like:

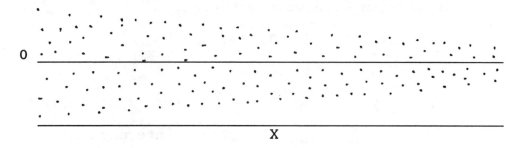

This is an indication of _____.

17.   Suppose the graph of the residuals looks like:

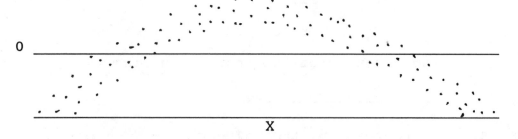

This is an indication of _____ in regression.

18.   Suppose the following data are used to determine the equation of the regression line given below:

    X: 2,   5, 11, 24, 31

    Y: 12, 13, 16, 14, 19

    $\hat{Y}$: = 12.224 + 0.1764 X

The residual for X = 11 is _____.

19.   The total of the residuals squared is called the

_____.

20. A standard deviation of the error of the regression model is called the _____ and is denoted by _____.

21. Suppose a regression model is developed for ten pairs of data resulting in S.S.E. = 1,203. The standard error of the estimate is _____.

22. A regression analysis results in the following data:

$\Sigma X = 276$ $\Sigma X^2 = 12,014$ $\Sigma XY = 2,438$

$\Sigma Y = 77$ $\Sigma Y^2 = 1,183$ $n = 7$

The value of S.S.E. is _____.

23. The value of S_e is computed from the data of question 22 is _____.

24. Suppose a regression model results in a value of $S_e = 27.9$. 95% of the residuals should fall within _____.

25. Coefficient of determination is denoted by _____.

26. _____ is the proportion of variability of the dependent variable accounted for or explained by the independent variable.

27. The value of r^2 always falls between _____ and _____ inclusive.

28. Suppose a regression analysis results in the following:

$b_1 = .19364$ $\Sigma Y = 1,019$

$b_0 = 59.4798$ $\Sigma Y^2 = 134,451$

$n = 8$ $\Sigma XY = 378,932$

The value of r^2 for this regression model is _____.

29.   Suppose the data below are used to determine the
equation of a regression line:

    X: 18, 14,   9,   6,   2

    Y: 14, 25, 22, 23, 27

The value of r^2 associated with this model is

_____.

30.   A researcher has developed a regression model from
sixteen pairs of data points. He wants to test to
determine if the slope is significantly different from
zero. He uses a two-tailed test and $\alpha = .01$. The
critical table t value is _____.

31.   The following data are used to develop a simple
regression model:

    X: 22, 20, 15, 15, 14, 9

    Y: 31, 20, 12, 9, 10, 6

The calculated t value used to test the slope of this
regression model is _____.

32.   If $\alpha = .05$ and a two-tailed test is being conducted,
the critical table t value to test the slope of the
model developed in question 31 is _____.

33.   The decision reached about the slope of the model
computed in question 31 is to _____ the null
hypothesis.

34.   The Pearson product-moment correlation coefficient is
denoted by _____.

35.   The value of r varies from _____.

36. Perfect positive correlation results in an r value of

    _____.

37. Squaring the value of the coefficient of correlation

    results in the value of _____.

38. The variance of X and Y together is called

    _____.

39. The value of the coefficient of correlation from the

    following data is _____.

         X: 19, 20, 26, 31, 34, 45, 45, 51

         Y: 78, 100, 125, 120, 119, 130, 145, 143

40. The value of r from the following data is _____.

         X: -10, -6,   1,   4, 15

         Y: -26, -44, -36, -39, -43

41. Regression analysis with one dependent variable and two

    or more independent variables is called _____

    regression.

42. Qualitative variables are sometimes referred to as

    _____ variables.

43. If a qualitative variable has "k" categories,

    _____ dummy variables must be created and

    used in the regression analysis.

44. Data gathered over a period of time are referred to as

    _____ data.

45. The long-term general direction of the data is referred

    to as _____.

46. The highs and lows of business volume within a
particular business cycle is called _____.

47. Suppose a researcher is given the time-series data
below:

Year	Sales (millions)
1983	2.7
1984	4.6
1985	5.3
1986	11.9
1987	12.0
1988	15.4
1989	19.1
1990	25.7
1991	28.1

The equation of the regression line to forecast sales

over time is _____.

V.   ANSWERS TO STUDY QUESTIONS

1. Correlation

2. Regression

3. Simple

4. Dependent

5. Independent

6. Scatter Plot

7. Slope

8. Y Intercept

9. Price of Gold

10. -0.626, 25.575

11. -1.253 + 2.425 X

12. Residual

13. Outliers

14. Homoscedasticity, Heteroscadasticity

15. Nonindependent

16. Nonconstant Error Variance

17. Nonlinearity

18. 14.1644

19. Sum of Squares of Error

20. Standard Error of the Estimate, S_e

21. 12.263

22. 20.0135

23. 2.00

24. 0 ± 55.8

25. r^2

26. Coefficient of Determination

27. 0, 1

28. .900

29. .578

30. 2.977

31. 4.72

32. ± 2.776

33. Reject

34. r

35. -1 to 0 to +1

36. +1

37. r^2

38. Covariance

39. .876

40. -.581

41. Multiple

42. Dummy

43. k - 1

44. Time-series

45. Trend

46. Seasonality

47. -6477 + 3.2667 X

VI. **SOLUTIONS TO ODD-NUMBERED PROBLEMS IN TEXT**

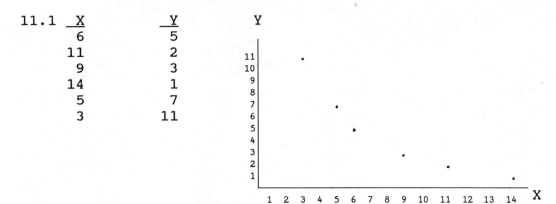

11.1

X	Y
6	5
11	2
9	3
14	1
5	7
3	11

$$11.3 \quad b_1 = \frac{SS_{XY}}{SS_X} = \frac{\Sigma XY - \dfrac{(\Sigma X)(\Sigma Y)}{n}}{\Sigma X^2 - \dfrac{(\Sigma X)^2}{n}} =$$

$$\frac{6,596 - \dfrac{(261)(148)}{9}}{11,219 - \dfrac{(261)^2}{9}} = \frac{2,304}{3,650} = 0.631$$

$$b_0 = \frac{\Sigma Y}{n} - b_1 \frac{\Sigma X}{n} = \frac{149}{9} - 0.631 \frac{261}{9} = -1.855$$

$$\boxed{\hat{Y} = -1.855 + 0.631\ X}$$

11.5

X	Y
12	17
21	15
28	22
8	19
20	24

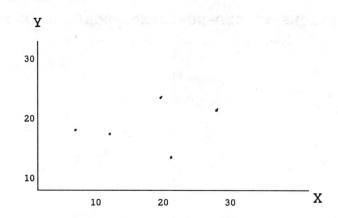

$\Sigma X = 89$ $\Sigma Y = 97$ $\Sigma XY = 1,767$

$\Sigma X^2 = 1,833$ $\Sigma Y^2 = 1,935$ $n = 5$

$$b_1 = \frac{\Sigma XY - \dfrac{(\Sigma X)(\Sigma Y)}{n}}{\Sigma X^2 - \dfrac{(\Sigma X)^2}{n}} = \frac{1,767 - \dfrac{(89)(97)}{5}}{1,833 - \dfrac{(89)^2}{5}} = 0.162$$

$$b_0 = \frac{\Sigma Y}{n} - b_1\frac{\Sigma X}{n} = \frac{97}{5} - 0.162\frac{89}{5} = 16.5$$

$$\boxed{\hat{Y} = 16.5 + 0.162 \, X}$$

11.7 <u>(Advertising) X</u>   <u>(Sales) Y</u>

X	Y
12.5	148
3.7	55
21.6	338
60.0	994
37.6	541
6.1	89
16.8	126
41.2	379

ΣX $= 199.5$ ΣY $= 2{,}670$ $\Sigma XY = 107{,}610.4$

ΣX^2 $= 7{,}667.15$ ΣY^2 $= 1{,}587{,}328$ $n = 8$

$$b_1 = \frac{\Sigma XY - \dfrac{(\Sigma X)(\Sigma Y)}{n}}{\Sigma X^2 - \dfrac{(\Sigma X)^2}{n}} = \frac{107{,}610.4 - \dfrac{(199.5)(2{,}670)}{8}}{7{,}667.15 - \dfrac{(199.5)^2}{8}}$$

$$b_1 = 15.240$$

$$b_0 = \frac{\Sigma Y}{n} - b_1 \frac{\Sigma X}{n} = \frac{2{,}670}{8} - 15.24 \frac{199.5}{8} = -46.29$$

$$\boxed{\hat{Y} = -46.29 + 15.24\ X}$$

11.9

CPI-W (X)	CPI-U (Y)
124.8	125.0
120.7	122.6
117.7	119.1
115.9	115.9
148.8	148.7
125.5	126.2
147.3	147.7
130.5	131.6

$\Sigma X = 1,031.2$ $\Sigma Y = 1,036.8$

$\Sigma X^2 = 134,048.86$ $\Sigma Y^2 = 135,445.36$

$\Sigma XY = 134,743.37$ $n = 8$

$$b_1 = \frac{\Sigma XY - \dfrac{\Sigma X \ \Sigma Y}{n}}{\Sigma X^2 - \dfrac{(\Sigma X)^2}{n}} = \frac{134,743.37 - \dfrac{(1,031.2)(1036.8)}{8}}{134,048.86 - \dfrac{(1,031.2)^2}{8}}$$

$b_1 = 0.976$

$$b_0 = \frac{\Sigma Y}{n} - b_1 \frac{\Sigma X}{n} = \frac{1036.8}{8} - 0.976 \frac{1,031.2}{8} = 3.825$$

$$\boxed{\hat{Y} = 3.825 + 0.976 \ X}$$

1036.8

$$134743.37 - \frac{(1,031.2)(1036.8)}{8}$$

11.11

METRO (X)	HOUSEHOLDS (Y)
8,602,100	1,630,000
8,813,600	1,230,000
6,214,400	1,070,000
4,385,400	820,000
4,934,900	720,000
3,778,200	670,000
2,849,500	620,000
3,244,600	580,000
2,669,900	500,000
2,481,900	440,000

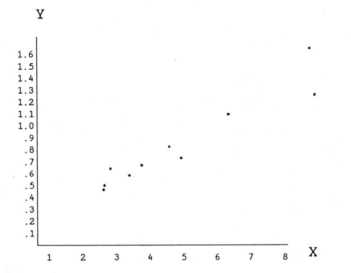

$\Sigma X = 47,974,500$

$\Sigma Y^2 = 2.8008947 \times 10^{14}$

$\Sigma Y = 8,280,000$

$\Sigma Y^2 = 8.1188 \times 10^{12}$

$\Sigma XY = 4.7267653 \times 10^{13}$

$n = 10$

$$b_1 = \frac{\Sigma XY - \dfrac{\Sigma X\ \Sigma Y}{n}}{\Sigma X^2 - \dfrac{(\Sigma X)^2}{n}} = \frac{4.7267653 \times 10^{13} - \dfrac{(47,974,500)(8,280,000)}{10}}{2.8008947 \times 10^{14} - \dfrac{(47,974,500)^2}{10}}$$

$b_1 = 0.151$

$$b_0 = \frac{\Sigma Y}{n} - b_1 \frac{\Sigma X}{n} = \frac{8,280,000}{10} - 0.151 \frac{47,974,500}{10} = 103,133.4$$

$$\boxed{\hat{Y} = 103,133.4 + 0.151\ X}$$

11.13

X	Y	Predicted $(\hat{Y})$	Residuals $(Y-\hat{Y})$
12	17	18.4582	-1.4582
21	15	19.9196	-4.9196
28	22	21.0563	0.9437
8	19	17.8087	1.1913
20	24	19.7572	4.2428

$$\hat{Y} = 16.5 + 0.162\ X$$

11.15

X	Y	Predicted $(\hat{Y})$	Residuals $(Y-\hat{Y})$
12.5	148	144.2053	3.7947
3.7	55	10.0953	44.9047
21.6	338	282.8873	55.1127
60.0	994	868.0945	125.9055
37.6	541	526.7236	14.2764
6.1	89	46.6708	42.3292
16.8	126	209.7364	-83.7364
41.2	379	581.5868	-202.5868

$$\hat{Y} = -46.29 + 15.24\ X$$

11.17

X	Y	Predicted ($\hat{Y}$)	Residuals ($Y-\hat{Y}$)
5	47	42.2756	4.7244
7	38	38.9836	-0.9836
11	32	32.3996	-0.3996
12	24	30.7537	-6.7537
19	22	19.2317	2.7683
25	10	9.3558	0.6442

$$\hat{Y} = 50.5056 - 1.6460\ X$$

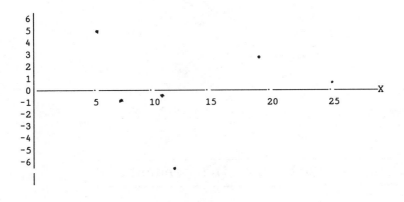

No apparent violation of assumptions

11.19

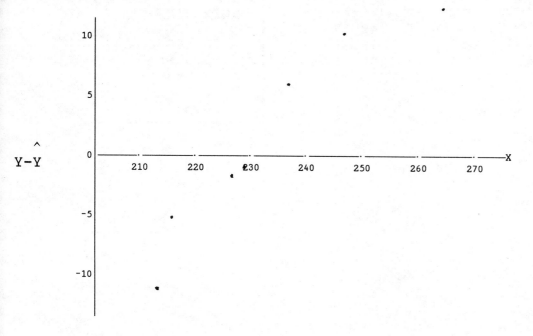

Error terms appear to be non independent.

11.21

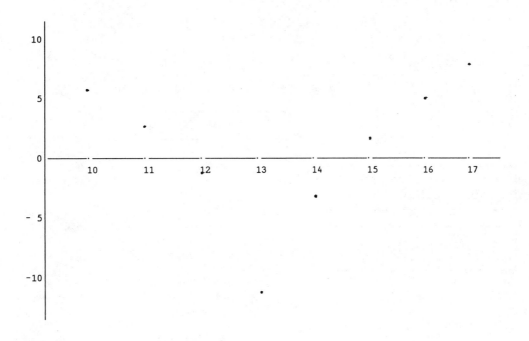

There appears to be nonlinear regression.

11.23 $SSE = \Sigma y^2 - b_0 \Sigma y - b_1 \Sigma XY$

$$= 45,154 - 144.414(498) - (-.89824)(30,099)$$

$$\boxed{SSE = 272.0}$$

$$SE = \sqrt{\frac{SSE}{n-2}} = \sqrt{\frac{272.0}{5}} = \boxed{7.376 = S_e}$$

$$\boxed{\begin{array}{l} \text{6 out of 7} = 85.7\% \\ \text{fall within } \pm 1S_e \end{array}}$$

$$\boxed{\begin{array}{l} \text{7 out of 7} = 100\% \\ \text{fall within } \pm 2S_e \end{array}}$$

11.25 $SSE = \Sigma y^2 - b_0 \Sigma y - b_1 \Sigma Xy$

$$= 524 - 15.46(48) - (-0.71462)(333)$$

$$\boxed{SSE = 19.8885}$$

$$SE = \sqrt{\frac{SSE}{n-2}} = \sqrt{\frac{19.8885}{3}} = \boxed{2.575 = S_e}$$

68% of the estimates are within 2.5759 of the actual rate for bonds. This amount of error is probably not acceptable to financial analysts.

11.27

$(Y-\hat{Y})$	$(Y-\hat{Y})$
.1023	.0105
-.0222	.0005
-.1128	.0127
.0506	.0026
-.0996	.0099
.1076	.0116
-.0962	.0093
.0702	.0049

$$\boxed{SSE = \Sigma(Y-\hat{Y})^2 = .0620}$$

$$S_e = \sqrt{\frac{SSE}{n-2}} = \sqrt{\frac{.0620}{6}} = \boxed{.1017 = S_e}$$

The model produces estimates that are ±.1017 or within about 10 cents 68% of the time. However, the range of milk costs is only 45 cents for this data.

11.29 $r^2 = 1 - \dfrac{SSE}{\Sigma Y^2 - \dfrac{(\Sigma Y)^2}{n}} = 1 - \dfrac{46.5692}{1,935 - \dfrac{(97)^2}{5}}$

$$r^2 = 1 - .875 = \boxed{.125}$$

This is a low value of r^2

11.31 $r^2 = 1 - \dfrac{SSE}{\Sigma Y^2 - \dfrac{(\Sigma Y)^2}{n}} = 1 - \dfrac{70,940}{1,587,328 - \dfrac{(2,670)^2}{8}}$

$$r^2 = \boxed{.898}$$

This value of r^2 is relatively high

11.33 $r^2 = 1 - \dfrac{SSE}{\Sigma Y^2 - \dfrac{(\Sigma Y)^2}{n}} = 1 - \dfrac{77.1384}{5,837 - \dfrac{(173)^2}{6}}$

$r^2 = \boxed{.909}$

This value is a relatively high value of r^2. Almost 91% of the variability of Y is accounted for by the X values.

11.35 $S_b = \dfrac{S_e}{\sqrt{\Sigma X^2 - \dfrac{(\Sigma X)^2}{n}}} = \dfrac{3.94}{\sqrt{1,833 - \dfrac{(89)^2}{5}}}$

$S_b = .2498$
$b_1 = 0.162$

$H_o: \quad \beta = 0$ $\qquad\qquad \alpha = .05$

$H_a: \quad \beta \neq 0$

Two-tail test, $\alpha/2 = .025$
df = n - 2 = 5 - 2 = 3
$t_{.025,3} = \pm 3.182$

$t = \dfrac{b_1 - \beta_1}{S_b} = \dfrac{0.162 - 0}{.2498} = \boxed{0.65}$

The calculated t = 0.65 < $t_{.025,3}$ = 3.182

$\boxed{\text{Fail to reject the null hypothesis}}$

11.37 $\quad S_b = \dfrac{S_e}{\sqrt{\Sigma X^2 - \dfrac{(\Sigma X)^2}{n}}} = \dfrac{108.7}{\sqrt{7{,}667.15 - \dfrac{(199.5)^2}{8}}}$

$S_b = 2.095$
$b_1 = 15.240$

$H_o:\quad \beta = 0 \qquad\qquad \alpha = .10$

$H_a:\quad \beta \neq 0$

Two-tail test, $\alpha/2 = .05$
df $= n - 2 = 8 - 2 = 6$
$t_{.05,6} = 1.943$

$t = \dfrac{b_1 - \beta_1}{S_b} = \dfrac{15{,}240 - 0}{2.095} = \boxed{7.27}$

The calculated $t = 7.27 > t_{.05,6} = 1.943$

$\boxed{\text{Reject the null hypothesis}}$

11.39 $X_0 = 25$
95% confidence
$\alpha/2 = .025$
$df = n - 2 = 5 - 2 = 3$
$t_{.025,3} = \pm 3.182$

$$\overline{X} = \frac{\Sigma X}{n} = \frac{89}{5} = 17.8$$

$\Sigma X = 89 \qquad\qquad \Sigma X^2 = 1,833$
$S_e = 3.94$
$\hat{Y} = 16.5 + 0.162(25) = 20.55$

$$\hat{Y} \quad \pm\ t_{\alpha/2,n-2}\ S_e\ \sqrt{\frac{1}{n} + \frac{(X_o - \overline{X})^2}{\Sigma X^2 - \dfrac{(\Sigma X)^2}{n}}}$$

$$20.55 \pm 3.182(3.94)\ \sqrt{\frac{1}{5} + \frac{(25-17.8)^2}{1,833 - \dfrac{(89)^2}{5}}}$$

$20.55 \pm 3.182(3.94)(.63903)$
20.55 ± 8.01

$$\boxed{12.54 \le E(Y_{25}) \le 28.56}$$

11.41 $X_0 = 20$
             98% confidence
             $\alpha/2 = .01$
             $df = n - 2 = 8 - 2 = 6$
             $t_{.01,6} = 3.143$

$$\overline{X} = \frac{\Sigma X}{n} = \frac{199.5}{8} = 24.9375$$

$\Sigma X = 199.5$ $\qquad\qquad$ $\Sigma X^2 = 7,667.15$

$S_e = 108.8$

$\hat{Y} = -46.29 + 15.24(20) = 258.51$

$$\hat{Y} \pm t_{\alpha/2,n-2}\, S_e \sqrt{\frac{1}{n} + \frac{(X_o - \overline{X})^2}{\Sigma X^2 - \frac{(\Sigma X)^2}{n}}}$$

$$258.51 \pm (3.143)(108.8) \sqrt{\frac{1}{8} + \frac{(20-24.9375)^2}{7.667.15 - \frac{(199.5)^2}{8}}}$$

$258.51 \pm (3.143)(108.8)(0.36614)$
258.51 ± 125.20

$$\boxed{133.31 \le E(Y_{20}) \le 383.71}$$

For single Y value:

$$\hat{Y} \pm t_{\alpha/2,n-2}\, S_e \sqrt{1 + \frac{1}{n} + \frac{(X_o - \overline{X})^2}{\Sigma X^2 - \frac{(\Sigma X)^2}{n}}}$$

$$258.51 \pm (3.143)(108.8) \sqrt{1 + \frac{1}{8} + \frac{(20-24.9375)^2}{7,667.15 - \frac{(199.5)^2}{8}}}$$

$258.51 \pm (3.143)(108.8)(1.06492)$
258.51 ± 364.16

$$\boxed{-105.65 \le Y \le 622.67}$$

The confidence interval for the single value of Y is wider
than the confidence interval for the average value of Y
because the average is more towards the middle and
individual values of Y can vary more than values of the
average.

11.43 $\Sigma X = 80$ $\Sigma X^2 = 1,148$
           $\Sigma Y = 69$ $\Sigma Y^2 = 815$
           $\Sigma XY = 624$ $n = 7$

$$r = \frac{\Sigma XY - \dfrac{(\Sigma X)(\Sigma Y)}{n}}{\sqrt{\left[\Sigma X^2 - \dfrac{(\Sigma X)^2}{n}\right]\left[\Sigma Y^2 - \dfrac{(\Sigma Y)^2}{n}\right]}}$$

$$r = \frac{624 - \dfrac{(80)(69)}{7}}{\sqrt{\left[1,148 - \dfrac{(80)^2}{7}\right]\left[815 - \dfrac{(69)^2}{7}\right]}} = \frac{-164.571}{\sqrt{(233.714)(134.857)}}$$

$$r = \frac{-164.571}{177.533} = \boxed{-0.927}$$

11.45 $\Sigma X = 1.087$ $\Sigma X^2 = 322,345$
           $\Sigma Y = 2,032$ $\Sigma Y^2 = 878,686$
           $\Sigma XY = 507,509$ $n = 5$

$$r = \frac{\Sigma XY - \dfrac{(\Sigma X)(\Sigma Y)}{n}}{\sqrt{\left[\Sigma X^2 - \dfrac{(\Sigma X)^2}{n}\right]\left[\Sigma Y^2 - \dfrac{(\Sigma Y)^2}{n}\right]}}$$

$$r = \frac{507,509 - \dfrac{(1,087)(2,032)}{5}}{\sqrt{\left[322,345 - \dfrac{(1,087)^2}{5}\right]\left[878,686 - \dfrac{(2,032)^2}{5}\right]}}$$

$$r = \frac{65,752.2}{\sqrt{(86,031.2)(52,881.2)}} = \frac{65,752.2}{67,449.5}$$

$$r = \boxed{.975}$$

11.47 $\Sigma X = 23,300$ $\Sigma X^2 = 60,381,796$
         $\Sigma Y = 31,695$ $\Sigma Y^2 = 111,746,863$
         $\Sigma XY = 82,031,036$ $n = 9$

$$r = \frac{\Sigma XY - \dfrac{(\Sigma X)(\Sigma Y)}{n}}{\sqrt{\left[\Sigma X^2 - \dfrac{(\Sigma X)^2}{n}\right]\left[\Sigma Y^2 - \dfrac{(\Sigma Y)^2}{n}\right]}}$$

$$r = \frac{82,031,036 - \dfrac{(23,300)(31,695)}{9}}{\sqrt{\left[60,381,796 - \dfrac{(23,300)^2}{9}\right]\left[111,746,863 - \dfrac{(31,695)^2}{9}\right]}}$$

$$r = \frac{-23,797.33}{\sqrt{(60,684.89)(127,638)}} = \frac{-23,797.33}{88,009.65}$$

$$r = \boxed{-.270}$$

This r value is quite small. It indicates that there may be a slight negative relationship between the T-bond index and the Dow-Jones Average.

$\boxed{r^2 = .073}$ very little predictability.

11.49   Correlation between 1985 and 1987:

$$\Sigma X = 17.09 \qquad \Sigma X^2 = 58.7911$$
$$\Sigma Y = 15.12 \qquad \Sigma Y^2 = 41.7054$$
$$\Sigma XY = 48.97 \qquad n = 8$$

$$r = \frac{\Sigma XY - \dfrac{(\Sigma X)(\Sigma Y)}{n}}{\sqrt{\left[\Sigma X^2 - \dfrac{(\Sigma X)^2}{n}\right]\left[\Sigma Y^2 - \dfrac{(\Sigma Y)^2}{n}\right]}}$$

$$r = \frac{48.97 - \dfrac{(17.09)(15.12)}{8}}{\sqrt{\left[58.7911 - \dfrac{(17.09)^2}{8}\right]\left[41.7054 - \dfrac{(15.12)^2}{8}\right]}}$$

$$r = \frac{16.6699}{\sqrt{(22.28259)(13.1286)}} = \frac{16.6699}{17.1038}$$

$$r = \boxed{.975}$$

          Correlation between 1987 and 1989:

$$\Sigma X = 15.12 \qquad \Sigma X^2 = 41.7054$$
$$\Sigma Y = 15.86 \qquad \Sigma Y^2 = 42.0396$$
$$\Sigma XY = 41.5934 \qquad n = 8$$

$$r = \frac{\Sigma XY - \dfrac{(\Sigma X)(\Sigma Y)}{n}}{\sqrt{\left[\Sigma X^2 - \dfrac{(\Sigma X)^2}{n}\right]\left[\Sigma Y^2 - \dfrac{(\Sigma Y)^2}{n}\right]}}$$

$$r = \frac{41.5934 - \dfrac{(15.12)(15.86)}{8}}{\sqrt{\left[41.7054 - \dfrac{(15.12)^2}{8}\right]\left[42.0396 - \dfrac{(15.86)^2}{8}\right]}}$$

$$r = \frac{11.618}{\sqrt{(13.1286)(10.59715)}} = \frac{11.618}{11.795}$$

$$r = \boxed{.985}$$

Correlation between 1985 and 1989:

$\Sigma X = 17.09$ $\Sigma X^2 = 58.7911$
$\Sigma Y = 15.86$ $\Sigma Y^2 = 42.0396$
$\Sigma XY = 48.5827$ $n = 8$

$$r = \frac{\Sigma XY - \dfrac{(\Sigma X)(\Sigma Y)}{n}}{\sqrt{[\Sigma X^2 - \dfrac{(\Sigma X)^2}{n}][\Sigma Y^2 - \dfrac{(\Sigma Y)^2}{n}]}}$$

$$r = \frac{48.5827 - \dfrac{(17.09)(15.86)}{8}}{\sqrt{[58.7911 - \dfrac{(17.09)^2}{8}][42.0396 - \dfrac{(15.86)^2}{8}]}}$$

$$r = \frac{14.702}{\sqrt{(22.2826)(10.5972)}} = \frac{14.702}{15.367}$$

$$r = \boxed{.957}$$

The years 1987 and 1989 are the most correlated with
r = .985.

11.51

Variable X_1 is a dummy variable as shown by the 0's and 1's. Examining the t ratio for variable X_1 reveals that this variable is not a significant predictor of Y in this model since the probability of X_1's t ratio is .145.

It appears that variables X_3 and X_4 are negatively related to Y based on the negative coefficients of these variables' slopes and the negative t ratios. However, caution must be exercised in reaching this conclusion. If either of these two variables were a single predictor of Y there is the possibility that they would not be negatively related to Y. This is because sometimes in multiple regression a variable will have a negative coefficient when taken in consideration as a predictor with other variables even though as a single predictor is has positive relationship. However, an examination of the raw data shows that particularly variable X_4 seems to have an inverse relationship with the Y values.

An examination of t ratios reveals that variables X_2 and X_4 are statistically significant predictors of Y in this model. Both t ratios produce probabilities less than .01.

The R^2 value of 92.5% means that this multiple regression model accounts for 92.5% of the variability of Y and only 7.5% of the variability of Y is unaccounted for by the model. The standard error of the estimate, s = 1.264. This also indicates the strength of the model. While the Y values vary from 2 to 17, the standard error of the estimate indicates that at least 68% of the estimates are within ±1s or ±1.264. This value is quite small given the range of Y values meaning that the model works quite well on this data.

Thus, the R^2 value is high and the s value is low indicating a strong amount of predictability with this model.

11.53

$$\Sigma X = 25,792 \qquad \Sigma X^2 = 51,171.510$$
$$\Sigma Y = 162 \qquad \Sigma Y^2 = 2,710$$
$$\Sigma XY = 321,760 \qquad n = 13$$

$b_1 = 1.934$
$b_0 = -3824.725$

$$\boxed{\begin{array}{l} \hat{Y} = -3824.725 + 1.934 \ X \\ \text{Where} \quad X = \text{Year} \\ \qquad \qquad Y = \text{Cost} \end{array}}$$

Let $X = 1992$

$$\hat{Y}_{1992} = -3824.725 \ 1.934(1992) =$$

$$\boxed{\hat{Y}_{1992} = 27.8}$$

11.55

a)

Year (X)	Treasury Securities (Y)
1960	24.1
1965	24.9
1970	31.1
1975	51.6
1980	133.0
1985	396.4

$\Sigma X = 11,835$ $\Sigma X^2 = 23,344,975$

$\Sigma Y = 661.1$ $\Sigma Y^2 = 179,652.55$

$\Sigma XY = 1,309,535.5$ $n = 6$

$b_1 = 12.60743$

$b_0 = -24757.9695$

$$\hat{Y} = -24757.9695 + 12.60743\ X$$

for X = 1990:

$$\hat{Y}_{1990} = -24757.9695 + 12.60743(1990)$$

$$\hat{Y}_{1990} = 330.8$$

b)

Year (X)	Mutual Funds (Y)
1960	17.0
1965	34.4
1970	44.5
1975	38.7
1980	52.1
1985	203.0

$\Sigma X = 11,835$ $\Sigma X^2 = 23,344,975$

$\Sigma Y = 389.7$ $\Sigma Y^2 = 48,873.71$

$\Sigma XY = 771,126.5$ $n = 6$

$b_1 = 5.58457$

$b_0 = -10,950.617$

$$\hat{Y} = -10,950.617 + 5.58457\ X$$

for X = 2000:

$$\hat{Y}_{2000} = -10,950.617 + 5.58457(2000) =$$

$$\hat{Y}_{2000} = 218.5$$

11.57

X	Y
5	8
7	9
3	11
16	27
12	15
9	13

$\Sigma X = 52$ $\Sigma X^2 = 564$ $b_1 = 1.2853$

$\Sigma Y = 83$ $\Sigma Y^2 = 1,389$

$\Sigma XY = 865$ $n = 6$ $b_0 = 2.6941$

a) $\boxed{\hat{Y} = 2.6941 + 1.2853\ X}$

b)

$\hat{Y}$ (Predicted Values)	$(Y-\hat{Y})$ residuals
9.1206	-1.1206
11.6912	-2.6912
6.5500	4.4500
23.2588	3.7412
18.1176	-3.1176
14.2618	-1.2618

c)

$(Y-\hat{Y})^2$
1.2557
7.2426
19.8025
13.9966
9.7194
1.5921

$SS_e = 53.6089$

$$S_e = \sqrt{\frac{SSE}{n-2}} = \sqrt{\frac{53.6089}{4}} = \boxed{3.661}$$

d) $r^2 = 1 - \dfrac{SSE}{\Sigma Y^2 \dfrac{(\Sigma Y)^2}{n}} = 1 - \dfrac{53.6089}{1,389 - \dfrac{(83)^2}{6}}$

$\boxed{r^2 = .777}$

e) H_o: $\beta = 0$ $\alpha = .01$

      H_a: $\beta \neq 0$

Two-tailed test, $\alpha/2 = .005$
df = n - 2 = 6 - 2 = 4
$t_{.005,4} = \pm4.604$

$$S_b = \frac{S_e}{\sqrt{\Sigma X^2 - \dfrac{(\Sigma X)^2}{n}}} = \frac{3.661}{\sqrt{564 - \dfrac{(52)^2}{6}}} = .34389$$

$$t = \frac{b_1 - \beta}{S_b} = \frac{1.2853 - 0}{.34389} = \boxed{3.74}$$

Calculated $t = 3.74 < t_{.005,4} = 4.604$

> Fail to reject the null hypothesis

f)   The $R^2 = 77.74\%$ is modest. There appears to be some
      prediction with this model. The slope of the regression
      line is not significantly different from zero using $\alpha = .01$.
      However, for $\alpha = .05$, the null hypothesis of a zero slope is
      rejected. The standard error of the estimate, $S_e = 3.661$ is
      not particularly small given the range of values for
      Y (11 - 3 = 8).

11.59 $\Sigma X = 1,263$ $\Sigma X^2 = 268,295$
            $\Sigma Y = 417$ $\Sigma Y^2 = 29,135$
            $\Sigma XY = 88,288$ $n = 6$

$$r = \frac{\Sigma XY - \frac{(\Sigma X)(\Sigma Y)}{n}}{\sqrt{[\Sigma X^2 - \frac{(\Sigma X)^2}{n}][\Sigma Y^2 - \frac{(\Sigma Y)^2}{n}]}}$$

$$= \frac{88,288 - \frac{(1,263)(417)}{6}}{\sqrt{[268,295 - \frac{(1,263)^2}{6}][29,135 - \frac{(417)^2}{6}]}}$$

$$= \frac{509.5}{\sqrt{(2,433.5)(153.5)}} = \frac{509.5}{611.18} = \boxed{.834}$$

Coefficient of determination $= r^2 = \boxed{.695}$

11.61   Let Water use = Y   and Temperature = X

$\Sigma X = 608$ $\Sigma X^2 = 49,584$ $b_1 = 2.40107$

$\Sigma Y = 1,025$ $\Sigma Y^2 = 152,711$

$\Sigma XY = 86,006$ $n = 8$ $b_0 = -54.35604$

$$\boxed{\hat{Y} = -54.35604 + 2.40107\ X}$$

$$\hat{Y}_{100} = -54.35604 + 2.40107(100) = \boxed{185.751}$$

$SSE = \Sigma Y^2 - b_0 \Sigma Y - b_1 \Sigma XY$

$SSE = 152,711 - (-54.35604)(1,025) - (2.40107)(86,006)$

$SSE = 1919.5146$

$$S_e = \sqrt{\frac{SSE}{n-2}} = \sqrt{\frac{1,919.5146}{8-2}} = \boxed{17.886}$$

$$r^2 = 1 - \frac{SSE}{\Sigma Y^2 - \frac{(\Sigma Y)^2}{n}} = 1 - \frac{1,919.5145}{152,711 - \frac{(1025)^2}{8}} = 1 - \frac{1,919.5146}{21,382.875}$$

$$r^2 = 1 - .09 = \boxed{.91}$$

Testing the slope:

H_o: $\beta = 0$ $\alpha \doteq .01$

H_a: $\beta \neq 0$

Two-tailed test, $\alpha/2 = .005$

$df = n - 2 = 8 - 2 = 6$

$t_{.005,6} = \pm 3.707$

$$S_b = \frac{S_e}{\sqrt{\Sigma X^2 - \frac{(\Sigma X)^2}{n}}} = \frac{17.886}{\sqrt{49,584 - \frac{(608)^2}{8}}}$$

$S_b = .30783$

$$t = \frac{b_1 - \beta_1}{S_b} = \frac{2.40107 - 0}{.30783} = \boxed{7.80}$$

The calculated $t = 7.80 < t_{.005,6} = 3.707$

$$\boxed{\text{Reject the null hypothesis}}$$

11.63
$$\Sigma X = 305.7 \qquad \Sigma X^2 = 24,943.27 \qquad b_1 = -1.07386$$
$$\Sigma Y = 6,801.7 \qquad \Sigma Y^2 = 7,442,829.39$$
$$\Sigma XY = 284,930.12 \qquad n = 7 \qquad b_0 = 1,019.8542$$

$$\boxed{\hat{Y} = 1,019.8542 - 1.07386\ X}$$

$$SSE = \Sigma Y^2 - b_0 \Sigma Y - b_1 \Sigma XY$$
$$SSE = 7442829.39 - (1019.8542)(6810.7) - (-1.07386)(284930.12)$$
$$SSE = 802,883.45$$

$$S_e = \sqrt{\frac{SSE}{n-2}} = \sqrt{\frac{802,883.45}{7-2}} = \boxed{400.72}$$

$$r^2 = 1 - \frac{SSE}{\Sigma Y^2 - \frac{(\Sigma Y)^2}{n}} = 1 - \frac{802,883.45}{7,442,829.39 - \frac{(6,810.7)^2}{7}}$$

$$r^2 = \boxed{.016}$$

Testing the slope:
$H_o: \quad \beta = 0 \qquad\qquad \alpha = .05$

$H_a: \quad \beta \neq 0$

Two-tailed test, $\alpha/2 = .025$
$df = n - 2 = 7 - 2 = 5$
$t_{.025,5} = \pm 2.571$

$$S_b = \frac{S_e}{\sqrt{\Sigma X^2 - \frac{(\Sigma X)^2}{n}}} = \frac{400.72}{\sqrt{24,993.27 - \frac{(305.7)^2}{7}}}$$

$$S_b = 3.71373$$

$$t = \frac{b_1 - \beta_1}{S_b} = \frac{-1.07386 - 0}{3.71373} = \boxed{-0.29}$$

Calculated $t = -0.29 > t_{.025,5} = -2.571$

$$\boxed{\text{Fail to reject the null hypothesis}}$$

11.65 ΣX = 36 ΣX^2 = 256
         ΣY = 44 ΣY^2 = 300
         ΣXY = 188   n = 7

$$r = \frac{\Sigma XY - \dfrac{(\Sigma X)(\Sigma Y)}{n}}{\sqrt{[\Sigma X^2 - \dfrac{(\Sigma X)^2}{n}][\Sigma Y^2 - \dfrac{(\Sigma Y)^2}{n}]}}$$

$$r = \frac{188 - \dfrac{(36)(44)}{7}}{\sqrt{[256 - \dfrac{(36)^2}{7}][300 - \dfrac{(44)^2}{7}]}}$$

$$r = \frac{-38.2857}{\sqrt{(70.8571)(23.42857)}} = \frac{-38.2857}{40.7441} = \boxed{-.940}$$

11.67 ΣX = 36.63 ΣX^2 = 217.137
         ΣY = 57.23 ΣY^2 = 479.3231
         ΣXY = 314.9091   n = 8

$$r = \frac{\Sigma XY - \dfrac{(\Sigma X)(\Sigma Y)}{n}}{\sqrt{[\Sigma X^2 - \dfrac{(\Sigma X)^2}{n}][\Sigma Y^2 - \dfrac{(\Sigma Y)^2}{n}]}}$$

$$r = \frac{314.9091 - \dfrac{(36.62)(57.23)}{8}}{\sqrt{[217.137 - \dfrac{(36.62)^2}{8}][479.3231 - \dfrac{(57.23)^2}{8}]}}$$

$$r = \frac{52.938775}{\sqrt{(49.50895)(69.91399)}} = \frac{52.938775}{58.83339}$$

$$r = \boxed{.90}$$

There is a strong positive relationship between the inflation rate and the thirty-year treasury yield.

11.69

	Abbott	Bausch & Lomb	Exxon	Motorola	Sara Lee	Tootsie Roll
Abbott	–	.999	.506	1.000	.998	1.000
Bausch & Lomb	.999	–	.536	.999	1.000	1.000
Exxon	.506	.536	–	.509	.553	.511
Motorola	1.000	.999	.509	–	.999	1.000
Sara Lee	.998	1.000	.553	.999	–	.999
Tootsie Roll	1.000	1.000	.511	1.000	.999	–

Most Correlated Stocks:

Abbott and Bausch & Lomb

Abbott and Motorola

Abbott and Sara Lee

Abbott and Tootsie Roll

Bausch & Lomb and Motorola

Bausch & Lomb and Sara Lee

Bausch & Lomb and Tootsie Roll

Motorola and Sara Lee

Motorola and Tootsie Roll

Sara Lee and Tootsie Roll

- each pair correlated near 1.00

11.71   Let: year = X   inflation rate = y

ΣX = 11,805 ΣX^2 = 23,226,775
ΣY = 27 ΣY^2 = 170.7926
ΣXY = 53,262.05   n = 6
b_1 = 0.31897 b_0 = -623.0763

$$\hat{Y} = -623.0763 + 0.31897 \ X$$

For X = 1985

$$\hat{Y}_{1985} = -623.0763 + 0.31897(1985) = \boxed{10.08}$$

The actual inflation rate through the 1980"s decreased, thus
resulting in a down turn or non linear regression
relationship. The regression model created with these
number through 1980 extrapolated a 1985 value based on a
linear relationship. Thus, the predicted value of 10.08%
was quite different than the actual figure of around 5% for
the 1980's.

11.73 a)   Let X = State Banks   Y = Total Banks

ΣX = 14,237 ΣX^2 = 21,475,129
ΣY = 145,914 ΣY^2 = 2,130,509,554
ΣXY = 207,050,511   n = 10
b_1 = -0.5699 b_0 = 15,402.7684

$$\hat{Y} = 15,402.7684 - 0.5699 \ X$$

b)   Let X = State Banks   Y = Mutual Savings

$$\Sigma X = 14,237 \qquad \Sigma X^2 = 21,475,129$$
$$\Sigma Y = 4,934 \qquad \Sigma Y^2 = 2,466,238$$
$$\Sigma XY = 7,139,287 \qquad n = 10$$

$$r = \frac{\Sigma XY - \dfrac{(\Sigma X)(\Sigma Y)}{n}}{\sqrt{\left[\Sigma X^2 - \dfrac{(\Sigma X)^2}{n}\right]\left[\Sigma Y^2 - \dfrac{(\Sigma Y)^2}{n}\right]}}$$

$$r = \frac{7,139,287 - \dfrac{(14,237)(4,934)}{10}}{\sqrt{\left[21,475,129 - \dfrac{(14,237)^2}{10}\right]\left[2,466,238 - \dfrac{(4,934)^2}{10}\right]}}$$

$$r = \boxed{.586}$$

c)   Let X = Year   Y = Mutual Savings

$$\Sigma X = 19,625 \qquad \Sigma X^2 = 38,516,125$$
$$\Sigma Y = 4,934 \qquad \Sigma Y^2 = 2,466,238$$
$$\Sigma XY = 9,676,045 \qquad n = 10$$
$$b_1 = -3.36 \qquad b_0 = 7.087.4$$

$$\boxed{\hat{Y} = 7,987.4 - 3.36\ X}$$

$$\hat{Y}_{1995} = 7087.4 - 3.36\ (1995) = \boxed{384.2}$$

11.75   Let   Y = rentals
                   X_1 = corner store or not
                   X_2 = number of competitors
                   X_3 = average family income

The regression equation is:

$$\hat{Y} = -62 + 149\ X_1 + 25.8\ X_2 + 10.4\ X_3$$

The value of the coefficient of determination is:

$$R^2 = 79.0\%$$

That is, seventy-nine percent of the variance of rentals is accounted for by this multiple regression model containing three predictor variables.

The F test for the existence of at least one significant predictor resulted in:

$$F = 10.01$$

with a probability of .004. This is statistically significant at α = .01. There exists at least one significant predictor of rentals.

Examining the t-ratios for individual slopes:
For the variable corner store:

$$t = 2.29 \text{ with a probability of } .052$$

For the variable, number of competitors:

$$t = 1.12 \text{ with a probability of } .294$$

For the variable family income:

$$\boxed{t = 4.36 \text{ with a probability of } .002}$$

The variable, family income has a slope that is significantly different from zero using a two-tail test and $\alpha = .01$. This variable seems to be the most significant predictor of rentals. The standard error of the estimate is:

$$\boxed{S_e = 84.46}$$

The standard error of the estimate is:

$$S_e = 84.46$$

That is, at least 68% of the estimates are within 84.46 rentals per day and 95% within $2(84.46) = 168.92$ rentals.

12

CHI-SQUARE AND OTHER NONPARAMETRIC STATISTICS

I. **CHAPTER OBJECTIVES**

The main objective of this chapter is to present several nonparametric statistics that can be used when the level of data is insufficient to warrant the use of parametric statistics, specifically enabling you to:

1. Recognize the advantages and disadvantages of nonparametric statistics.

2. Understand the chi-square goodness-of-fit test and how to use it.

3. Analyze data using contingency analysis.

4. Know when and how to use the Mann-Whitney U Test, the Wilcoxon matched-pairs signed rank test, and the Kruskal-Wallis test.

5. Correlate data using Spearman's rank correlation coefficient.

II.   **CHAPTER OUTLINE**

12.1   Chi-Square Goodness-of-Fit Test

                          Chi-Square Distribution

12.2   Chi-Square Test of Independence

12.3   Mann-Whitney U Test

12.4   Wilcoxon Matched-Pairs Signed Rank Test

12.5   Kruskal-Wallis Test

12.6   Spearman's Rank Correlation

III.   **KEY WORDS**

Parametric Statistics   Contingency Analysis
Nonparametric Statistics   Mann-Whitney U Test
Chi-Square Goodness-of-Fit Test   Wilcoxon Matched-Pairs
Chi-Square Distribution   Signed Rank Test
Chi-Square Test of Independence   Kruskal-Wallis Test
Contingency Table   Spearman's Rank
                                             Correlation

IV. STUDY QUESTIONS

1. Statistical techniques based on assumptions about the population from which the sample data are selected are called _____ statistics.

2. Statistical techniques based on fewer assumptions about the population and the parameters are called _____ statistics.

3. A chi-square goodness-of-fit test is being used to determine if the observed frequencies from seven categories are significantly different from the expected frequencies from the seven categories. The degrees of freedom for this test are _____.

4. A value of alpha = .05 is used to conduct the test described in question 3. The critical table chi-square value is _____.

5. A variable contains five categories. It is expected that data are uniformly distributed across these five categories. To test this, a sample of observed data is gathered on this variable resulting in frequencies of 27, 30, 29, 21, 24. A value of .01 is specified for alpha. The degrees of freedom for this test are _____.

6. The critical table chi-square value of the problem presented in question 5 is _____.

7. The calculated chi-square value for the problem
    presented in question five is _____. Based
    on this value and the critical chi-square value, a
    researcher would decide to _____ the null
    hypothesis.

8. A researcher believes that a variable is Poisson
    distributed across six categories. To test this, a
    random sample of observations is made for the variable
    resulting in the following data:

Number of arrivals	Observed
0	47
1	56
2	38
3	23
4	15
5	12

    Suppose alpha is .10, the critical table chi-square
    value used to conduct this chi-square goodness-of-fit
    test is _____.

9. The value of the calculated chi-square for the data
    presented in question 8 is _____.
    Based on this value and the critical value determined
    in question 8, the decision of the researcher is to
    _____ the null hypothesis.

10. The degrees of freedom used in conducting a chi-square
    goodness-of-fit test to determine if a distribution is
    normally distributed are _____.

11. In using the chi-square goodness-of-fit test, a statistician needs to make certain that none of the expected values are less than _____.

12. The chi-square _____ is used to analyze frequencies of two variables with multiple categories.

13. A two-way frequency table is sometimes referred to as a _____ table.

14. Suppose a researcher wants to use the data below and the chi-square test of independence to determine if variable one is independent of variable two.

Variable One

		A	B	C
Variable Two	D	25	40	60
	E	10	15	20

The expected value for the cell of D and B is

_____.

15. The degrees of freedom for the problem presented in question 14 are _____.

16. If alpha is .05, the critical chi-square value for the problem presented in question 14 is _____.

17. The calculated value of chi-square for the problem presented in question 14 is _____. Based on this calculated value of chi-square and the critical chi-square value determined in question 16, the

researcher should decide to _____ the null

hypothosis that the two variables are independent.

18. A researcher wants to statistically determine if

variable three is independent of variable four using

the observed data given below:

Variable Three

	A	B
C	92	70
D	112	145

Variable Four

If alpha is .01, the critical chi-square table value

for this problem is _____.

19. The calculated chi-square value for the problem

presented in question 18 is _____.

Based on this value and the critical value determined

in question 18, the researcher should decide to

_____ the null hypothesis.

20. The nonparametric counterpart of the t test to compare

the means of two independent populations is called

_____.

21. Suppose a Mann-Whitney U test is being used to test to determine if two populations are different or not. A value of alpha = .05 is used. Random samples of size 16 are gathered from each population and the resulting data are given below:

    Sample 1:   19, 27, 23, 29, 22, 20, 29, 31,
                25, 17, 26, 23, 18, 28, 28, 33

    Sample 2:   27, 35, 33, 28, 24, 33, 30, 31,
                38, 39, 29, 41, 33, 34, 36, 34

    The critical table value of Z for this problem is

    _____.

22. In the problem presented in question 21 if sample one is designated as group one, the value of W is _____.

23. In the problem presented in question 21, the value of U is _____.

24. For the problem presented in question 21, the calculated value of Z is _____. Based on this value and the critical value determined in question 21, the decision should be to _____ the null hypothesis.

25. The nonparametric alternative to the t test for two related samples or matched-pairs is _____.

26. The Wilcoxon matched-pairs signed rank test uses a _____ statistic to analyze the data.

27. Suppose the following samples of paired data are gathered and the Wilcoxon matched-pairs signed is used to determine if there is a significant difference in the two populations from which the samples are were gathered.

Sample 1	Sample 2
109	98
103	100
111	107
98	102
105	99
108	96
101	100
102	104
100	93
97	98
106	100
112	108
104	105
105	101
109	101

Let alpha be .10. The critical value of Z for this problem is _____.

28. The value of T for the problem presented in question 27 is _____.

29. The mean value of T for the sample size of the problem presented in question 27 is _____.

The standard deviation of T for this sample size is _____.

30. The calculated Z value for the problem presented in question 27 is _____. Based on the critical value determined in question 27 and the calculated

value of Z, a statistician would decide to

_____ the null hypothesis.

31. The nonparametric alternative to the one-way analysis of variance is the _____ test.

32. The value of K computed in the Kruskal-Wallis test is distributed approximately as a _____ value.

33. Suppose a researcher desires to analyze the data below using a Kruskal-Wallis test to determine if there is a significant difference in the populations from which the four samples were taken.

Sample 1	Sample 2	Sample 3	Sample 4
113	97	105	109
124	99	108	106
117	98	100	105
118	101	98	108
122		103	110

The degrees of freedom associated with the Kruskal-Wallis test of this data are _____.

34. The critical value of chi-square used to test the data for the problem in question 33 using $\alpha = .05$ is

_____.

35. The calculated value of chi-square for the data of the problem in question 33 is _____.   Using this value and the critical value determined in question 34, a researcher would decide to _____ the null hypothesis.

36. A nonparametric alternative to Pearson's product-moment correlation coefficient, r, is _____.

37. The data below have been gathered in pairs from two variables:

    X: 12, 19, 21, 34, 50, 69, 70

    Y: 8, 17, 15, 29, 31, 45, 39

    The value of Spearman's rank correlation for this data is _____.

38. The data below have been gathered in pairs from two variables:

    X: 29,   13,   11,   9,   5,   -1,   -3,   -4, -11

    Y: -12, -13, -16, -25, -26, -18, -20, -44, -90

    The value of Spearman's correlation for this data is

    _____.

39. The data below have been gathered in pairs from two variables:

    X: 230, 221, 190, 130, 124, 109

    Y: 107, 150, 134, 138, 166, 178

    The value of Spearman's rank correlation for this data is _____.

40. If the value of Spearman's rank correlation is near -1, the two variables have _____ correlations. If the value of a Spearman's rank correlation is near 0, the two variables have _____ correlation.

V.   **ANSWERS TO STUDY**

1. Parametric Statistics

2. Nonparametric Statistics

3. 6

4. 12.592

5. 4

6. 13.277

7. 2.091,   fail to reject

8. 7.779

9. 16.4,   Reject

10. K-3

11. 5

12. Test of Independence

13. Contingency

14. 40.44

15. 2

16. 5.991

17. .19,   Fail to Reject

18. 6.635

19. 6.945,   Reject

20. Mann-Whitney U Test

21. $\pm$ 1.96

22. 164.5

23. 227.5

24. 3.75,   Reject

25. Wilcoxon Matched-Pairs Signed Rank Test

26.   Z

27.   ± 1.645

28.   15.5

29.   60,   17.61

30.   -2.53,   Reject

31.   Kruskal-Wallis test

32.   Chi-square

33.   3

34.   7.815

35.   15.11,   Reject

36.   Spearman's Rank Correlation

37.   .929

38.   .867

39.   -.829

40.   High Negative,   Little or No

VI.   SOLUTIONS TO ODD-NUMBERED PROBLEMS IN TEXT

12.1

f_o	f_e	$\dfrac{(f_0-f_e)^2}{f_e}$
53	68	3.309
37	42	0.595
32	33	0.030
28	22	1.636
18	10	6.400
15	8	6.125

H_o: The observed distribution is the same
         as the expected distribution.

H_a: The observed distribution is not the same
         as the expected distribution.

Calculated $\chi^2 = \Sigma \dfrac{(f_o-f_e)^2}{f_e} = \;= \boxed{18.095}$

df = k - 1 = 6 - 1 = 5
α = .05

$\chi^2_{.05,5} = 11.070$

Calculated $\chi^2 = 18.095 > \chi^2_{.05,5} = 11.070$

$\boxed{\text{Reject the null hypothesis}}$

The observed frequencies are not distributed the same as the
expected frequencies.

12.3

Number	f_o	Number x f_o
0	28	0
1	17	17
2	11	22
3	5	15
		54

H_o: The frequency distribution is Poisson.
H_a: The frequency distribution is not Poisson.

$$\lambda = \frac{54}{61} = 0.9$$

Number	Expected Probability	Expected Frequency
0	.4066	24.803
1	.3659	22.312
2	.1647	10.047
≥ 3	.0628	3.831

Since f_e for ≥ 3 is less than 5 collapse categories:

Number	f_o	f_e	$\frac{(f_o - f_e)^2}{f_e}$
0	28	24.803	0.412
1	17	22.312	1.265
≥ 2	16	13.878	0.324
	61	60.993	2.001

df = k - 2 = 3 - 2 = 1
α = .05

$$\chi^2_{.05,1} = 3.841$$

Calculated $\chi^2 = \Sigma \frac{(f_o - f_e)^2}{f_e} = = \boxed{2.001}$

Since calculated $\chi^2 = 2.001 < \chi^2_{.05,1} = 3.841$

$\boxed{\text{Fail to Reject the null hypothesis}}$

There is insufficient evidence to reject the observed frequency distribution as Poisson distributed. The conclusion is that the observed distribution is Possson distributed.

12.5

Definition	f_o	Proportion expected	f_e	$\frac{(f_o-f_e)^2}{f_e}$
Happiness	42	.39	223(.39)= 88.53	24.46
Sales/Profit	95	.12	227(.12)= 27.24	168.55
Helping Others	27	.18	40.86	4.70
Achievement/ Challenge	63	.31	70.34	0.77
	227			198.48

H_o: The observed frequencies are distributed the same as the expected frequencies.

H_a: The observed frequencies are not distributed the same as the expected frequencies.

Calculated χ^2 = 189.48

df = k - 1 = 4 - 1 = 3

α = .05

$\chi^2_{.05,3}$ = 7.815

Calculated χ^2 = 198.48 > $\chi^2_{.05,3}$ = 7.815

$$\boxed{\text{Reject the null hypothesis}}$$

The observed frequencies for men are not distributed the same as the expected frequencies which are based on the responses of women.

12.7

Age	f_o	M	fm	fm^2
10-20	16	15	240	3,600
20-30	44	25	1,100	27,500
30-40	61	35	2,135	74,725
40-50	56	45	2,520	113,400
50-60	35	55	1,925	105,875
60-70	19	65	1,235	80,275
	231		$\Sigma fm = 9,155$	$\Sigma fm^2 = 405,375$

$$\overline{X} = \frac{\Sigma fm}{n} = \frac{9,155}{231} = 39.63$$

$$S = \sqrt{\frac{\Sigma fm^2 - \frac{(\Sigma fm)^2}{n}}{n-1}} = \sqrt{\frac{405,375 - \frac{(9,155)^2}{231}}{230}}$$

$$S = 13.6$$

H_o: The observed frequencies are normally distributed.
H_a: The observed frequencies are not normally distributed.

For Category 10-20	P

$$Z = \frac{10 - 39.63}{13.6} = -2.18 \qquad\qquad .4854$$

$$Z = \frac{20 - 39.63}{13.6} = -1.44 \qquad\qquad \underline{-.4251}$$

expected prob.   .0603

For Category 20-30	P

for $X = 20$, $Z = -1.44$ \qquad\qquad .4251

$$Z = \frac{30 - 39.63}{13.6} = -0.71 \qquad\qquad \underline{-.2611}$$

expected prob.   .1640

For Category 30-40	P
for X = 30, Z = -0.71	.2611
$Z = \frac{40 - 39.63}{13.6} = 0.03$	+.0120
expected prob.	.2731

For Category 40-50	P
$Z = \frac{50 - 39.63}{13.6} = 0.76$	.2764
for X = 40, Z = 0.03	-.0120
expected prob.	.2644

For Category 50-60	P
$Z = \frac{60 - 39.63}{13.6} = 1.50$	.4332
for X = 50, Z = 0.76	-.2764
expected prob.	.1568

For Category 60-70	P
$Z = \frac{70 - 39.63}{13.6} = 2.23$	.4871
for X = 60, Z = 1.50	-.4332
expected prob.	.0539

For < 10:
Probability between 10 and the mean
    = .0603 + .1640 + .2611 = .4854
Probability < 10 = .5000 - .4854 = .0146

For > 70:
Probability between 70 and the mean
    = .0120 + .2644 + .1568 + .0539 = .4871
Probability > 70 = .5000 - .4871 = .0129

Age	Probability		f_e
< 10	.0146	(.0146)(231) =	3.37
10-20	.0603	(.0603)(231) =	13.93
20-30	.1640		37.88
30-40	.2731		63.09
40-50	.2644		61.08
50-60	.1568		36.22
60-70	.0539		12.45
> 70	.0129		2.98

Categories < 10 and > 70 are less than 5.   Collapse the < 10 into 10-20 and > 70 into 60-70.

Age	f_o	f_e	$\dfrac{(f_o-f_e)^2}{f_e}$
10-20	16	17.3	0.10
20-30	44	37.88	0.99
30-40	61	63.09	0.07
40-50	56	61.08	0.42
50-60	35	36.22	0.04
60-70	19	15.43	0.83
			2.45

df = k - 3 = 6 - 3 = 3

α = .05

$\chi^2_{.05,3}$ = 7.815

Calculated χ^2 = $\boxed{2.45}$

Calculated χ^2 = 2.45 < $\chi^2_{.05,3}$ = 7.815

$\boxed{\text{Fail to reject the null hypothesis}}$

No reason to reject that the observed frequencies are normally distributed.

12.9

Variable Two

Variable One			
	24	59	83
	13	43	56
	20	35	55
	57	137	194

H_o: Variable one is independent of Variable Two.
H_a: Variable one is not independent of Variable Two.

$$e_{11} = \frac{(83)(57)}{194} = 24.39$$

$$e_{12} = \frac{(83)(13)}{194} = 58.61$$

$$e_{21} = \frac{(56)(57)}{194} = 16.45$$

$$e_{22} = \frac{(56)(137)}{194} = 39.55$$

$$e_{31} = \frac{(55)(57)}{194} = 16.16$$

$$e_{32} = \frac{(55)(137)}{194} = 38.84$$

Variable Two

Variable One			
	(24.39) 24	(58.61) 59	83
	(16.45) 13	(39.55) 43	56
	(16.16) 20	(38.84) 35	55
	57	137	194

$$\chi^2 = \frac{(24-24.39)^2}{24.39} + \frac{(59-58.61)^2}{58.61} +$$

$$\frac{(13-16.45)^2}{16.45} + \frac{(43-39.55)^2}{39.55} +$$

$$\frac{(20-16.16)^2}{16.16} + \frac{(35-38.84)^2}{38.84} =$$

$$\chi^2 = .01 + .00 + .72 + .30 + .91 + .38 = \boxed{2.32}$$

$\alpha = .05$

$df = (c-1)(r-1) + (2-1)(3-1) = 2$

$\chi^2_{.05,2} = 5.991$

Calculated $\chi^2 = 2.32 < \chi^2_{.05,2} = 5.991$

$$\boxed{\text{Fail to reject the null hypothesis}}$$

Variable One is independent of Variable Two.

12.11

Variable
Two

24	13	47	58	142
93	59	187	244	583
117	72	234	302	725

Variable One (row label at left)

H_o: Variable One is independent of Variable Two.
H_a: Variable One is not independent of Variable Two.

$$e_{11} = \frac{(142)(117)}{725} = 22.92$$

$$e_{12} = \frac{(142)(72)}{725} = 14.10$$

$$e_{13} = \frac{(142)(234)}{725} = 45.83$$

$$e_{14} = \frac{(142)(302)}{725} = 59.15$$

$$e_{21} = \frac{(583)(117)}{725} = 94.08$$

$$e_{22} = \frac{(583)(72)}{725} = 57.90$$

$$e_{23} = \frac{(583)(234)}{725} = 188.17$$

$$e_{24} = \frac{(583)(302)}{725} = 242.85$$

Variable
Two

(22.92) 24	(14.10) 13	(45.83) 47	(59.15) 58
(94.08) 93	(57.90) 59	(188.17) 187	(242.85) 244

Variable
One

$$\chi^2 = \frac{(24-22.92)^2}{22.92} + \frac{(13-14.10)^2}{14.10} + \frac{(47-45.83)^2}{45.83}$$

$$+ \frac{(58-59.15)^2}{59.15} + \frac{(93-94.08)^2}{94.08} +$$

$$\frac{(59-57.90)^2}{57.90} + \frac{(188-188.17)^2}{188.17} + \frac{(244-242.85)^2}{242.85}$$

$$\chi^2 = .05 + .09 + .03 + .02 + .01 + .02 + .01 + .01 =$$

$$\chi^2 = \boxed{0.24}$$

$$\alpha = .01$$

$$df = (c-1)(r-1) + (4-1)(2-1) = 3$$

$$\chi^2_{.01,3} = 11.345$$

Calculated $\chi^2 = 0.24 < \chi^2_{.01,3} = 11.345$

Fail to reject the null hypothesis

Variable One is independent of Variable Two.

12.13

Type of Music Preferred

		Rock	Soul	Country	Classical	
	NE	140	32	5	18	195
Region	S	135	41	52	8	235
	W	154	27	8	13	202
		428	100	65	39	632

H_o: Type of music preferred is independent of region.
H_a: Type of music preferred is not independent of region.

$$e_{11} = \frac{(195)(428)}{632} = 132.06 \qquad e_{23} = \frac{(235)(65)}{632} = 24.17$$

$$e_{12} = \frac{(195)(100)}{632} = 30.85 \qquad e_{24} = \frac{(235)(39)}{632} = 14.50$$

$$e_{13} = \frac{(195)(65)}{632} = 20.06 \qquad e_{31} = \frac{(202)(428)}{632} = 136.80$$

$$e_{14} = \frac{(195)(39)}{632} = 12.03 \qquad e_{32} = \frac{(202)(100)}{632} = 31.96$$

$$e_{21} = \frac{(235)(428)}{632} = 159.15 \qquad e_{33} = \frac{(202)(65)}{632} = 20.78$$

$$e_{22} = \frac{(235)(100)}{632} = 37.18 \qquad e_{34} = \frac{(202)(39)}{632} = 12.47$$

Type of Music Preferred

		Rock	Soul	Country	Classical	
	NE	(132.06) 140	(30.85) 32	(20.06) 5	(12.03) 18	195
Region	S	(159.15) 134	(37.18) 41	(24.17) 52	(14.50) 8	235
	W	(136.80) 154	(31.96) 27	(20.78) 8	(12.47) 13	202
		428	100	65	39	

$$\chi^2 = \frac{(140-132.06)^2}{132.06} + \frac{(32-30.85)^2}{30.85} + \frac{(5-20.06)^2}{20.06} +$$

$$\frac{(18-12.03)^2}{12.03} + \frac{(134-159.15)^2}{159.15} + \frac{(41-37.18)^2}{37.18}$$

$$\frac{(52-24.17)^2}{24.17} + \frac{(8-14.50)^2}{14.50} + \frac{(154-136.80)^2}{136.80} +$$

$$\frac{(27-31.96)^2}{31.96} + \frac{(8-20.78)^2}{20.78} + \frac{(13-12.47)^2}{12.47} =$$

$$\chi^2 = .48 + .04 + 11.31 + 2.96 + 3.97 + .39 +$$
$$32.04 + 2.91 + 2.16 + .77 + 7.86 + .02 =$$

$$\chi^2 = \boxed{64.91}$$

$\alpha = .01$

$df = (c-1)(r-1) = (4-1)(3-1) = 6$

$\chi^2_{.01,6} = 16.812$

Calculated $\chi^2 = 64.91 > \chi^2_{.01,6} = 16.812$

$$\boxed{\text{Reject the null hypothesis}}$$

Type of music preferred is not independent of region of the country.

12.15

	Car Telephone Yes	No	
Physician	42	39	81
Lawyer	21	34	55
Accountant	13	38	51
	76	111	187

Profession

H_o: Having a car phone is independent of profession.
H_a: Having a car phone is not independent of profession.

$$e_{11} = \frac{(81)(76)}{187} = 32.92 \qquad e_{22} = \frac{(55)(111)}{187} = 32.65$$

$$e_{12} = \frac{(81)(111)}{187} = 48.08 \qquad e_{31} = \frac{(51)(76)}{187} = 20.73$$

$$e_{21} = \frac{(55)(76)}{187} = 22.35 \qquad e_{32} = \frac{(51)(111)}{187} = 30.27$$

	Car Telephone Yes	No
Physician	(32.92) 42	(48.08) 39
Lawyer	(22.35) 21	(32.65) 34
Accountant	(20.73) 13	(30.27) 38

Profession

$$\chi^2 = \frac{(42-32.92)^2}{32.92} + \frac{(39-48.08)^2}{48.08} + \frac{(21-22.35)^2}{22.35} +$$

$$\frac{(34-32.65)^2}{32.65} + \frac{(13-20.73)^2}{20.73} + \frac{(38-30.27)^2}{30.27} =$$

$$\chi^2 = 2.50 + 1.71 + .08 + .06 + 2.88 + 1.97 =$$

$$\chi^2 = \boxed{9.20}$$

$\alpha = .10$
$df = (c-1)(r-1) = (2-1)(3-1) = 2$

$\chi^2_{.10,2} = 4.605$

Calculated $\chi^2 = 9.20 > \chi^2_{.10,2} = 4.605$

$$\boxed{\text{Reject the null hypothesis}}$$

Having a car phone or <u>not</u> is not independent of profession.

12.17

$$H_o: \quad \mu_1 - \mu_2 = 0$$

$$H_a: \quad \mu_1 - \mu_2 \neq 0$$

Value	Rank	Group
11	1	1
13	2.5	1
13	2.5	2
14	4	2
15	5	1
17	6	1
18	7.5	1
18	7.5	2
21	10	1
21	10	1
21	10	2
22	12.5	1
22	12.5	2
23	14.5	2
23	14.5	2
24	16	2
26	17.5	1
26	17.5	2
27	19	2
29	20	1

$n_1 = 10$
$n_2 = 10$

$$W_1 = 1 + 2.5 + 5 + 6 + 7.5 + 10 + 10 + 12.5 + 17.5 + 20 = 92$$

$$\mu = \frac{n_1 \cdot n_2}{2} = \frac{(10)(10)}{2} = 50$$

$$\sigma = \sqrt{\frac{n_1 \cdot n_2 (n_1 + n_2 + 1)}{12}} = \sqrt{\frac{(10)(10)(21)}{12}} = 13.23$$

$$U = n_1 \cdot n_2 + \frac{n_1(n_1+1)}{2} - W_1$$

$$= (10)(10) + \frac{(10)(11)}{2} - 92 = 63$$

$$Z = \frac{U-\mu}{\sigma} = \frac{63-50}{13.23} = \boxed{0.98}$$

$\alpha = .05$ $\qquad\qquad \alpha/2 = .025$
$Z_{.025} = \pm 1.96$

Calculated $Z = 0.98 < Z = 1.96$

Fail to reject the null hypothesis

12.19 H_o: $\mu_1 - \mu_2 \geq 0$
             H_a: $\mu_1 - \mu_2 < 0$

Contacts	Rank	Group
1	1	1
3	2	1
4	3	1
5	4	2
6	6	1
6	6	1
6	6	2
7	8.5	1
7	8.5	2
8	10.5	1
8	10.5	2
9	13.5	1
9	13.5	1
9	13.5	2
9	13.5	2
10	15	2
11	17	1
11	17	2
11	17	2
12	19	2
13	20	2
13	21	2

$n_1 = 10$
$n_2 = 12$

$W_1 = 1 + 2 + 3 + 6 + 6 + 8.5 + 10.5 + 13.5 + 13.5 + 17 = 81$

$\mu = \dfrac{n_1 \cdot n_2}{2} = \dfrac{(10)(12)}{2} = 60$

$$\sigma = \sqrt{\frac{n_1 \cdot n_2(n_1+n_2+1)}{12}} = \sqrt{\frac{(10)(12)(23)}{12}} = 15.17$$

$$U = n_1 \cdot n_2 + \frac{n_1(n_1+1)}{2} - W_1$$

$$= (10)(12) + \frac{(10)(11)}{2} - 81 = 94$$

$$Z = \frac{U-\mu}{\sigma} = \frac{94-60}{15.17} = \boxed{2.24}$$

$\alpha = .01$

$Z_{.01} = -2.33$

$Z = 2.24 < |Z_{10} = -2.33|$

$$\boxed{\text{Fail to reject the null hypothesis}}$$

12.21

$H_o: \mu_1 - \mu_2 \leq 0$

$H_a: \mu_1 - \mu_2 > 0$

Earnings	Rank	Gender
$28,900	1	F
31,400	2	F
36,600	3	F
40,000	4	F
40,500	5	F
41,200	6	F
42,300	7	F
42,500	8	F
44,500	9	F
45,000	10	M
47,500	11	F
47,800	12.5	F
47,800	12.5	M
48,000	14	F
50,100	15	M
51,000	16	M
51,500	17.5	M
51,500	17.5	M
53,850	19	M
55,000	20	M
57,800	21	M
61,100	22	M
63,900	23	M

$n_1 = 11$

$n_2 = 12$

$W_1 = 10 + 12.5 + 15 + 16 + 17.5 + 17.5 + 19 + 20 + 21 + 22 + 23 = 193.5$

$$\mu = \frac{n_1 \cdot n_2}{2} = \frac{(11)(12)}{2} = 66$$

$$\sigma = \sqrt{\frac{n_1 \cdot n_2(n_1+n_2+1)}{12}} = \sqrt{\frac{(11)(12)(24)}{12}} = 16.25$$

$$U = n_1 \cdot n_2 + \frac{n_1(n_1+1)}{2} - W_1$$

$$= (11)(12) + \frac{(11)(12)}{2} - 193.5 = 4.5$$

$$Z = \frac{U-\mu}{\sigma} = \frac{4.5-66}{16.25} = \boxed{-3.78}$$

$\alpha = .01$

$Z_{.01} = 2.33$

Calculated $Z = |-3.78| > Z_{.01} = 2.33$

$$\boxed{\text{Reject the null hypothesis}}$$

12.23

H_o: The population differences = 0

H_a: The population differences $\neq$ 0

1	2	d	Rank
212	179	33	15
234	184	50	16
219	213	6	7.5
199	167	32	13.5
194	189	5	6
206	200	6	7.5
234	212	22	11
225	221	4	5
220	223	-3	- 3.5
218	217	1	1
234	208	26	12
212	215	-3	-3.5
219	187	32	13.5
196	198	-2	-2
178	189	-11	-9
213	201	12	10

n = 16

T_- = 3.5 + 3.5 + 2 + 9 = 18

T = 18

$\mu = \dfrac{(n)(n+1)}{4} = \dfrac{(16)(17)}{4} = 68$

$\sigma = \sqrt{\dfrac{n(n+1)(2n+1)}{24}} = \sqrt{\dfrac{16(17)(33)}{24}} = 19.34$

$Z = \dfrac{T-\mu}{\sigma} = \dfrac{18-68}{19.34} = \boxed{-2.59}$

α = .10 $\alpha/2$ = .05

$Z_{.05}$ = ±1.645

Calculated Z = -2.59 < $Z_{.05}$ = -1.645

Reject the null hypothesis

12.25 H_o: The population differences $\geq$ 0
                       H_a: The population differences < 0

Before	After	d	Rank
10,500	12,600	-2,100	-11
8,750	10,660	-1,790	-9
12,300	11,890	410	3
10,510	14,630	-4,120	-17
5,570	8,580	-3,010	-15
9,150	10,115	-965	-7
11,980	14,320	-2,370	-12
6,740	6,900	-160	-2
7,340	8,890	-1,550	-8
13,400	16,540	-3,140	-16
12,200	11,300	900	6
10,570	13,330	-2,760	-13
9,880	9,990	-110	-1
12,100	14,050	-1,950	-10
9,000	9,500	-500	-4
11,800	12,450	-650	-5
10,500	13,450	-2,950	-14

n = 17

$T+$ = 3 + 6 = 9

T = 9

$\mu = \dfrac{(n)(n+1)}{4} = \dfrac{(17)(18)}{4} = 76.5$

$\sigma = \sqrt{\dfrac{n(n+1)(2n+1)}{24}} = \sqrt{\dfrac{(17)(18)(35)}{24}} = 21.12$

$Z = \dfrac{T-\mu}{\sigma} = \dfrac{9-76.5}{21.12} = \boxed{-3.20}$

α = .05

$Z_{.05}$ = -1.645

Calculated $Z = -3.20 < Z_{.05} = -1.645$

Reject the null hypothesis

12.27 H_o: The population differences ≥ 0
H_a: The population differences < 0

1990	1992	d	Rank
49	54	-5	-7.5
27	38	-11	-15
39	38	1	2
75	80	-5	-7.5
59	53	6	11
67	68	-1	-2
22	43	-21	-20
61	67	-6	-11
58	73	-15	-18
60	55	5	7.5
72	58	14	16.5
62	57	5	7.5
49	63	-14	-16.5
48	49	-1	-2
19	39	-20	-19
32	34	-2	-4.5
60	66	-6	-11
80	90	-10	-13.5
55	57	-2	-4.5
68	58	10	13.5

$n = 20$

$T+ = 2 + 11 + 7.5 + 16.5 + 7.5 + 13.5 = 58$

$T = 58$

$$\mu = \frac{(n)(n+1)}{4} = \frac{(20)(21)}{4} = 105$$

$$\sigma = \sqrt{\frac{n(n+1)(2n+1)}{24}} = \sqrt{\frac{(20)(21)(41)}{24}} = 26.79$$

$$Z = \frac{T-\mu}{\sigma} = \frac{58-105}{26.79} = \boxed{-1.75}$$

$\alpha = .10$

$Z_{.10} = -1.28$

Calculated $Z = -1.75 < Z_{.10} = -1.28$

Reject the null hypothesis

12.29 H_o: The C populations are identical
         H_a: At least one of the C populations is different

1	2	3	4	5
157	165	219	286	197
188	197	257	243	215
175	204	243	259	235
174	214	231	250	217
201	183	217	279	240
203		203		233
				213

BY RANKS

	1	2	3	4	5
	1	2	18	29	7.5
	6	7.5	26	23.5	15
	4	12	23.5	27	21
	3	14	19	25	16.5
	10.5	5	16.5	28	22
			10.5		20
					13
T_j	33.5	40.5	113.5	132.5	115
n_j	6	5	6	5	7

$$\Sigma \frac{T_j^2}{n_j} = \frac{(33.5)^2}{6} + \frac{(40.5)^2}{5} + \frac{(113.5)^2}{6} + \frac{(132.5)^2}{5} + \frac{(115)^2}{7}$$

$$= 8,062.67$$

n = 29

$$K = \frac{12}{n(n+1)} \Sigma \frac{T_j^2}{n_j} - 3(n+1) = \frac{12}{29(30)}(8,062.67) - 3(30) =$$

K = $\boxed{21.21}$

$\alpha = .01$
df = c - 1 = 5 - 1 = 4

$\chi^2_{.01,4} = 13.277$

Calculated K = 21.21 > $\chi^2_{.01,4}$ = 13.277

$\boxed{\text{Reject the null hypothesis}}$

12.31 H_o: The C populations are identical
         H_a: At least one of the C populations is different

Region 1	Region 2	Region 3	Region 4
$1,200	$225	$ 675	$1,075
450	950	500	1,050
110	100	1,100	750
800	350	310	180
375	275	660	330
200			680
			425

By Ranks

	Region 1	Region 2	Region 3	Region 4
	23	5	15	21
	12	19	13	20
	2	1	22	17
	18	9	7	3
	10	6	14	8
	4			16
				11
T_j	69	40	71	96
n_j	6	5	5	7

$$\Sigma \frac{T_j^2}{n_j} = \frac{(69.5)^2}{6} + \frac{(40)^2}{5} + \frac{(71)^2}{5} + \frac{(96)^2}{7} = 3,438.27$$

$n = 23$

$$K = \frac{12}{n(n+1)} \Sigma \frac{T_j^2}{n_j} - 3(n+1) = \frac{12}{23(24)}(3,428.27) - 3(24) =$$

$$K = \boxed{2.75}$$

$\alpha = .05$
$df = c - 1 = 4 - 1 = 3$

$\chi_{.05,3}^2 = 7.815$

Calculated $K = 2.75 < \chi_{.05,3}^2 = 7.815$

$\boxed{\text{Fail to reject the null hypothesis}}$

12.33 H_o: The C populations are identical
           H_a: At least one of the C populations is different

Amusement Parks	Lake Area	City	National Park
0	3	2	2
1	2	2	4
1	3	3	3
0	5	2	4
2	4	3	3
1	4	2	5
0	3	3	4
	5	3	4
	2	1	
		3	

By Ranks

Amusement Parks	Lake Area	City	National Park
2	20.5	11.5	11.5
5.5	11.5	11.5	28.5
5.5	20.5	20.5	20.5
2	33	11.5	28.5
11.5	28.5	20.5	20.5
5.5	28.5	11.5	33
2	20.5	20.5	28.5
	33	20.5	28.5
	11.5	5.5	
		20.5	

T_j 34   207.5   154.0   199.5

n_j 7   9   10   8

$$\Sigma \frac{T_j^2}{n_j} = \frac{(34)^2}{7} + \frac{(207.5)^2}{9} + \frac{(154)^2}{10} + \frac{(199.5)^2}{8} = 12,295.80$$

$n = 34$

$$K = \frac{12}{n(n+1)} \Sigma \frac{T_j^2}{n_j} - 3(n+1) = \frac{12}{34(35)}(12,295.80) - 3(35) =$$

$K = \boxed{18.99}$

$\alpha = .05$

$df = c - 1 = 4 - 1 = 3$

$\chi^2_{.05,3} = 7.815$

Calculated $K = 18.99 > \chi^2_{.05,3} = 7.815$

Reject the null hypothesis

12.35

X	Y	X Ranked	Y Ranked	d	d^2
23	201	3	2	1	1
41	259	10.5	11	-.5	.25
37	234	8	7	1	1
29	240	6	8	-2	4
25	231	4	6	-2	4
17	209	1	3	-2	4
33	229	7	5	2	4
41	246	10.5	9	1.5	2.25
40	248	9	10	-1	1
28	227	5	4	1	1
19	200	2	1	1	1

$$\Sigma d^2 = 23.5$$

$$n = 11$$
$$r_s = 1 - \frac{6\Sigma d^2}{n(n^2-1)} = 1 - \frac{6(23.5)}{11(120)} = \boxed{.893}$$

12.37

X	Y	X Ranked	Y Ranked	d	d^2
99	108	8	2	6	36
67	139	4	5	-1	1
82	117	6	3	3	9
46	168	1	8	-7	49
80	124	5	4	1	1
57	162	3	7	-4	16
49	145	2	6	-4	16
91	102	7	1	6	36

$$\Sigma d^2 = 164$$

$$n = 8$$
$$r_s = 1 - \frac{6\Sigma d^2}{n(n^2-1)} = 1 - \frac{6(164)}{8(63)} = \boxed{-.95}$$

12.39

Budget	Income	Budget Ranked	Income Ranked	d	d^2
24	210	2	8	-6	36
53	53	8	4	4	16
45	83	6.5	6	.5	.25
45	79	6.5	5	1.5	2.25
30	121	5	7	-2	4
20	14	1	3	-2	4
28	7	4	1	3	9
25	11	3	2	1	1

$$\Sigma d^2 = 72.5$$

$$n = 8$$
$$r_s = 1 - \frac{6\Sigma d^2}{n(n^2-1)} = 1 - \frac{6(72.5)}{8(63)} = \boxed{.137}$$

12.41

Firms	Pop.	Ranked Firms	Ranked Pop.	d	d^2
56.7	3.353	10	9	1	1
47.0	0.371	9	3	6	36
23.0	7.353	8	10	-2	4
16.0	1.698	7	7	0	0
15.2	0.941	6	5	1	1
10.4	1.070	5	6	-1	1
10.2	0.211	4	1	3	9
9.7	0.245	3	2	1	1
8.2	0.511	2	4	-2	4
7.8	2.978	1	8	-7	49

$$\Sigma d^2 = 106$$

$$n = 10$$

$$r_s = 1 - \frac{6\Sigma d^2}{n(n^2-1)} = 1 - \frac{6(106)}{10(99)} = \boxed{.358}$$

12.43

H_o: The observed frequencies are distributed the same as the expected frequencies.

H_a: The observed frequencies are not distributed the same as the expected frequencies.

f_o	f_e	$\dfrac{(f_o-f_e)^2}{f_e}$
205	208	0.04
195	200	0.13
166	156	0.64
108	110	0.04
157	148	0.55
174	182	0.35
180	180	0.00
		1.75

Calculated χ^2 = $\boxed{1.75}$

α = .01

df = k - 1 = 7 - 1 = 6

$\chi^2_{.01,6}$ = 16.812

Calculated χ^2 = 1.75 < $\chi^2_{.01,6}$ = 16.812

$\boxed{\text{Fail to reject the null hypothesis}}$

There is not enough evidence to reject the claim that the distribution of observed frequencies is the same as the distribution of expected frequencies.

12.45

Number	f_o	(f_o) (Number)
0	6	0
1	11	11
2	29	58
3	17	51
4	10	40
5	7	35
6	5	30
	$\Sigma f_o = 85$	$\Sigma(f_o)$ (Number) $= 225$

$$\lambda = \frac{\Sigma(f_o)(\text{Number})}{\Sigma f_o} = \frac{225}{85} = 2.6$$

H_o: The observed frequencies are Poisson distributed.
H_a: The observed frequencies are not Poisson distributed.

Number	Probability	(f_o) (Number)
0	.0743	$(.0743)(85) = 6.32$
1	.1931	$(.1931)(85) = 16.41$
2	.2510	21.34
3	.2176	18.50
4	.1414	12.02
5	.0735	6.25
6 or more	.0490	4.17

f_o	f_e	$\dfrac{(f_o - f_e)^2}{f_e}$
6	6.32	0.02
11	16.41	1.78
29	21.34	2.75
17	18.50	0.12
10	12.02	0.34
7	6.25	0.09
5	4.17	0.17
		5.27

Calculated $\chi^2 = \boxed{5.27}$
$\alpha = .10$
df $= k - 2 = 7 - 2 = 5$

$\chi^2_{.10,5} = 9.236$

Calculated $\chi^2 = 5.27 < \chi^2_{.10,5} = 9.236$

$\boxed{\text{Fail to reject the null hypothesis}}$

Not enough evidence to reject the claim that the observed frequencies are Poisson distributed.

12.47 H_0: The distribution of observed frequencies is the same as the distribution of expected frequencies.

H_a: The distribution of observed frequencies is not the same as the distribution of expected frequencies.

Soft Drink	f_o	proportions		f_e	$\dfrac{(f_o-f_e)^2}{f_e}$
Classic Coke	361	.200	(.200)(1726) =	345.2	0.72
Pepsi	340	.188	(.188)(1726) =	324.49	0.74
Diet Coke	192	.093		160.52	6.17
Diet Pepsi	153	.088		151.89	0.01
Dr. Pepper	82	.049		84.57	0.08
Sprite	40	.037		63.86	8.91
Others	558	.345		595.47	2.36
	$\Sigma f_o = 1,726$				18.99

Calculated $\chi^2 = \boxed{18.99}$

$\alpha = .05$
df $= k - 1 = 7 - 1 = 6$

$\chi^2_{.05,6} = 12.592$

Calculated $\chi^2 = 18.99 > \chi^2_{.05,6} = 12.592$

$\boxed{\text{Reject the null hypothesis}}$

The observed frequencies are not distributed the same as the expected frequencies from the national poll.

12.49

Variable Two

6	18	22	46
19	38	45	102

Variable One

25   56   67   148

H_o: Variable One is independent of Variable Two.
H_a: Variable One is not independent of Variable Two.

$$e_{11} = \frac{(46)(25)}{148} = 7.77 \qquad e_{21} = \frac{(102)(25)}{148} = 17.23$$

$$e_{12} = \frac{(46)(56)}{148} = 17.41 \qquad e_{22} = \frac{(102)(56)}{148} = 38.59$$

$$e_{13} = \frac{(46)(67)}{148} = 20.82 \qquad e_{23} = \frac{(102)(67)}{148} = 46.18$$

Variable Two

(7.77) 6	(17.41) 18	(20.82) 22	46
(17.23) 19	(38.59) 38	(46.18) 45	102

Variable One

25   56   67   148

$$\chi^2 = \frac{(6-7.77)^2}{7.77} + \frac{(18-17.41)^2}{17.41} + \frac{(22-20.82)^2}{20.82} +$$

$$\frac{(19-17.23)^2}{17.23} + \frac{(38-38.59)^2}{38.59} + \frac{(45-46.18)^2}{46.18} =$$

$$\chi^2 = .40 + .02 + .07 + .18 + .01 + .03 = \boxed{.71}$$

$\alpha = .01$
df $= (c - 1)(r - 1) = (3 - 1)(2 - 1) = 2$

$$\chi^2_{.01,2} = 9.210$$

Calculated $\chi^2 = 0.71 < \chi^2_{.01,2} = 9.210$

Fail to reject the null hypothesis

Variable One is not independent of Variable Two.

12.51

Type of College or University

Number of Children		Community College	Large University	Small College	
	0	25	178	31	234
	1	49	141	12	202
	2	31	54	8	93
	≥ 3	22	14	6	42
		127	387	57	571

H_o: Number of Children is independent of Type of College or University.

H_a: Number of Children is not independent of Type of College or University.

$$e_{11} = \frac{(234)(127)}{571} = 52.05 \qquad e_{31} = \frac{(93)(127)}{571} = 20.68$$

$$e_{12} = \frac{(234)(387)}{571} = 158.60 \qquad e_{32} = \frac{(93)(387)}{571} = 63.03$$

$$e_{13} = \frac{(234)(57)}{571} = 23.36 \qquad e_{33} = \frac{(93)(57)}{571} = 9.28$$

$$e_{21} = \frac{(202)(127)}{571} = 44.93 \qquad e_{41} = \frac{(42)(127)}{571} = 9.34$$

$$e_{22} = \frac{(202)(387)}{571} = 136.91 \qquad e_{42} = \frac{(42)(387)}{571} = 28.47$$

$$e_{23} = \frac{(202)(57)}{571} = 20.16 \qquad e_{43} = \frac{(42)(57)}{571} = 4.19$$

Type of College or University

		Community College	Large University	Small College	
	0	(52.05) 25	(158.60) 178	(23.36) 31	234
Number of Children	1	(44.93) 49	(136.91) 141	(20.16) 12	202
	2	(20.68) 31	(63.03) 54	(9.28) 8	93
	≥ 3	(9.34) 22	(28.47) 14	(4.19) 6	42
		127	387	57	571

$$\chi^2 = \frac{(25-52.05)^2}{52.05} + \frac{(178-158.6)^2}{158.6} + \frac{(31-23.36)^2}{23.36} +$$

$$\frac{(49-44.93)^2}{44.93} + \frac{(141-136.91)^2}{136.91} + \frac{(12-20.16)^2}{20.16} +$$

$$\frac{(31-20.68)^2}{20.68} + \frac{(54-63.03)^2}{63.03} + \frac{(8-9.28)^2}{9.28} +$$

$$\frac{(22-9.34)^2}{9.34} + \frac{(14-28.47)^2}{28.47} + \frac{(6-4.19)^2}{4.19} =$$

$$\chi^2 = 14.06 + 2.37 + 2.50 + .37 + .12 + 3.30 + 5.15 +$$

$$1.29 + .18 + 17.16 + 7.35 + .78 = \boxed{54.63}$$

$\alpha = .05$

$df = (c - 1)(r - 1) = (3 - 1)(4 - 1) = 6$

$\chi^2_{.05,6} = 12.592$

Calculated $\chi^2 = 54.63 > \chi^2_{.05,6} = 12.592$

Reject the null hypothesis

Numbers of children is not independent of type of College or University.

12.53

	Location		
	NE	W	S

Customer		NE	W	S	
	Industrial	230	115	68	413
	Retail	185	143	89	417
		415	258	157	830

$$e_{11} = \frac{(413)(415)}{830} = 206.5 \qquad e_{21} = \frac{(417)(415)}{830} = 208.5$$

$$e_{12} = \frac{(413)(258)}{830} = 128.38 \qquad e_{22} = \frac{(417)(258)}{830} = 129.62$$

$$e_{13} = \frac{(413)(157)}{830} = 78.12 \qquad e_{23} = \frac{(417)(157)}{830} = 78.88$$

	Location		
	NE	W	S

Customer		NE	W	S	
	Industrial	(206.5) 230	(128.38) 115	(78.12) 68	413
	Retail	(208.5) 185	(129.62) 143	(78.88) 89	417
		415	258	157	

$$\chi^2 = \frac{(230-206.5)^2}{206.5} + \frac{(115-128.38)^2}{128.38} + \frac{(68-78.12)^2}{78.12} +$$

$$\frac{(185-208.5)^2}{208.5} + \frac{(143-129.62)^2}{129.62} + \frac{(89-78.88)^2}{78.88} =$$

$$\chi^2 = 2.67 + 1.39 + 1.31 + 2.65 + 1.38 + 1.30 = \boxed{10.70}$$

$\alpha = .10$

$df = (c - 1)(r - 1) = (3 - 1)(2 - 1) = 2$

$\chi^2_{.10,2} = 4.605$

Calculated $\chi^2 = 10.70 > \chi^2_{.10,2} = 4.605$

Reject the null hypothesis

Type of customer is not independent of geographic region.

12.55 H_o: $\mu_1 - \mu_2 = 0$

        H_a: $\mu_1 - \mu_2 \neq 0$

Value	Rank	Group
41	1	1
42	2	2
43	3.5	1
43	3.5	1
44	5	1
46	6	2
47	7	2
48	8.5	1
48	8.5	2
49	10.5	1
49	10.5	2
50	12	1
51	13.5	1
51	13.5	2
52	15	2
53	16	2
54	17	2
55	18	2
56	19	1
57	20	1
58	21	2
59	22	1

$n_1 = 11$
$n_2 = 11$

$W_1 = 1 + 3.5 + 3.5 + 5 + 8.5 + 10.5 + 12 + 13.5 +$

      $19 + 20 + 22 = 118.5$

$\mu = \dfrac{n_1 \cdot n_2}{2} = \dfrac{(11)(11)}{2} = 60.5$

$\sigma = \sqrt{\dfrac{n_1 \cdot n_2 (n_1 + n_2 + 1)}{12}} = \sqrt{\dfrac{(11)(11)(23)}{12}} = 15.23$

$U = n_1 \cdot n_2 + \dfrac{n_1(n_1 + 1)}{2} - W_1$

   $= (11)(11) + \dfrac{(11)(12)}{2} - 118.5 = 68.5$

$Z = \dfrac{U - \mu}{\sigma} = \dfrac{68.5 - 60.5}{15.23} = \boxed{0.53}$

$\alpha = .05 \qquad \alpha/2 = .025$

$Z_{.025} = \pm 1.96$

Calculated $Z = 0.53 < Z_{.025} = 1.96$

Fail to reject the null hypothesis

12.57 H_0: $\mu_1 - \mu_2 = 0$

H_a: $\mu_1 - \mu_2 \neq 0$

Value	Rank	Group
1.98	1	2
2.30	2	1
2.39	3	1
2.65	4	1
2.72	5	2
2.74	6	2
2.75	7	2
2.78	8	2
2.87	9	2
2.98	10	2
3.02	11	1
3.04	12	2
3.07	13	1
3.13	14	1
3.16	15	2
3.34	16	1
3.38	17	2
3.45	18	1
3.61	19	2
4.01	20	2
4.09	21	2
4.11	22.5	1
4.11	22.5	2
4.12	24	1
4.23	25	1

$n_1 = 11$
$n_2 = 14$

$W_1 = 2 + 3 + 4 + 11 + 13 + 14 + 16 + 18 +$
$\quad 22.5 + 24 + 25 = 152.5$

$$\mu = \frac{n_1 \cdot n_2}{2} = \frac{(11)(14)}{2} = 77$$

$$\sigma = \sqrt{\frac{n_1 \cdot n_2 (n_1 + n_2 + 1)}{12}} = \sqrt{\frac{(11)(14)(26)}{12}} = 18.27$$

$$U = n_1 \cdot n_2 + \frac{n_1 (n_1 + 1)}{2} - W_1$$

$$= (11)(14) + \frac{(11)(12)}{2} - 152.5 = 67.5$$

$$Z = \frac{U - \mu}{\sigma} = \frac{67.5 - 77}{18.27} = \boxed{-0.52}$$

$$\alpha = .01 \qquad \alpha/2 = .005$$

$$Z_{.005} = \pm 2.575$$

Calculated $Z = -0.52 > Z_{.005} = -2.575$

$$\boxed{\text{Fail to reject the null hypothesis}}$$

12.59 H_o: $\mu_1 - \mu_2 \leq 0$
          H_a: $\mu_1 - \mu_2 > 0$

Rating	Rank	Group
16	1	2
17	2	2
19	3.5	2
19	3.5	2
20	5	2
21	6.5	2
21	6.5	1
22	9	1
22	9	1
22	9	2
23	11.5	1
23	11.5	2
24	13	2
25	15.5	1
25	15.5	1
25	15.5	1
25	15.5	2
26	19	1
26	19	1
26	19	2
27	21	1
28	22	1

$n_1 = 11 \quad n_2 = 11$

$W_1 = 6.5 + 9 + 9 + 11.5 + 15.5 + 15.5 + 15.5 +$
$\qquad 19 + 19 + 21 + 22 = 163.5$

$$\mu = \frac{n_1 \cdot n_2}{2} = \frac{(11)(11)}{2} = 60.5$$

$$\sigma = \sqrt{\frac{n_1 \cdot n_2(n_1+n_2+1)}{12}} = \sqrt{\frac{(11)(11)(23)}{12}} = 15.23$$

$$U = n_1 \cdot n_2 + \frac{n_1(n_1+1)}{2} - W_1$$

$$= (11)(11) + \frac{(11)(12)}{2} - 163.5 = 23.5$$

$$Z = \frac{U - \mu}{\sigma} = \frac{23.5 - 60.5}{15.23} = \boxed{-2.43}$$

$\alpha = .05$
$Z_{.05} = 1.645$
Calculated $Z = |-2.43| > Z_{.05} = 1.645$

$\boxed{\text{Reject the null hypothesis}}$

12.61 H_o: $\mu_1 - \mu_2 \leq 0$
                         H_a: $\mu_1 - \mu_2 > 0$

Sales	Rank	Type of Dispenser
92	1	M
105	2	M
106	3	M
109	4	M
110	5	A
114	6	M
117	7	M
118	8.5	A
118	8.5	M
122	10	M
125	11	M
126	12	M
128	13	A
129	14	M
137	15	A
143	16	A
144	17	A
146	18	A
151	19	A
152	20	A
153	21	A
168	22	A

$n_1 = 11$ $n_2 = 11$

$W_1 = 5 + 8.5 + 13 + 15 + 16 + 17 + 18 +$
$\quad\quad 19 + 20 + 21 + 22 = 174.5$

$\mu = n_1 \cdot n_2 = \dfrac{(11)(11)}{2} = 60.5$
$\quad\quad\quad 2$

$\sigma = \sqrt{\dfrac{n_1 \cdot n_2 (n_1 + n_2 + 1)}{12}} = \sqrt{\dfrac{(11)(11)(23)}{12}}\ 15.23$

$U = n_1 \cdot n_2 + \dfrac{n_1(n_1+1)}{2} - W_1 = (11)(11) + \dfrac{(11)(12)}{2} - 174.5 = 12.5$

$Z = \dfrac{U - \mu}{\sigma} = \dfrac{12.5 - 60.5}{15.23} =$ $\boxed{-3.15}$

$\alpha = .01$
$Z_{.01} = 2.33$

Calculated value $Z = |-3.15| > Z_{.01} = 2.33$

$\boxed{\text{Reject the null hypothesis}}$

12.63 H_0:   The population differences = 0

             H_a: The population differences ≠ 0

Group 1	Group 2	d	Rank
111	116	-5	-9.5
87	90	-3	-5.5
96	95	1	1.5
103	100	3	5.5
102	115	-13	-15
97	107	-10	-13
113	111	2	3.5
95	80	15	16.5
97	96	1	1.5
90	79	11	14
101	105	-4	-7.5
100	91	9	12
93	97	-4	-7.5
88	82	6	11
104	109	-5	-9.5
94	79	15	16.5
107	109	-2	-3.5

n = 17

T- = 9.5 + 5.5 + 15 + 13 + 7.5 + 7.5 + 9.5 + 3.5 = 71

T+ = 1.5 + 5.5 + 3.5 + 16.5 + 1.5 + 14 + 12 + 11 + 16.5 = 82

T = 71

$$\mu = \frac{(n)(n+1)}{4} = \frac{(17)(18)}{4} = 76.5$$

$$\sigma = \sqrt{\frac{n(n+1)(2n+1)}{24}} = \sqrt{\frac{(17)(18)(35)}{24}} = 21.12$$

$$Z = \frac{T-\mu}{\sigma} = \frac{71 - 76.5}{21.12} = \boxed{-0.26}$$

$\alpha = .01$, $\alpha/2 = .005$

$Z_{.005} = \pm2.575$

Calculated Z = -0.26 > $Z_{.005}$ = -2.575

Fail to reject the null hypothesis

12.65 H_o: The population differences $\geq$ 0
                   H_a: The population differences < 0

Before	After	d	Rank
430	465	-35	-16
485	475	10	6.5
520	535	-15	-10
360	410	-50	-17
440	425	15	10
500	505	-5	-2.5
425	450	-25	-14.5
470	480	-10	-6.5
515	520	-5	-2.5
430	430	0	OMIT
450	460	-10	-6.5
495	500	-5	-2.5
540	530	10	6.5
460	475	-15	-10
400	420	-20	-12.5
420	445	-25	-14.5
385	380	5	2.5
455	475	-20	-12.5

n = 17

T+ = 6.5 + 10 + 6.5 + 2.5 = 25.5

T = 25.5

$$\mu = \frac{(n)(n+1)}{4} = \frac{(17)(18)}{4} = 76.5$$

$$\sigma = \sqrt{\frac{n(n+1)(2n+1)}{24}} = \sqrt{\frac{(17)(18)(35)}{24}} = 21.12$$

$$Z = \frac{T-\mu}{\sigma} = \frac{25.5 - 76.5}{21.12} = \boxed{-2.41}$$

α = .01
$Z_{.01}$ = -2.33

Calculated Z = -2.41 < $Z_{.01}$ = -2.33

Reject the null hypothesis

12.67 H_o: The population differences = 0

               H_a: The population differences $\neq$ 0

With	Without	d	Rank
1180	1209	-29	-6
874	902	-28	-5
1071	862	209	18
668	503	165	15
889	974	-85	-12.5
724	675	49	9
880	821	59	10
482	567	-85	-12.5
796	602	194	16
1207	1097	110	14
968	962	6	1
1027	1045	-18	-4
1158	896	262	20
670	708	-38	-8
849	642	207	17
559	327	232	19
449	483	-34	-7
992	978	14	3
1046	973	73	11
852	841	11	2

n = 20

T_- = 6 + 5 + 12.5 + 12.5 + 4 + 8 + 7 = 55

T = 55

$\mu = \dfrac{(n)(n+1)}{4} = \dfrac{(20)(21)}{4} = 105$

$\sigma = \sqrt{\dfrac{n(n+1)(2n+1)}{24}} = \sqrt{\dfrac{(20)(21)(41)}{24}} = 26.79$

$Z = \dfrac{T-\mu}{\sigma} = \dfrac{55 - 105}{26.79} = \boxed{-1.87}$

$\alpha = .01, \quad \alpha/2 = .005$
$Z_{.005} = \pm 2.575$

Calculated Z = -1.87 > $Z_{.005}$ = -2.575

Fail to reject the null hypothesis

12.69 H_o: The C populations are identical.
          H_a: At least one of the C populations is different.

Sample 1	Sample 2	Sample 3
1057	1109	1078
1049	1120	1090
1066	1092	1099
1023	1083	1101
1071	1089	1103
1026	1117	1100
	1095	1113
		1108

By Ranks

Sample 1	Sample 2	Sample 3
4	18	7
3	21	10
5	11	13
1	8	15
6	9	16
2	20	14
	12	19
		17

T_j 21   99   111

n_j 6   7   8

$$\sum \frac{T_j^2}{n_j} = \frac{(21)^2}{6} + \frac{(99)^2}{7} + \frac{(111)^2}{8} = 3,013.77$$

$n = 21$

$$K = \frac{12}{n(n+1)} \left(\sum \frac{T_j^2}{n_j} \right) - 3(n+1) =$$

$$\frac{12}{(21)(22)} (3,013.77) - 3(22) = \boxed{12.29}$$

$\alpha = .05$
$df = (c - 1) = 3 - 1 = 2$

$\chi^2_{.05,2} = 5.991$

Calculated $K = 12.29 > \chi^2_{.05,2} = 5.991$

Reject the null hypothesis

12.71 H_o: The C populations are identical.
          H_a: At least one of the C populations is different.

1	2	3	4	5
23.14	14.58	20.17	18.56	23.21
21.48	19.87	20.50	20.14	22.97
22.39	20.13	20.90	19.74	21.19
22.57	18.51	19.99	19.34	22.39
23.00	17.75	19.36	20.17	22.95
21.78		20.48	18.86	22.01
22.69		19.73		22.87
21.38				22.92
				22.41

By Ranks

	1	2	3	4	5
	34	1	14.5	4	35
	21	10	17	13	32
	24.5	12	18	9	19
	27	3	11	6	24.5
	33	2	7	14.5	31
	22		16	5	23
	28		8		29
	20				30
					26
T_j	209.5	28	91.5	51.5	249.5
n_j	8	5	7	6	9

$$\sum \frac{T_j^2}{n_j} = \frac{(209.5)^2}{8} + \frac{(28)^2}{5} + \frac{(91.5)^2}{7} + \frac{(51.5)^2}{6} + \frac{(249.5)^2}{9}$$

$$= 14,197.85$$

$$n = 35$$

$$K = \frac{12}{n(n+1)} \left(\sum \frac{T_j^2}{n_j}\right) - 3(n+1) =$$

$$= \frac{12}{35(36)}(14,197.85) - 3(36) = \boxed{27.22}$$

$$\alpha = .05$$
$$df = c - 1 = 5 - 1 = 4$$

$$\chi^2_{.05,4} = 9.488$$

Calculated $K = 27.22 > \chi^2_{.05,4} = 9.488$

Reject the null hypothesis

12.73 H_o: The C populations are identical
             H_a: At least one of the C populations is different

3-day	Quality	Mgmt. Inv.
9	27	16
11	38	21
17	25	18
10	40	28
22	31	29
15	19	20
6	35	31

By Ranks

	3-day	Quality	Mgmt. Inv.
	2	14	6
	4	20	11
	7	13	8
	3	21	15
	12	17.5	16
	5	9	10
	1	19	17.5
T_j	34	113.5	83.5
n_j	7	7	7

$$\sum \frac{T_j^2}{n_j} = \frac{(34)^2}{7} + \frac{(113.5)^2}{7} + \frac{(83.5)^2}{7} = 3,001.5$$

$n = 21$

$$K = \frac{12}{n(n+1)} \left(\sum \frac{T_j^2}{n_j}\right) - 3(n+1) =$$

$$= \frac{12}{21(22)}(3,001.5) - 3(22) = \boxed{11.96}$$

$\alpha = .10$
$df = c - 1 = 3 - 1 = 2$

$\chi^2_{.10,2} = 4.605$

Calculated $K = 11.96 > \chi^2_{.10,2} = 4.605$

Reject the null hypothesis

12.75

Var. 1	Var. 2	Ranked Var. 1	Ranked Var. 2	d	d^2
35	91	1	7	-6	36
42	88	3	5	-2	4
50	86	5	3	2	4
55	90	6	6	0	0
39	87	2	4	-2	4
48	80	4	2	2	4
65	73	7	1	6	36
				$\Sigma d^2 =$	88

$n = 7$

$$r_s = 1 - \frac{6\Sigma d^2}{n(n^2-1)} = 1 - \frac{6(88)}{7(48)} = \boxed{-0.571}$$

12.77

1	2	d	d^2
1	4	-3	9
2	1	1	1
3	3	0	0
4	5	-1	1
5	2	3	9
6	7	-1	1
7	8	-1	1
8	6	2	4
		$\Sigma d^2 =$	26

$n = 8$

$$r_s = 1 - \frac{6\Sigma d^2}{n(n^2-1)} = 1 - \frac{6(26)}{8(63)} = \boxed{.690}$$

12.79

Cups	Stress	Ranked Cups	Ranked Stress	d	d^2
25	80	6	8	-2	4
41	85	9	9	0	0
16	35	4	3	1	1
0	45	1	5	-4	16
11	30	3	2	1	1
28	50	7	6	1	1
34	65	8	7	1	1
18	40	5	4	1	1
5	20	2	1	1	1
				$\Sigma d^2 =$	26

$n = 9$

$$r_s = 1 - \frac{6\Sigma d^2}{n(n^2-1)} = 1 - \frac{6(26)}{9(80)} = \boxed{.783}$$